D0853198

Wallace Library	DUE DATE (stamped in blue) RETURN DATE (stamped in black)

GABRIELE D'ANNUNZIO
IN FRANCE

GABRIELE D'ANNUNZIO IN FRANCE

IN FRANCE

A Study in Cultural Relations

GIOVANNI GULLACE

SYRACUSE UNIVERSITY PRESS

LIBRARY

Copyright © 1966 by Syracuse University Press
Syracuse, New York   ALL RIGHTS RESERVED

FIRST EDITION 1966

Library of Congress Catalog Card: 66-20233

PQ
4804
G8

Manufactured in the United States of America

To
Rose and Gina

Acknowledgment

Without the encouragement and the generous help of my friend and colleague Antonio Pace of Syracuse University this work would perhaps never have reached its final form. To him my deepest gratitude. All errors and misjudgments are exclusively mine. I am also indebted to my dear colleague Carrol F. Coates for his careful reading of the proofs.

Contents

Introduction

GABRIELE D'ANNUNZIO was perhaps the only modern Italian writer to find in France immediate and widespread acceptance. When introduced to the French public in 1892 he was still unknown outside Italy; but through the brilliant success of his novels in the French translation by Georges Hérelle, he unexpectedly emerged as a European literary figure, thus acquiring a high stature even in his own country where his works had previously been regarded with suspicion if not scorn. The publication of the trilogy of the "romans de la rose" (*L'Intrus, L'Enfant de volupté, Le Triomph de la mort*) in the early and middle 1890's produced an immediate sensation. D'Annunzio's lyrical expression, his ardent sensuality, the refined atmosphere surrounding his characters, delighted the French readers, who had grown weary of the vulgarity of naturalism and of the somber psychology of northern literatures. The enthusiasm for the young Italian writer went beyond proportion: Melchior de Vogüé hailed him as the flag bearer of a "Latin renaissance." Although his subsequent novels did not win the general acclaim of his early ones, his prestige as a novelist remained uncontested.

Later in the 1890's D'Annunzio suddenly revealed himself as a dramatist; his first plays (*Il Sogno d'un mattino di primavera, La Ville morte*) were seen in the French theater even before they became known in Italy. Other dramatic works (*Le Martyre de Saint Sébastien, La Pisanelle, Le Chèvrefeuille*) were not only presented in France first, but they were written directly in French. His dramas, permeated by intense lyricism and strongly marked by an antirealistic tendency, were widely discussed and, despite their structural defects, their presentation was always an important event of the theatrical season. The most renowned actresses—Eleonora Duse, Sarah Bernhardt, Suzanne Desprès, and later the Russian dancer Ida Rubinstein—were proud to incarnate D'Annunzio's roles. The French theaters, such as the Théâtre de la Renaissance, the Théâtre de l'Oeuvre, the Gymnase, the Théâtre de la Porte Saint-Martin, the Théâtre du Châtelet, L'Opéra, and finally the Comédie-Française, welcomed his plays.

As a poet, however, D'Annunzio was little known in France owing to the difficulty of translating his poetry into another language. Of his vast poetic production, only one volume of selections appeared in French (1912), and it does not include any of *Le Laudi* which represents the highest achievement in modern Italian poetry. The four books of *Le Laudi* became known to the French public through fragments published from time to time in periodicals. Only in 1947 did the first book, *Laus Vitae,* appear in its entirety. Thus, while for the Italians D'Annunzio was the foremost poet of his time, for the French he remained, above all, the novelist and the dramatist—two manifestations of his artistic talent that they were able to understand and appreciate better than the author's own compatriots.

His wide success and reputation in France were definitely unique, and they astonished the Italians at the beginning. In 1902 Ernest Tissot remarked that D'Annunzio was still "plus admiré et mieux compris de ce côté-ci des Alpes que de l'autre."[1] But when D'Annunzio's novels and plays no longer claimed the attention of the public, he was able to win French admiration anew, this time as a war hero, a fervent friend, an ardent advocate of Latin brotherhood. His long stay in France (March 1910–May 1915), his French works, the role he played in the intervention of Italy into the war on the side of France, his extensive connections in the French artistic, literary, and political worlds, the quarrel with the French government over Fiume at the end of the First World War—these made him a well-known figure on the other side of the Alps. France was his "seconda patria" in the sincerest and most profound sense of the term, despite the disappointment and bitterness of the period following the First World War.

His impact is eloquently shown by the huge number of articles and essays on his personality and art, and the many translations of his own works. The bibliography by Joseph Fucilla and Joseph Carrière, *D'Annunzio Abroad* (2 vols., 1935–37) lists well over one thousand critical and biographical items and some 120 translations appearing in France. Many more have been published since, even though general interest in the author has almost completely died over the years. No other Italian writer, with the exception of Dante, attracted so much attention and aroused so much discussion in French literary circles.

But the critics interested in D'Annunzio's relations with France have neglected to consider his immense literary fortune there. In fact, to my knowledge, no work exists on this important aspect of his literary

career. In the past, attention was primarily focused on the French influences on the author; and research in this direction reached an unpleasant climax at the end of the last century. In January 1896 Enrico
Thovez, an Italian critic animated by a caustic and polemic spirit,
launched a clamorous accusation of plagiarism against D'Annunzio in
La Gazzetta letteraria (Turin).[2] Thovez' revelations, according to
which the "Imaginifico" had plundered a great number of Italian and
foreign authors—especially French—triggered a bitter controversy
which resulted in an intensive inquiry into the author's literary sources.
Some French critics had already vaguely pointed out, rather complacently, certain possible influences on D'Annunzio, but they had not yet
become aware of the extent of his borrowings from their literature.
They joined with the Italians and, in malignant delight, made every
effort to detect D'Annunzio's alleged "thefts" and to belittle his stature
as a writer.[3] The long list of authors from whom he was accused of
having stolen included, besides the Italians, the classics, and the Bible,
the names of Hugo, Gautier, Musset, Baudelaire, Flaubert, Maupassant,
Zola, Coppée, Paul Alexis, Banville, Jean Lorrain, Péladan, Verlaine,
Maeterlinck, Verhaeren, Amiel, Barrès, Régnier, Mendès, Mauclair,
Schwob, as well as Poe, Shelley, Wilde, Mary Robinson, Swinburne,
Hauptman, Nietzsche, Dostoevsky, Korolenko, and Ibsen.

But this logomachy over D'Annunzio's plagiarisms had no positive
results. That the author had reproduced in his early poetic works a
certain atmosphere reminiscent of Baudelaire, that he had borrowed
plots and ideas from Maupassant[4] for his short stories, or that he had
used some phrases from Flaubert[5] did not constitute great literary
offenses. The most reliable critics—Benedetto Croce,[6] Charles Maurras,[7]
Ernest Bovet,[8] and many others—maintained in fact that there was no
plagiarism in D'Annunzio, since whatever he drew from other writers
was completely transformed by his strong literary personality and bore
his own unmistakable imprint—his sumptuous expression and his intensely sensual lyricism. The real problem from the critical point of
view was not so much to uncover the sources as to study the use made
of them by the author and to determine whether he had merely inserted
the borrowed elements or fused them into an original and well-unified
whole. An analysis of this sort would clearly show that D'Annunzio's
occasional use of literary sources never compromised his originality.

When the polemic on the plagiarisms came to an end, studies on

D'Annunzio's literary relations with France subsided for several years. A thorough appraisal of the impact of French literature on his works is still lacking and whatever exists on the subject is only fragmentary.[9] In 1946 Guy Tosi, the most active D'Annunzio scholar in France,[10] announced as in progress a comprehensive study—*Gabriele d'Annunzio et la France*—covering mainly the French influences and other related problems; but as far as I know it has not yet appeared. A book by Jole Nardi, *D'Annunzio e alcuni scrittori francesi,* was published in 1951; it deals with analogies between the poet and some French writers, but the supporting material is often unconvincing, and the similarities shown in most cases appear to be unrelated and purely coincidental.

However, if the book promised by Guy Tosi is published, as is hoped, it will certainly satisfy this need. There would remain a more serious gap—that concerning D'Annunzio's fortune in France—which the present work is intended to fill, at least partially. An attempt has been made to explain the reasons for the author's literary success in that country against the background of the general reaction to naturalism at the turn of the century. Influences on him have not been discussed, except occasionally, since Tosi's work will cover that aspect of the problem. Nor can I say that I have dealt with D'Annunzio's literary influences on French writers, since his works seem to have exerted little, if any, directly. He was an author "à la mode" who enjoyed great popularity for a long period, but who left no durable imprint. The main interest of the present volume has been to discuss the critical reaction to his works, the problem of translation, the theatrical presentation of his plays, his French writings, his extraliterary relations with France, and other pertinent questions. I hope that this modest study of D'Annunzio's relations with France will give some new perspectives on the career of an author whose name filled an entire epoch in Italian literature, and who was the first among modern Italian writers to acquire an international reputation.

GIOVANNI GULLACE

Binghamton, New York
January 1966

Part I
THE NOVELIST

1. The Enthusiastic Reception: *L'Intrus*

D'ANNUNZIO's name appeared in the French literary press for the first time in March 1887 when Vittorio Pica, a Neapolitan critic, published in the *Revue indépendante* a sympathetic article devoted particularly to the *Intermezzo di rime*,[1] a collection of poems which had aroused most of the Italian critics against the mad sensuality of the young poet. A second article by Pica, devoted this time to another of D'Annunzio's poetic works—*L'Isottèo*[2]—was published in the same periodical in October 1890. But the poet failed in both instances to capture the attention of the French public; and despite his growing popularity in Italy he remained completely unknown on the other side of the Alps until 1892 when the translation of one of his prose works revealed him quite suddenly to France and brought him unexpectedly more fame there than he had thus far enjoyed in Italy. This work was *L'Innocente,* a novel serialized under the title *L'Intrus*[3] in the weekly *Le Temps* beginning with the issue of September 24, 1892. Strangely enough D'Annunzio's novel, turned down by the Italian published Emilio Treves (Milan) on a question of literary decency,[4] gave the author that artistic consecration which France accords only to geniuses.

It was D'Annunzio's rare good luck to find in Georges Hérelle a translator of great competence, capable of giving new life to his works.[5] Hérelle's contribution to the extraordinary fortune of the Italian writer in France is an acknowledged fact. In a letter of May 2, 1894, D'Annunzio wrote him: "Désormais votre nom est lié pour toujours au mien; nous sommes désormais en France une seule personne."[6] French critics have never failed to point out Hérelle's incontestable merits as D'Annunzio's translator or to place special emphasis on the quality of his work. It was even suggested that the translations were, if anything, superior to the original texts, and that D'Annunzio's great success in France was largely due to the excellence of Hérelle's work. Most critics, however, seemed well aware that a writer of D'Annunzio's stature

1

would sooner or later have imposed himself upon the French reading public even without the services of the gifted professor of philosophy from Cherbourg. In any case, the meeting of the two men formed a rare combination of talents, and the warm friendship which soon developed between them led to a fruitful literary association lasting many years. Their correspondence reveals the important part Hérelle had in the literary career of the Italian author.[7] D'Annunzio fondly referred to him as his "révélateur" and his "auteur," fully acknowledging the translator's contribution to his own success abroad. Although their relations were not always completely smooth, owing to certain differences in their artistic temperament and taste, their occasional dissension never impaired their deep friendship.

Georges Hérelle began his career as a translator at the age of forty-five when, by pure chance, he happened upon D'Annunzio's *L'Innocente*. During the summer of 1891, while vacationing in Naples, he became interested in the literary pages of *Il Corriere di Napoli*, and on leaving Italy bought a six-month subscription to the paper in order to improve his still limited knowledge of the Italian language. The literary page of the daily had for some time been carrying a banal adventure novel, but when it ended in the autumn of that year Hérelle's attention was suddenly drawn to the first installment of a new serial story. It was D'Annunzio's *L'Innocente*. Hérelle described thus his immediate reaction to it: "Dès le premier feuilleton je fus ébloui et ma surprise, mon admiration ne firent que s'accroître avec les feuilletons suivants. Le nom de l'auteur m'était inconnu et je m'en étonnais. Comment était-il possible qu'un écrivain de ce talent n'eût point acquis déjà la célébrité."[8] D'Annunzio's brilliant prose prompted Hérelle to translate some pages for pure delectation. He read his translations to his friends, who shared his admiration for the newly discovered writer and suggested that he translate the whole novel and publish it. Their encouragement led Hérelle to seek permission for the work. He wrote to the unknown author, addressing the letter to *Il Corriere di Napoli*, and he did not have to wait long for D'Annunzio's answer which was affirmative as well as enthusiastic: "Votre lettre m'est arrivée hier comme un cadeau de Noël inattendu. ... J'avais déjà pensé à faire publier en France mon nouveau roman. Mais j'hésitais sur le choix du traducteur. Certaines recherches de style et de nombreuses subtilités d'analyse rendent la traduction très difficile. Mais rien qu'à lire votre lettre, je devine votre valeur."[9]

This answer was dated Christmas Day 1891. The translation was completed in the following summer and was immediately accepted by *Le Temps*. The novel met with unexpected acclaim and opened the door to the author's European success. D'Annunzio had followed the translation with the closest attention and, on the whole, he was well satisfied with it. However, his preoccupation with stylistic perfection led him, in the course of the work, to argue about a host of linguistic minutiae. So concerned was he with the peculiar nature of his own style that in many instances he expected Hérelle to disregard the very character of the French language in order to comply with the high-flown expression of the original. After reading a part of the translation, he wrote, in fact: "Puisque les plus récents stylistes de France, surtout les jeunes, se rapprochent beaucoup de l'ampleur de certaines constructions latines et ne répugnent pas à quelques italianismes, je crois qu'il ne serait pas mauvais de laisser çà et là dans la traduction l'étrange saveur de l'original."[10] About a month later, upon receiving another portion of the work, he returned once more to the subject, formulating in clear-cut terms his ideas concerning art and stressing the necessity of rendering his phrases in French as musical as they were in Italian. To emphasize his view he often pointed to the example of the "divin Flaubert."[11] In time he became so exacting as to demand that the structure of the French language be molded to suit his own artistic audacity: "Il ne faut pas avoir peur de certaines phrases un peu longues. Je sais que la phrase longue, avec beaucoup d'incidents, n'est pas française; mais les stylistes contemporains ont renouvelé leur syntaxe. Et je désire que mes phrases soient rendues dans leur totalité et non morcelées en trois ou quatre phrases au grand détriment de l'effet."[12] He complained about "consonances désagréables" which would destroy "certaines délicatesses de forme de l'original"; he asked Hérelle to retain "tel quel le mot *multanime* et même *multanimité* (Italianisms) and to delete from the work all the "pour ainsi dire" which to his mind encumbered his phrases and weakened their effectiveness.

Hérelle was not always docile; often he had to take a firm stand against D'Annunzio's unreasonable demands. However, there were times when he had to admit the fairness of the author's observations. The problem of translation—the most delicate in their relations—is discussed again and again in their correspondence. D'Annunzio had always emphatically defined himself as being, above all, a stylist: "Confrontez une page de moi," he wrote, "avec n'importe quel écrivain italien contemporain et vous verrez la différence."[13] And, when Hérelle pointed out that the main objective in translating should be to render ideas faithfully, he answered that he could not conceive of a difference between content and form, stressing that content can acquire its full value only in a perfect form.[14]

What D'Annunzio asked of the translator was not only the faithful rendering of the meaning of the Italian words, but the reproduction of their external features as well; he constantly urged Hérelle to choose the French words closest to Italian in their orthography, etymology, and musical qualities. He felt Hérelle at times to be too timid, and he boasted that he himself never sacrificed an artistic effect for the sake of conforming to common usage of the language. But Hérelle, whose notion of the language was based on common usage, objected strongly, and in most cases justifiably, to D'Annunzio's suggestions. The author's aim was to attract the French public through the uncommon refinement of his style and his distinctive taste for artistic beauty—the very characteristics which had caught the attention of the Italian readers—even though, for various reasons, they never accepted his works unreservedly.

But the problem of translation was not the only one obsessing D'Annunzio; he detested the editors of journals, often too ready with pencils in attempts to tone down his work. He was constantly distressed by the thought of possible editorial cuts, and he passionately defended the integrity of his manuscripts against any alterations or deletions. He claimed for himself exclusively the right to modify his writings in any way. Despite his protective efforts, however, he could not prevent bowdlerizations. *L'Intrus,* which *Le Temps* had accepted only on condition that some of the boldest passages be eliminated, was actually published in a mutilated form. D'Annunzio's irritation is clearly shown by a letter to Hérelle after reading the first installments of the novel: "Avez-vous vu le massacre que le *Temps* fait de mon pauvre roman? Ils ont coupé deux chapitres entiers et pourtant ces deux chapitres ne sont pas parmi les plus audacieux. Que feront-ils pour le reste? ... Ces suppressions sont vraiment faites d'une façon barbare. Je ne comprends pas pour quelle raison le *Temps* a accepté mon roman, s'il avait l'intention de le dévaster de cette façon."[15]

Despite the numerous omissions the novel found widespread success; a chorus of enthusiastic praise arose on every side. D'Annunzio's work was something of a revelation; it brought to the literary world a fresh note of originality, soon interpreted as the signal for an artistic rebirth after the brutal experience of naturalism. His somber lyricism and his refined sensuality pleased the public greatly, while the elegance of his style and his studied expression aroused the keen interest of the literary elite. Upon reading a part of *L'Intrus* in *Le Temps*, Paul Calmann-Lévy, in a letter to Hérelle,[16] solicited authorization to publish the novel in book form. When D'Annunzio was informed of the publisher's request, he immediately asked Hérelle to restore the work to its original form and to prevent deletions. But Calmann-Lévy, too, was to exasperate the author by demanding further "adoucissements" of the text for his edition. The danger of more cutting prompted D'Annunzio to write Hérelle a vehement letter, stressing that his prose should not be tailored to please "la bêtise agglomérée"—the "grand Public." And he added:

> A la pensée que mon oeuvre doive être châtrée pour une fin commerciale, j'éprouve la même indignation que si quelqu'un venait me faire une proposition honteuse. Dans mon livre, tout est calculé, médité, exécuté avec un art sévère. Mes intentions ont toujours été pures et hautes. Mon livre, comme vous l'avez reconnu dès le début, est moral. ... Et en France, au pays de la grande liberté intellectuelle, l'éditeur de Charles Baudelaire me demande "des adoucissements!" En France, où désormais est définitivement acceptée la devise de Ernest Hello, celle qu'il faut écrire en tête du Code de la République des Lettres: LE STYLE EST INVIOLABLE![17]

However, D'Annunzio's reluctance was overcome. The novel was published early in 1893, and he had once again to resign himself to the "adoucissements" requested by Calmann-Lévy.

If the moral scruples of the editor of *Le Temps* and of the publisher Calmann-Lévy angered the author, the warm reception of his work filled him with enthusiasm. Amédée Pigeon,[18] in a letter of November, 1892, had spoken of *L'Intrus* with great admiration, pointing out artistic qualities which no one had yet discovered. D'Annunzio's reaction to Pigeon's appreciations can be read in a letter to Hérelle: "Comme je suis heureux qu'en France mon oeuvre enfin soit comprise! Ici, en Italie, l'ignorance générale, l'indifférence stupide et l'insuffisante culture empêchent qu'une oeuvre d'art soit appréciée pour ses qualités les plus hautes. ... Deux ou trois critiques à peine ont compris l'esprit véritable de l'oeuvre."[19] But what intrigued D'Annunzio mainly in

Pigeon's letter was the flattering remark that the author of *L'Intrus* must necessarily be also a musician:

> Personne encore n'avait noté cette musicalité de mon livre. Et cette musicalité, précisément, a été ma principale recherche d'art et la plus attentive. En effet, j'ai introduit dans ma prose jusqu'au *Leit motiv* comme dans le drame wagnérien. ... Naturellement, il était impossible de conserver la musique originale dans la traduction. Mais Pigeon a eu l'intuition de mon dessein profond.[20]

Remy de Gourmont, in taking issue with the criticism leveled by Luigi Capuana[21] at the cumbersome lyricism of D'Annunzio's novels, commented: "C'est précisément ce lyrisme brumeux que j'aime en M. d'Annunzio. Le roman ne relève d'une autre esthétique que le poème. Le roman original fut en vers. ... L'ère du roman instructif étant close pour quelques lustres, qu'on nous permette de nous amuser à des poèmes."[22] A long article by Pigeon—the first comprehensive study on D'Annunzio to be published in France—appeared in the *Revue hebdomadaire,* June 24, 1893, with an autobiographical sketch of the author. In discussing the merits of *L'Intrus,* Pigeon pointed to two main influences: "M. Gabriele d'Annunzio," he said, "est un psychologue. ... Il a certainement lu beaucoup Shakespeare et Tolstoï. C'est Shakespeare, j'imagine, qui lui a enseigné ce qu'on pourrait appeler la beauté artistique du crime. ... C'est Tolstoï peut-être, autant que Shakespeare, qui l'a penché sur toutes les plaies du coeur, et lui a montré, à l'origine de la plupart des grands crimes, une faiblesse des sens."[23] He remarked, however, that the influences of the North had not prevailed on D'Annunzio and, although they had contributed to his intellectual development, they had not altered his Latin originality. He added further that D'Annunzio was "un Latin à l'âme slave" whose psychological complexity deserved the attention of the French public who had shown so much interest in the Russian novelists.[24] Pigeon's pertinent remarks explain D'Annunzio's literary success in France in the light of the cultural atmosphere of the time. *L'Intrus* seemed to combine the Latin taste for artistic beauty with the Slavic psychological depth found in the Russian novels. An article by Émile Soinet in the *Union universitaire* of July 1 and in *Plume* of July 15, 1893, lavished praise on D'Annunzio's work and its translator: "N'est-ce pas le triomphe même de l'ecrivain que de concrétiser les mots et les phrases en ces sensations cérébrales si intenses et que normalement seule la musique peut donner? Ce triomphe, M. Hérelle le partage avec d'Annunzio. Car sa traduction, qui avant tout est une merveille de fidélité, a cependant la valeur intrinsèque d'une oeuvre littéraire française."[25] *Le Figaro* put the novel at the head of the list of books recommended for vacation reading, and an article by Philippe Gille in the same journal (August 18, 1893) led its editor to ask D'Annunzio for the manuscript of *Il Trionfo della morte*, which Hérelle had just begun to translate. *L'Intrus* was discussed or mentioned in nearly all of the reviews and newspapers. In a letter of September 28, 1893, D'Annunzio informed Hérelle that he had received about seventy clippings concerning his novel and that he had been asked permission to have a play adapted from it for the Théâtre Libre. The *National* of November 18, 1893, carried an article by Pierre Mercieux beginning with these words: "— Avez-vous lu Baruch? — demandait le bon La Fontaine à tous ceux qu'il recontrait sur la route. — Avez-vous lu l'*Intrus?* — demandent en ce moment à leurs amis et connaissances, etc. ... Non? Et bien! lisez-le. Voilà une oeuvre admirable. C'est plus fort que du Bourget. ..."[26] Someone went so far as to propose to D'Annunzio a new version of the book; but the author was quite satisfied with Hérelle's work and the proposal was turned down.[27]

In *La Liberté*, July 12, 1893, however, D'Annunzio was reproached for having used the same device for killing an infant as that employed by Maupassant in his short story, *La Confession*. In both *L'Intrus* and Maupassant's "nouvelle," in fact, the presence of an infant was an obstacle to the protagonist's plans or desires, and in both cases he was eliminated by deliberate exposure to icy air from an open window. D'Annunzio defended himself against the accusation: "Je ne connais pas la nouvelle de Maupassant," he wrote Hérelle, "je désire même savoir par curiosité dans quel volume elle se trouve."[28] Nevertheless, his denial does not prove his innocence. The similarity between *La Confession* and the entire denouement in *L'Intrus* eloquently attests to the fact that D'Annunzio had borrowed the idea from Maupassant. But it would be difficult to speak of plagiarism. D'Annunzio's works are so strongly marked by his personal imprint that even the most obvious borrowings appear in a new and original light. In Maupassant's story the protagonist kills in order to remove an obstacle to an advantageous social situation; in *L'Intrus* Tullio Hermil commits the same crime in order to free himself from the sexual obsession aroused in him by the presence of the infant. The motivation and the treatment of the crime are here typically D'Annunzian.

However, this minor criticism did not in any away reflect upon the artistic value of *L'Intrus*. The author wrote to Hérelle on November 16, 1893, that in the clippings he had received from the *Courrier de la presse* he had noticed that some journals (*L'Art social, La Revue blanche*) had used lines from his novel as "épigraphe à des écrits remarquables par la finesse de la forme et de la pensée." And he concluded: "Voilà un signe qui fait plaisir. Frapper profondément et obséder quelques esprits choisis, voilà mon ambition."[29] He had achieved his first goal: he now had to push his initial success.

2. The D'Annunzian Vogue: *Episcopo et Cie, L'Enfant de volupté, Le Triomphe de la mort*

THE ACCLAIM won by *L'Intrus* prompted both author and translator to publish other works without delay. Hérelle suggested the translation of a volume of selected short stories, but D'Annunzio was at first opposed to this idea; he felt that his stories, written in his early youth, would add nothing to his reputation from the artistic point of view. Furthermore, they were far removed in character from *L'Intrus* and the other novels he had since written or was then writing. D'Annunzio's early prose works are imitations of the French and Italian naturalist schools. In his stories there was, as he himself pointed out,[1] a sort of "naturalisme maniéré" which in content was no less brutal than the naturalism of Maupassant whose influence on him was easily detectable.[2]

D'Annunzio finally consented to Hérelle's suggestion on condition that the dates of composition be clearly indicated in the publication in order to justify any artistic weaknesses. He even furnished notes for a preface which would explain his artistic evolution as a prose writer. The stories began to appear in periodicals in the fall of 1893,[3] and were assembled in a volume published by Calmann-Lévy in 1895 under the title *Episcopo et Cie*. The volume contained the short novel *Giovanni Episcopo* and nine stories taken from D'Annunzio's three published collections—*Terra vergine* (1882), *Il Libro delle vergini* (1884), and *San Pantaleone* (1886). These new translations also met with wide success. Paul Bourget, for example, after reading *Giovanni Episcopo* in the *Revue de Paris* of February 1 and 15, 1894, wrote to Hérelle: "Mes compliments pour ta belle traduction de cet admirable D'Annunzio. *Giovanni Episcopo* est un chef-d'oeuvre."[4]

During the year 1894 author and translator worked relentlessly on *Il Piacere* and *Il Trionfo della morte*. D'Annunzio intended to give the latter to *Le Figaro*, which had already requested it. But, since no immediate action was decided upon, Brunetière stepped in to propose publication of the novel in the *Revue des Deux Mondes*.[5] This unexpected step astonished D'Annunzio, the more so since Brunetière had earlier refused *Episcopo*, feeling it to be too gloomy. To the author's mind *Il Trionfo della morte* was, if anything, even gloomier: "Est-il possible," he wrote to Hérelle, "que les lecteurs de la *Revue des Deux Mondes* aient acquis un estomac plus résistant?"[6] D'Annunzio, however, could not resist the offer of a critic such as Brunetière, whom he esteemed highly. There was, of course, a serious obstacle to be overcome—that of editorial cuts in the text. The word "coupures" filled him with apprehension. Would Brunetière publish the novel in its original form, or would he demand the suppression of entire pages? D'Annunzio could never repress his indignation against anyone's impairing the integrity of his work. While he wished to be kind to Brunetière, he could not disregard the fact that his novel was completely unlike anything heretofore published by the *Revue des Deux Mondes*. The general tone of *Il Trionfo della morte* was extremely sensual, and he suspected that Brunetière would require some "adoucissements"; he realized too late their extent.

As for *Il Piacere*, agreement was quickly reached with the *Revue de Paris*. While this journal also suggested cuts, on the whole it was not too demanding, and negotiations were carried out smoothly. In fact this novel appeared in French before *Il Trionfo della morte*.

In August 1894 D'Annunzio and Hérelle met for the first time in Venice. This meeting sealed a warm friendship which was to last their lifetime. The unassuming Hérelle, who had gone to Venice filled with uneasiness at the thought of having to face a pretentious and tyrannical author, was delighted to find instead that D'Annunzio was far different from what he had imagined. The young writer's elegant appearance, his expressive eyes, his caressing voice, and his cordial reception enchanted him. During their two weeks in Venice they were constantly together, discussing future plans and working on the translation of *Il Trionfo della morte,* which was to be published the following January. In the course of their work Hérelle was impressed by the author's wide literary knowledge. He noticed that, while D'Annunzio's French pronunciation was rather poor and his syntax hesitant, he was thoroughly familiar with French literature, especially with Flaubert whom he admired and cited almost constantly. They left Venice promising to have another meeting in the Abruzzi the following year, and on parting D'Annunzio gave Hérelle as a gift a copy of the engraving *Il Zodiaco* described in *Il Piacere.*[7]

After Hérelle's departure D'Annunzio became increasingly impatient to see his works in French translation. He wrote him the following November:

> Il faut battre le fer pendant qu'il est chaud. Ainsi, en vérité, voilá notre grande bataille. Dans quelques semaines, *Episcopo et Cie* verra le jour; le 15 décembre commencera la publication de l'*Enfant de volupté;* en janvier celle du *Triomphe;* et en février René Doumic fera sa conférence à la Sorbonne. ... Je vous demande, en cette occasion, la fleur de votre intelligence et de vos meilleurs efforts. Il faut faire vite et bien. Le succès de l'*Enfant de volupté* dépend da la forme. C'est purement un roman de forme, et il faut lui laisser aussi ce je ne sais quoi d'affecté dans le raffinement.[8]

While D'Annunzio showed little concern for the critics' judgment of his works and reacted vehemently only when attacked on moral grounds, he was possessed completely by the problem of translation. But once the translation had been completed to his satisfaction and the editorial scissors had not damaged the manuscript too much, nothing could disturb his conscience as an artist.[9] What often distressed him about Hérelle's work was the use of commonplace expressions and trite phrases. He demanded choice phraseology at all times, even in the rendering of the most ordinary thoughts. He felt in this respect that the translation of *Il Trionfo della morte* was less accurate than that of *L'Intrus.*[10] Hérelle's main concern was, of course, to follow the original as closely as possible; but he intended, above all, to give his translation the character proper to the French language. In Hérelle's lucid expression D'Annunzio at times could not recognize his own style. "C'est de l'excellent Hérelle, mais ce n'est pas du d'Annunzio." A studied refinement was the very essence of his style; therefore, he insisted that this characteristic—even if a defect—should not be obliterated. "Par mon goût singulier," he pointed out to Hérelle, "entre deux expressions également efficaces dont l'une est commune et l'autre insolite, je choisis toujours l'insolite. Or, vous supprimez, avec trop de sévérité, les expressions insolites dont la phrase est hérissée."[11] Evidently, in order to satisfy the author's demands, the translator was expected to *dannunzieggiare*.

Brunetière agreed with Hérelle that the translation had to be, above all, in good French and free from exotic flavor. And so in the course of the work on *Il Trionfo della morte*, D'Annunzio also had Brunetière to contend with. He suspected the editor of the *Revue des Deux Mondes* of wanting to offer his readers not a translation but an adaptation of the novel. "Il faudrait donc écrire en sous titre," he said ironically to Hérelle, "*ad usum Francorum* puisque d'après Brunetière il existe une si profonde différence entre l'homme du nord et l'homme du sud."[12] The obstinacy with which D'Annunzio defended his point of view on the matter of translation revealed his general incompetence and his lack of understanding of the very nature of the French language.[13] He strove at all costs to prevent the Gallicizing of his work, feeling that it had to be offered to the public with the same qualities and whatever defects existed in the original. The literal translation in his opinion would have been the ideal; consequently, instead of paraphrasing in the interest of clarity, he kept insisting that the text be closely followed. He was strongly opposed to the rules of common usage. The French language, he reasoned, was the language of audacities. Why, then, should Hérelle be so timid?

The problem of translation arose again and again, and with each new work it became increasingly delicate and difficult; the more so since D'Annunzio's artistic creation gradually emptied itself of content to become pure stylistic exercise. Unquestionably Hérelle did tend to Gallicize the Italian text, and as a result D'Annunzio felt that his own artistic skill was obscured: hence his resistance to the translator's tendencies.

Il Piacere began to appear in the *Revue de Paris* of December 15, 1894, under the title *L'Enfant de volupté*—a title which D'Annunzio chose in preference to others proposed, such as *Le Dilettantisme, La Jouissance, Le Plaisir*. The text did not suffer much damage; suppressions were limited to about forty pages, which the author approved. On the suggestion of Louis Ganderax, the editor of the review, D'Annunzio reshaped the novel, changing its original architecture. As a result, *L'Enfant de volupté* differs greatly from *Il Piacere* as published by Treves in 1889. In the Italian edition the work was divided into sixteen chapters; the French version was divided into four parts and the number of chapters brought to thirty. Finally, the chapters were disposed in the chronological order of events. In this new arrangement what was "past" or "remembered" in *Il Piacere* became "present" in *L'Enfant de volupté*. Of these changes D'Annunzio retained only the division into four books for subsequent Italian editions, in which he reestablished the original number of chapters and the former order. Thus the Italian volume does not correspond to the French, published by Calmann-Lévy in 1895. In the French translation D'Annunzio eliminated passages which he himself judged too bold and affected, and whose esthetic principle was already outworn. In *L'Enfant de volupté* the licentious traits were attenuated; the author shortened certain supper meetings of Sperelli and his friends with vulgar and dissolute women. He also left out the French phrase he had used in the Italian text: "Ludovic, ne faites pas ça en dansant, je frisonne toute." Strangely enough the suppressed passages correspond more or less to borrowings he had made from Joséphin Péladan's *Initiation sentimentale,* which led critics to suspect that the cutting was prompted by practical rather than esthetic or moral considerations.

The publication of *L'Enfant de volupté* met with resounding success. In the *Gil Blas,* December 16, 1894, Jean Ciseaux wrote: "Eh! bien, oui, cela est saisissant, et, depuis Musset, nous n'avons rien lu de si éperdu et fiévreux que cette première partie de l'*Enfant.*"[14] Ganderax in a long letter to D'Annunzio assured him "qu'on admire beaucoup la première partie de cet admirable *Enfant de volupté.*"[15] In a perceptive study on D'Annunzio, Melchior de Vogüé spoke of the author in these words: "Imaginez du Baudelaire plus chaud, aussi grave, moins mystique; une impudeur effrénée, jamais vulgaire, et qui se fait pardonner par un accent d'antiquité si naturel, si peu suspect de pastiche, que ces pages semblent purifiées par un recul de vingt siècles."[16] He ended his article by expressing his joy "de saluer en Italie un présage certain de Renaissance latine."[17] The "D'Annunzitis" which France had caught with the publication of *L'Intrus* was reaching its acute stage, and for some years D'Annunzio's works delighted a French public greedy for new sensations, somber passions, and artistic refinement.

Despite the generally enthusiastic reception of *L'Enfant de volupté,* a critical reaction began to rise against its excessive sensuality. The novel displeased a number of readers whose moral scruples led them to consider the lewdness in it to be a threat to public morals. Ganderax wrote Hérelle on February 14, 1895, that letters of protest had been sent to the review after the appearance of the second installment. A member of the administrative council of the Calmann-Lévy Publishing Company, to which the *Revue de Paris* belonged, threatened to resign if the publisher persisted in the new trend. "Pour le public français, pour le public de revue," observed Ganderax, "nous sommes allés jusqu'à l'extrême limite."[18] Hérelle informed D'Annunzio of Ganderax' letter, and the author replied: "Demandez à l'aimable Ganderax la photographie de certain membre du Conseil d'Administration. Je désire en orner mon bureau afin que sa présence me maintienne dans le pur sentier de la vertu."[19]

On the other hand *L'Enfant de volupté* brought the author a flood of admiring letters from women. All seemed to express the same reaction—French women were identifying themselves with Maria Ferrès, the ideal creature who, in the novel, contrasted sharply with the extremely sensual Elena Muti, the woman who had exasperated Andrea Sperelli's sensibility. D'Annunzio therefore commented in a letter to Hérelle: "Vraiment seules les femmes ne se scandalisent jamais."[20]

On February 23, 1895, a lecture on D'Annunzio by René Doumic took place at the Sorbonne under the auspices of the Société d'Études Italiennes. Doumic's lecture, published in the *Revue bleue* of March 30, contributed greatly to the success of D'Annunzio's novels. It came most opportunely between the last installment of *L'Enfant de volupté* and the first of *Le Triomphe de la mort*. Although *L'Enfant de volupté* had in some instances been received with certain moral reservations, neither critics nor moralists on the whole judged it too severely. In Italy, on the contrary, critics had been rather violent against D'Annunzio's sensuality. His works were regarded as highly immoral. The aphrodisiac madness displayed in his *Intermezzo di rime* (1884) had aroused a bitter controversy around his name. Prominent critics intervened in the debate, and in the end a volume entitled *Alla ricerca della verecondia* (The Search for Decency)[21] was devoted to their vain logomachy. The volume contained articles by Chiarini, Lodi, Nencioni, and Panzacchi, previously published in periodicals. But these attacks resulted only in spreading the author's reputation. After the *Intermezzo* came *Il Piacere* and *L'Innocente,* arousing a new wave of adverse criticism. "La critique en Italie est misérable," D'Annunzio remarked later in a letter to Hérelle.[22] And in order to take vengeance against the malevolence of the critics, he wrote a volume of verses entitled *Margaritae ante porcos*—a title he changed later to *Poema paradisiaco* so that it could be published. As for the *Margaritae ante porcos*, he wrote to Hérelle in 1893: "Le titre est insolent, mais le public italien mérite pire encore."[23] At the time of his triumphs in France, the Italian public had still not changed its attitude toward him. D'Annunzio was looked upon with disfavor not only because of the impudicity of his works, but also because of his private life which seemed to challenge the most common rules of moral behavior. Moreover, even his style and his orthography irritated the Italian reader. Departing from the common practice of the language, D'Annunzio preferred to write, for example, *de le* instead of *delle, a le* instead of *alle*—unbearable affectations in the Italian, which disappeared in French translation.

On the other hand, it was inevitable that his novels should meet with more success in France than in Italy. His unrestrained sensuality, while pleasing the highly refined and mundane Parisians, could not be accepted by the more conservative and modest Italian public. D'Annunzio, in fact, well aware of this, preferred the French to the Italian readers. In an interview allegedly accorded to Diego Angeli and published in *Le Journal,* May 11, 1895, D'Annunzio is reported to have said: "Je dois avouer qu'à présent j'écris un peu pour la France. C'est le seul pays qui m'ait compris dans les moindres détails. Et je vous assure que quelquefois je serai presque tenté de faire publier mes oeuvres tout droit en France et porté à défendre que de mon vivant elles soient publiées dans une autre langue y compris la mienne."[24] He denied that this interview ever took place. It is certain, however, that he felt more at ease in France than in Italy, especially after the triumph of his novels in Hérelle's translation; the same novels had been received with scorn or indifference in Italy. D'Annunzio felt himself to be a victim of prejudice. Since he was regarded as a licentious writer, the Italian public seemed to find moral impurity even in the inoffensive pages of his works. "Après l'*Intermezzo,* même mes sonnets chrétiens paraissent immoraux en Italie."[25]

Ernest Tissot, in an article published in *La Quinzaine,* September 16, 1902, gave a significant account of the Italian public's hostile attitude toward D'Annunzio even after the enthusiastic acclaim he received in France. In one of the most prominent literary circles in Florence,

Tissot related, he had the imprudence to express his happiness at finding a copy of the first edition of *Il Piacere*. This caused him to be considered indiscreet and cost him some valuable acquaintances. Such a situation sharply contrasted with the favorable atmosphere surrounding D'Annunzio's works in France. When *L'Intrus* appeared in *Le Temps*, Tissot wrote:

> La révélation fut complète. Et bientôt la *Revue de Paris* en publiant *Episcopo et Cie*, l'*Enfant de volupté;* la *Revue des Deux Mondes* en donnant des traductions adroitement tronquées du *Triomphe de la mort* et des *Vierges aux rochers*, nous apprirent à conaître, c'est-à-dire à admirer l'un des plus brillants artistes qu'ait produits le dernier quart du XIXe siècle. Rarement concert d'éloges fut plus unanime. Des revues universitaires aux journaux du boulevard; de M. René Doumic à M. Jean Lorrain, il n'y eut qu'un mode—et ce fut le mode thébain—pour saluer le poète nouveau. Enfin M. de Vogüé sonna le coup de cloche définitif en découvrant en M. d'Annunzio un présage certain de renaissance latine.[26]

If Italy had discovered D'Annunzio, the poet, undoubtedly it was France that revealed the novelist. It was in the latter country, in fact, that his novels enjoyed public favor and won for him European renown. And it was from there that his novels returned to Italy to impose themselves upon the Italian readers who had followed with great astonishment D'Annunzio's literary fortune across the Alps. To account for the regrettable attitude of the Italians toward the author, Tissot remarked: "D'intelligence, de développement et de goût, M. Gabriele d'Annunzio paraît plus Français qu'Italien. Ses premiers modèles furent nos écrivains. Bourget n'a pas eu de disciple préférable. Nos poètes suscitèrent ses enthousiasmes juvéniles."[27] However questionable this statement may be, it contains a substratum of truth. After his first literary success, D'Annunzio underwent many French influences. Between 1881 and 1889 he studied and absorbed several French authors, borrowing from them psychology, plots, and techniques. Baudelaire, Flaubert, Maupassant, Bourget, and many others contributed much in forming his literary taste. But these influences never erased from his mind the first deep imprints left by his Italian masters, especially Carducci. As for Bourget, D'Annunzio had always shown a certain aversion for him, contending that in his works the scientific element overshadows art.

These close or remote affinities between D'Annunzio and French writers were a source of concern for both the author and the translator who, after the publication of *L'Enfant de volupté*, began to fear some adverse critical reaction. They were well aware that critics often acted spinelessly—after singing a chorus of praise, they could easily intone one of blame. In fact, while the general public continued to read D'Annunzio with increasing interest, the question of influences began to be brought up with vague hints of plagiarisms. In order to prevent possible attacks against his works, D'Annunzio suggested that Hérelle write a preface to *Le Triomphe de la mort* which was about to be serialized in the *Revue des Deux Mondes*. This preface should explain in a clear and firm manner the main qualities of the novel and the artistic intentions of its author; it should be the manifesto of D'Annunzio's art, defining his position in relation to other writers of the time, and stressing that he was above all a stylist and the substance of his art consisted solely in his style. D'Annunzio had already written a similar preface for the Italian edition of the novel and it had been published in the *Revue bleue*, August 1894, in a poor translation by Victor Barrucand (among other things the expression "sede dell'arte severa" had been ridiculously rendered by "chaise de l'art sévère"). He felt that it was more appropriate to furnish some notes to Hérelle and have him write a new preface. But the notes were never written and the preface never prepared. The success of the novel was nonetheless brilliant.

The *Triomphe de la mort* crowned the trilogy of the "Novels of the Rose" which included also *L'Enfant de volupté* and *L'Intrus*. The rose was for D'Annunzio the symbol of sensual pleasure—the dominant element in the three novels. The *Triomphe de la mort* is undoubtedly the best of the three and perhaps the best novel D'Annunzio ever wrote. It had been highly praised by French critics even before its publication in translation. In 1894 Paul Bourget wrote to Hérelle: "J'ai entendu plusieurs personnes, entre autres Eugène Melchior de Vogüé, parler du *Triomphe de la mort* comme d'un chef-d'oeuvre, ce qui ne m'a pas étonné après ce que j'ai lu de Gabriele d'Annunzio."[28] Brunetière, in a letter to D'Annunzio, expressed the opinion that the second part of *Le Triomphe de la mort*, entitled "La maison paternelle," was a masterpiece and that he expected it to make a great impression on the readers. D'Annunzio had no doubt concerning the success of the novel, but as the time for publication approached, he became more and more fearful that Brunetière would slash the text. From hints which Hérelle had conveyed to D'Annunzio, it was clear that the editor of the *Revue des Deux Mondes* was contemplating "textual improvements." The mixed feelings aroused by *L'Enfant de volupté* on moral grounds caused Brunetière, as a moralist critic, to take special precautions to forestall adverse criticism; the more so since the previous novel had already created a certain prejudice regarding the nature of D'Annunzio's works. The *Triomphe* began to appear on June 1, 1895. D'Annunzio had to yield reluctantly to Brunetière's pressure concerning what he called "brutal suppressions." But this was not all. In addition to authorized cuts many others not approved by D'Annunzio were made, and the novel was published frightfully mutilated. In all, more than one hundred pages were amputated from the text. D'Annunzio was greatly upset, but he realized the futility of trying to prevent Brunetière's censorship. Thus in a resigned but deeply annoyed tone he wrote to Hérelle:

> Il est inutile que je prenne aujourd'hui la défense des chapitres incriminés. ... M. Brunetière a gardé mon livre en main pendant un an. Pourquoi ses observations viennent-elles avec ce retard et à l'improviste? Et, de plus, est-il permis de soumettre une oeuvre au découpage comme un saucisson quelconque? ... Avoir travaillé pendant quinze ans avec une fière obstination contre tous les obstacles, et s'entendre opposer maintenant "le public" et le "commun des lecteurs." ... Je laisse volontiers aux Theuriet, aux Berkeley et Mme Caro l'honneur de la première page dans la *Revue des Deux Mondes*.[29]

Nevertheless, D'Annunzio could not long conceal his resentment, and in a note to Brunetière he declared that he would never again deal with him in matters of publication.

In October of that year D'Annunzio met in Venice Viscount Georges d'Avenel, of the editorial board of the *Revue des Deux Mondes,* who expressed his personal admiration for the novel and his regret at the deletions made in the text. D'Avenel indicated that they had been made over the opposition of the editorial staff, and he agreed with D'Annunzio that the *Triomphe* should have been published in its entirety or not at all. But after the tide of anger receded, D'Annunzio obviously agreed to some of the omissions, since in the publication of the work in book form (Calmann-Lévy, 1896) he did not entirely restore the passages eliminated in the *Revue des Deux Mondes.*

Despite mutilations the *Triomphe de la mort* made a deep impression on the public. Édouard Rod devoted a full article to the novel in the *Journal des débats;* De Vogüé had already given a perceptive analysis in the *Revue des Deux Mondes,* January 1, 1895, just a few months before publication. Referring to the imaginative power and the richness of the language in the work, he said: "Les lecteurs trouveront très prochainement ici une traduction du roman, au moins ce qu'on en peut traduire. Aucune publication française n'a osé donner intégralement les inventions de ce terrible homme. Il faut couper des pages, parfois des chapitres. ... La langue italienne a le privilège ... de braver dans ces mots tout ce que brave le latin."[30] René Doumic, in his lecture at the Sorbonne, expressed himself in these terms:

> Le *Triomphe de la mort* est jusqu'ici l'oeuvre la plus complète qu'on doive à M. d'Annunzio, celle où il a réalisé son effort le plus vigoureux, où il a mis le plus de pensée et d'art. ... Nou sommes assez loin de la peinture légère et superficielle de la volupté. Ayant commencé par ne décrire que le plaisir et que les joies des sens, d'Annunzio en arrive à nous faire toucher ce qu'il y a de troublant et de fatal dans la passion.[31]

Some passages of the novel were reprinted in the *Annales politiques et littéraires* with this introductory note: "Nous offrons à la curiosité de nos lecteurs, une des rares pages qui se puissent détacher du dernier roman de M. Gabriele d'Annunzio. ... C'est un hymne à la nature, un tableau rustique d'une exquise et poétique fraîcheur."[32]

The trilogy of the "Novels of the Rose" brought D'Annunzio widespread popularity in France, and his literary production was followed with close interest by the French critics. His ardent sensuality impassioned the mundane; his brilliant style pleased the literati. In the French admiration for D'Annunzio there was, as René Doumic put it: "... une sorte d'étonnement. Car ces transports de la volupté physique nous déconcertent quelque peu. L'amour est chez nous plus raisonnable, plus disert, plus spirituel, plus tendre aussi, plus recueilli et plus intimement douloureux."[33] In D'Annunzio love is not merely an abstract feeling or an idea born from the contemplation of eternal beauty: it is an all-inclusive sentiment conceived as physical and psychological torture and delight. It is at times even perversion. D'Annunzio's works contain elements and attitudes which liken him to Baudelaire—for example, a mingled Catholicism and debauchery, sensuality and religious emotion, sometimes even spiced with incestuous overtones. In *L'Enfant de volupté,* Andrea Sperelli's room, which was the setting for his perverted love affairs, had the appearance of a chapel, adorned with religious images and sacramentals. Tullio Hermil, in *L'Intrus,* tries to convince himself that Giuliana is not his wife, but his sister, as he called her, so that their love relation might acquire the illicit charm of incest.

D'Annunzio's perverted notions of love produced conflicting reactions in the readers in accordance with their own predispositions. Most of them took great pleasure in these licentious pictures, since the sincerity of tone in which characters expressed themselves rendered quite plausible even the excesses of physical voluptuousness. Beside the perverted creatures one often finds the pure ones who spiritualize whatever they touch. Such was Maria Ferrès in *L'Enfant de volupté*, whose creation atoned for all of the sensuality D'Annunzio displayed in the book. Those who did not approve of the author's morbid sensuality were nevertheless compelled to acknowledge the artistic qualities of his work. Adolphe Brisson wrote: "Tous les hommes, et aussi beaucoup de femmes s'éprennent de ces récits, où s'étale et déborde une sensualité effrénée. Les hardiesses de Maupassant sont dépassées. Il y aurait, dans ces peintures, quelque chose de bestial et de répugnant, si la brutalité n'en était atténuée par l'éclat admirable des descriptions et un profond amour de la nature."[34]

3. D'Annunzio and the "Latin Renaissance"

THE RAPID SUCCESS of D'Annunzio in France was witnessed with astonishment by the Italian public which had theretofore looked with distaste upon the unrestrained licentiousness of his works. But, unacceptable as D'Annunzio was in Italy, so much more enthusiastically was he received in France. In his eulogistic article of 1895 Melchior de Vogüé wrote: "Quelques fragments de son oeuvre, traduits en français, ont fait instantanément à M. d'Annunzio un nom célèbre à Paris et dans tous les cercles lettrés d'Europe."[1] Romain Rolland sadly gave this picture of the D'Annunzio craze in France in the nineties:

> A peine eut-il paru, habillé par Hérelle, son tailleur français, qu'il fut le lion de Paris, A l'*Enfant de volupté,* les femmes ouvrirent leurs rêves, faute de pouvoir ouvrir leur lit. Et le plus beau de l'affaire fut qu'aussi bien que les caillettes, les esthètes, le monde des "libertins" ... le monde aussi des "bien-pensants" et des académiciens revendiqua l'homme au nom d'ange. L'aigre et funèbre Doumic paraphrasait en chaire l'éloge du *Triomphe de la mort.* Chacun y trouvait son compte, les hommes du plaisir et ceux de la pénitence. Les deux revues rivales, la *Revue des Deux Mondes* et la *Revue de Paris,* se disputaient ses prémices.[2]

It is to be noted, however, that the strong French interest in D'Annunzio, while short-lived, was not pure whim: it stemmed from the lassitude and dissatisfaction with existing cultural trends and from a profound desire for a literary revival and change. The naturalist writers had strictly practiced the narrow theories of their school, which aimed at reproducing certain external aspects of the bourgeois and rustic world. The result was a superficial and coarse picture of life; and despite the talent of such artists as Zola and Maupassant the prose representing this movement lacked real appeal. The interminable descriptions of almost geographical precision, and the abuse of so-called local expressions made it colorless and tedious. Furthermore, the contemporary reaction against science facilitated the rapid infiltration of the literature of the North which accelerated the dissolution of naturalism. English, Germans, Russians, and Scandinavians, representing quite diverse tendencies, were received in France without discrimination. A wave of spiritualism passed into literature, transforming perceptibly the brutal atmosphere of naturalism. With the introduction of Russian literature by E. Dupuy and Eugène-Melchior de Vogüé[3] a sentiment of pity and evangelic charity, a desire for human solidarity invaded the literary domain, thus attenuating the coarseness, vulgarity, and indifference of naturalism toward the human creature. Writers threw themselves with enthusiasm and passion into this spiritualistic wave which swept over Europe, and turned now to Renan, who became their guide in the reaction against naturalism. Beginning with *A rebours,* Huysmans rejected materialistic theories and turned to mysticism; Bourget, in his *Le Disciple,* showed the disastrous effects of Taine's theories. In Italy, Verga asserted that naturalism was, after all, a method and that nothing prevented the conceiving of a mystical novel in naturalist form. Capuana, who had at first declared himself an atheist, became a believer and acknowledged the emptiness of science and its failure to satisfy the profound exigencies of the human spirit. Matilde Serao affirmed that science had stifled artistic imagination and that the time had come to free oneself from its yoke.[4]

But most of the writers lacked the strong literary education which would have permitted them to produce living works. While eager to renew themselves they were hampered by the lack of a new literary style. The poverty of the naturalist school weighed like an hereditary taint upon young writers. René Doumic, in a study devoted to the "Jeunes," often complained that writers of talent were unable to create great literary works because of the wide gaps in their classical education; hence, a large number of mediocre pieces, and not one living work. The invasion of northern literatures, however, aroused in turn a similar reaction. About 1890 the public appeared to have had enough not only of naturalism but also of Russians, Scandinavians, Slavic evangelism, and Nordic mistiness. D'Annunzio became known in France at the most favorable moment. "Ce Latin," wrote René Doumic, "nous arrive au moment où nous commençons à nous fatiguer de ce qu'on appelle d'un mot et en bloc: les littératures du Nord. ... Nous nous tournons vers ceux qui sont du Midi. Nous soupirons après une Renaissance latine. Il nous semble que M. d'Annunzio peut être l'un des ouvriers de cette renaissance."[5] This aspiration toward a "Latin renaissance," which in poetry found expression in the "École romane française," manifested itself as a tendency to revive the cult of formal beauty, of the classic spirit, and of national tradition. The movement stemmed also from a sort of national pride. Many French writers felt that to seek inspiration in the literature of the North was to depart from the national literary tradition and become slaves of foreign literatures. At a time when France aspired to national revenge, the idea of a "Latin renaissance"—the awakening of the classic spirit and art—was to find many enthusiastic adherents, especially during the last decade of the century when the nationalists and the democrats engaged in the long and bitter polemic of the "Affaire Dreyfus." It seems that nationalism was esthetic before being political, and although D'Annunzio had not yet shown any political tendency, the antidemocrats saw in him the awakening of the Latin spirit. When Enrico Thovez in January 1896 accused the author of plagiarism in the Gazzetta letteraria of Turin, it was the proponents of the "Latin renaissance" who undertook D'Annunzio's defense in France—Charles Maurras in the Revue encyclopédique of February 8, and Gaston Deschamps in Le Temps of January 26 and February 2.

Jules Lemaître, in a patriotic article published in the Revue des Deux Mondes, December 15, 1894, expressed his hatred for the literary influence of the North and predicted a rebirth of the Latin spirit as reaction to that influence. He pointed out that the Russians and the Scandinavians had nothing new to offer: they were merely giving back to France what they had received from her earlier in a different form. Lemaître's article provided Melchior de Vogüé with the opportunity to state, in his essay on D'Annunzio, the problem of the "Latin renaissance," a subject of much discussion in literary circles. In analyzing the works of the Italian writer he tried to show that Lemaître's prediction was already more than half acomplished. According to Vogüé, however, there was "renaissance et non pas réaction contre le Nord," and this was clearly proved by D'Annunzio's works. "Nous sommes bien obligés de constater," he said, "par les aveux mêmes du porte-bannière de cette renaissance, que le plus latin des génies latins a été influencé et foncièrement modifié par les littératures du Nord."[6]

Although the two points of view differed, it is nonetheless clear that the need for a literary revival in the Latin world was strongly felt. Théodore de Wyzewa expressed the same aspiration toward a "Latin renaissance" in an article in the Revue des Deux Mondes, September 15, 1895. "Aucune espérance," he wrote, "ne saurait nous être plus chère, en effet, que celle d'un prochain renouveau du génie latin."[7] And after pointing out that the literatures of the North had not offered "la satisfaction durable et profonde que nous en avions attendue," he added: "Si quelque forme de beauté nouvelle doit nous venir du dehors, nous avons l'impression que seules les races méridionales pourront garder en dépôt ces précieuses vertus classiques, la clarté, la mesure, la simplicité, dont le goût renaît chez nous tous les jours plus vif."[8] D'Annunzio's novels seemed to have broken the spell which for many years had prevented French readers from taking an interest in the "littératures des pays latins." It remained to be seen, in Wyzewa's opinion, whether D'Annunzio's works were the independent manifestation of a powerful artistic personality, or the sign of a general revival of the Latin spirit, as Vogüé believed.

It was in particular the great literary activity in Italy which aroused hope for the awakening of the Latin world. After 1870, with the problems of the Risorgimento no longer existing, Italian literature seemed to acquire a new and growing vitality. The number of schools and tendencies—verism, regionalism, socialism, individualism, mysticism— attested to a wide range of literary endeavors. The works of Fogazzaro, Serao, Giacosa, and many others were received in France with much interest. Was this the prelude to a literary renaissance in the Third Italy? In which direction was Italian literature moving? Hoping to find an answer to these questions, Ugo Ojetti undertook to conduct an inquiry in 1894, similar to that of Jules Huret in France three years earlier. The results, published in 1895 under the title Alla scoperta dei letterati (Milan: Dumolard), were significant. Of the twenty-six prominent writers interviewed by Ojetti nearly all felt the need for a change in literary trends. Even the verists Verga, Capuana, and Serao were forced to admit that naturalism as they had practiced it was at a dead end, and that, in order to revitalize literature, it was necessary to return to religion and idealism. All acknowledged further the necessity of restoring formal beauty, although some felt that Italy did not yet have a language capable of expressing new ideas and emotions.

But what was the novelty in D'Annunzio's works, if not the refined taste for formal beauty? It was this quality which made him the "présage certain" of a Latin renaissance. Perhaps he was the only one among the young writers in Italy to possess a decisively personal language and style, free from naturalistic coarseness or any form of academic jargon. If in his first novels there is a morbid and decadent atmosphere, there is as well a marked taste for classical perfection, for clarity and balance, which are the signs of the "Latin renaissance." The language he had created for himself, rich in ornate phrases and in uncommon rhythms, was a powerful artistic instrument. In addition, D'Annunzio introduced a new notion of art as the search for pure expression (a notion which Benedetto Croce was to theorize extensively), and he set the example for a sort of modern classicism tending to condense romantic sensibility into a plastic form. While drawing most of his inspiration from Russian evangelism and Nietzschean individualism, he strove constantly to be, above all, an artist, a creator of images, and a master of style. Most of the Italians, even those he strongly influenced, deliberately denied him merit. There are even today those who question whether D'Annunzio was truly a great artist. But it was precisely the literary qualities which his compatriots disliked that conquered the French public. Sensuality and lyricism acquired a new form in his works and gave a lively impression of art and beauty. His novels proved that the literature of the North was a rich source of inspiration. He had undergone many influences, and the mark of each was clearly perceptible in his works: in his short articles his indebtedness to Maupassant is evident; in *Il Piacere* he echoes Bourget to some extent; in *Giovanni Episcopo* and *L'Innocente* he is dominated by the Russian novel; and in his *Vergini delle rocce* he is a disciple of Nietzsche. But none of his relations with foreign cultures had substantially altered the traits of his personality. The depth of Northern thought and the sensuality of Latin temperament are fused in him without lessening his artictic originality. Into the mistiness of the North he seems to have injected light from Italian poetry, and by so doing transformed the nature of whatever he borrowed.

D'Annunzio's example provided the opportunity in France for examining the problem of intellectual exchange between European countries. Was foreign literary infiltration endangering the character of the national literature? Jules Lemaître believed that it was, and he insisted, in his article against the literatures of the North, on the necessity of a revival of the Latin tradition in order to resist this nordic "invasion." Vogüé and Doumic held the opposite view; and they used D'Annunzio, one of the most eclectic of artists, as the example to prove their point. The Latin renaissance which Vogüé and Doumic advocated, and which they foresaw in D'Annunzio, was a question of form rather than content. D'Annunzio personified the intellectual cosmopolitanism of the time; his works represented the synthesis of the trends dominating European literature—dilettantism, sensuality, egotism, the worship of beauty, and so forth. His originality consisted in his stylistic refinement. "L'art de M. d'Annunzio, et c'est ce qui lui constitue une espèce d'originalité," wrote François Carry, "est d'avoir su fondre toutes ces influences diverses dans le fin creuset de son imagination latine et d'avoir tiré de cet alliage d'éléments disparates un métal éclatant."[9] What one might consider "Latin" in D'Annunzio was his style, which in the words of Carry, "possède la limpidité et la sonorité du cristal."[10]

This, however, did not suffice to make of him the standard-bearer for the "Latin renaissance." And the opponents of this pretended literary rebirth contended that to point to D'Annunzio as the expression of the Latin spirit meant to take into account only the stylistic aspect of his works. As for anything else, they argued, he lacked the strong personality capable of motivating a renaissance. Pure sensuality and plastic beauty alone could not bring about a literary renewal. Only a powerful and unsophisticated genius could produce such a miracle, and D'Annunzio, in their opinion, was not that genius. To some critics the question of a "Latin renaissance," ignited by D'Annunzio's introduction into France, was but a deliberate move to discredit certain French authors and to arouse nationalistic feelings. In order to believe that this renaissance was definitely "Latin," one would have to find in D'Annunzio less influence from the North and less hostility from his compatriots. Remy de Gourmont saw in this alleged revival of the Latin world a mere attempt at propaganda, and after having praised D'Annunzio in 1893 in the *Mercure de France*,[11] he turned against him three years later. In a letter to D'Annunzio, Gourmont wrote:

... Je vous crois trop intelligent pour admettre la sincérité d'un enthousiasme touchant la Renaissance latine; vous savez, ayant lu Tolstoï,
Nietzsche, Ibsen, et les Français et les Anglais, vous savez qu'il n'y a
pas plus, à cette heure, d'esprit latin qu'il n'y a d'esprit russe ou d'esprit
scandinave; il y a un esprit européen et, ici et là, des individus qui s'af-
firment uniques, personnels et entiers. Alors la prétention d'une Renaissance latine se dévêt et la voici nue: joujou mal fait avec lequel on
voulait amuser le public. ... Prenez un lys et mettez-vous à la tête du
cortège: nous célébrerons dignement les funérailles de la Renaissance
latine.[12]

The letter continued in a sharp and ironical tone against Vogüé
(who, according to Gourmont, disesteemed in Baudelaire, Maeterlinck,
and Verlaine the very qualities he praised in D'Annunzio) and against
Gaston Deschamps and René Doumic: "... Et que fait M. Gaston
Deschamps et que font les doumicoulets sinon de vivre à même d'au-
trui?" Wishing to strike at his literary enemies, Gourmont lashed at
their idol, who had little to do with the idea of the "Latin renaissance."
In fact, ironically enough, D'Annunzio himself disagreed with Vogüé.
This becomes clear from a conversation he had with Ernest Tissot in
Milan in May 1896. "Bien qu'il évite de se pronouncer," reported
Tissot, "M. d'Annunzio ne paraît point aussi persuadé de cette renaissance que son éloquent critique" (Vogüé).[13] The polemic on the subject did not last long, however. D'Annunzio's works had revealed no
new truth hidden within the soul of the Latin race. In addition, his
esthetics soon underwent some deviations. His art lost more and more
in content to become pure form. This artistic effort toward the realization of formal beauty placed him beyond the narrow limits of any
national tradition in a higher domain where all national distinctions
vanish.

4. The Novels for the Elite: *Les Vierges aux rochers,*
   Le Feu

AFTER the cycle of the "Novels of the Rose," or sensual pleasure,
D'Annunzio conceived a new trilogy—that of the "Novels of the
Lily," or intellectual pleasure, which was to comprise *Le Vergini delle
rocce, La Grazia,* and *L'Annunciazione.* But of this trilogy the first

novel alone was written; the others remained in the preparatory stage. If the "Novels of the Rose" are characterized by a strong note of sensuality, ardent lyricism, and a certain tendency to psychological analysis, *Le Vergini delle rocce* was of an entirely different nature. Here the author tried to realize his artistic ideal—form. He was not a psychologist, and if he used psychological analysis in his previous novels, he did so as a mere pretext for giving expression to his artistic ideal. Critics in fact never took his psychology seriously: they studied instead his stylistic method resulting in such unusual literary effects.

Le Vergini delle rocce was published in Italy in October 1895 by Treves after being serialized in the periodical *Convito*. Ernest Tissot and Édouard Rod devoted two articles to the novel, in the *Revue bleue*, October 26, and the *Journal des débats*, November 15, respectively, in order to acquaint the French public with the new work. By that time most of it had been translated by Hérelle and negotiations had begun for its publication in France. The *Revue de Paris* and the *Revue des Deux Mondes* had already made advances, but after the mutilation of *Le Triomphe de la mort* and the cuts, though minor, in the other works, D'Annunzio decided to remain firm before any "brunetièresques" or "ganderaxiennes" attempts. "Je ne renoncerai," he wrote Hérelle, "ni à une ligne, ni à un mot, jamais, même au prix de ne jamais publier le roman. Je considère les *Vierges aux rochers* comme mon premier livre; et j'ai composé ceci avec une terrible rigueur de pensée et de style."[1] He stressed that he was not concerned with the reaction of the average reader, since he did not intend to become "un amuseur du public." He felt, therefore, that no understanding could be reached either with Brunetière or with Ganderax.

Despite his hostility to Brunetière's methods, D'Annunzio finally agreed to give the novel to the *Revue des Deux Mondes*, while he promised another work—*Il Fuoco*, which he had just begun to write —to the *Revue de Paris*. The translation of *Le Vergini delle rocce* required careful work because of its stylistic luxuriance. But Hérelle brilliantly overcame the many difficulties in the text, and the French Academy bestowed upon him the Prix Langlois in May 1897 in recognition of his translation. In style the book was rich and oratorical. The long and complicated sentences, reminiscent of Latin construction, gave more eloquence to his prose. But the old problem of translation arose again; and D'Annunzio was more exacting than ever, especially in *Le Vergini delle rocce*, considered by him to be a stylistic *tour de force* in which he strove to realize fully his idea of art as pure expression. The avowed aim of his book was to capture the refined reader.

While Hérelle did not care much for the work, his preference being for the "Novels of the Rose," D'Annunzio was extremely proud of his new form of artistic expression, for it was closer to his temperament as a man of letters. He remarked to Hérelle: "Beaucoup me sont reconnaissants d'avoir osé écrire un grand poème en cette époque dominée par les Zola, les Marcel Prévost et les Georges Ohnet."[2] D'Annunzio did not at all expect to meet the same popular success with *Le Vergini delle rocce* as with his previous novels in France. The work had been written for the cultivated elite, and they alone could appreciate the stylistic beauty, the rare and refined expression, which the author strove to achieve in his constant and laborious effort toward pure form. This was for D'Annunzio one more reason to insist upon close translation. He demanded that "la solennité et l'ampleur latines," and the "caractère un peu oratoire" be preserved, and he pointed to Bossuet as an example for Hérelle to follow. Although he seemed to be satisfied with the translation in a general way, he never ceased to complain. "... Je constate aujourd'hui que la traduction est d'autant plus faible que vous vous éloignez davantage de la lettre. Souvent—pour cette raison—la musique des phrases et leur signification sont totalement détruites."[3] What would remain of such a book if "l'énergie et la beauté du style" were destroyed? He strongly reminded Hérelle of the fact that he meant to write "un poème et non un roman: ou, plus précisément un roman dans le sens poétique du mot."[4]

But while D'Annunzio concerned himself this time only with the translation (not anticipating any cuts, since the novel was in no way objectionable from the moral point of view), Brunetière was quietly contemplating the usual editorial "improvements." After keeping the manuscript for a long time without comment, he began to demand changes when the moment for publication approached. He made revisions, not for reasons of decency, but only to lighten the tone of the book for the general public—the public about which D'Annunzio cared the least. Brunetière was, of course, acting in the interest of the *Revue des Deux Mondes,* which aimed at reaching as many readers as possible rather than confining itself to the refined élite alone. In a letter to Hérelle, immediately made known to D'Annunzio, he asked merely for the suppression of the "Prologue" which made up the first part of the novel. Since *Le Vergini delle rocce* was to be followed by

L'*Annunciazione* and *La Grazia*, also promised to the *Revue des Deux Mondes*, Brunetière felt that the prologue could be understood only after reading the last book of the "trilogy"; there was, therefore, the danger that the public, failing to grasp the meaning of it, would judge the entire work from the prologue and dispense with reading any further. Moreover, after the stir which had burst out in January 1896 over D'Annunzio's plagiarisms, it became necessary to proceed cautiously. D'Annunzio, on the other hand, was not disturbed in the least by possible attacks that Brunetière anticipated; he argued that his enemies would always be enemies with or without the suppression of the first part of the novel. "J'ai beaucoup d'ennemis, mais les ennemis sont et seront ma force."[5] In any case Brunetière was concerned with the public's reaction to the novel, and he was not optimistic, even after the prologue had been eliminated and some other parts of the work had undergone the customary "adoucissements." In a letter to Hérelle, in fact, he clearly pointed out his preoccupations: "Il ne faut pas nous dissimuler que, si l'on attend impatiemment les *Vierges aux rochers*, il n'entre dans cette impatience que très peu de bienveillance. On ferait volontiers payer à l'auteur la rapidité de son succès; et, pour peu qu'il y prête, nous en aurons pour deux ou trois ans alors à remonter le courant."[6] He indicated also that if D'Annunzio agreed to the sacrifice of the prologue there would be little to eliminate in the rest of the novel: "... et je ne lui demanderai d'adoucissements—moi Français! —qu'en ce qui touche la personnalité de ce pauvre roi Humbert."[7]

Evidently this time he did not wish to displease D'Annunzio and he did not appear to be so unyielding as he had been with *Le Triomphe de la mort*. Nevertheless, D'Annunzio did not surrender easily. "Y a-t-il donc vraiment quelque chose d'extraordinaire et d'intolérable dans ces pages? Ou bien paraîtront-elles simplement ennuyeuses? Pauvre littérature, réduite à amuser les imbéciles et les dames!"[8] He complained to Brunetière that the question of the "Prologue" should have been brought up at the time of the agreement concerning the publication of the novel. But as usual he finally left it to Brunetière to do whatever he chose, though he did not stop grumbling: "Je le laisse libre de faire de mon oeuvre le massacre qu'il lui plaira, mais je ne puis donner mon consentiment. Qu'il agisse à son gré, mais sans me consulter."[9]

Les Vierges aux rochers began to appear on September 1, 1896; the following year it was published in book form by Calmann-Lévy, and the "Prologue" omitted in the *Revue des Deux Mondes* was restored.

D'Annunzio, however, chose to leave out a second prologue which Brunetière had retained.

The novel was not as well received as his previous ones. There were in *Les Vierges aux rochers* none of the things the readers had admired in the trilogy of the "Novels of the Rose." But this relative unsuccess did not discourage D'Annunzio, who had no illusions concerning the average reader's preferences. *Les Vierges aux rochers* unfolds on a higher sphere, in a world of mystery and art where only the elite can penetrate. The general public, therefore, unable to appreciate the artistic qualities of the work as conceived by the author, found it thoroughly boring. In the preface of the *Trionfo della morte* D'Annunzio had already announced his literary theories, the realization of which rendered his writings accessible only to a small number of "élus." His artistic aim was in fact to create a work of poetry and beauty in plastic and symphonic prose, rich in images and music. The ideal work of modern prose would be, to his mind, the one possessing the musical rhythm of a poem, combining the most diverse qualities of the written word, harmonizing all forms of knowledge and dreams, fusing the precision of science with the seduction of mystery, appearing not to imitate but to continue the work of nature. This artistic ideal he tried to realize for the first time in *Le Vergini delle rocce*. "Le mérite le moins incontestable des *Vierges aux rochers*," wrote François Carry, "quoiqu'il échappe au lecteur français, réside dans la perfection du style."[10] André Maurois has expressed thus his admiration for D'Annunzio's artistic talent: "L'une des plus fortes émotions de mon adolescence a été la première lecture en italien des *Vierges aux rochers*. Jamais, fût-ce dans les plus grands poètes, je n'avais trouvé langue plus belle, ni phrases plus musicales."[11]

This novel marked an artistic evolution in the author. He departed from the psychological and sensual novel and yielded to the influence of Nietzsche's philosophy and to his own fundamental tendencies. In this novel he developed a sort of esthetic symbolism. His characters lacked psychological truth and became pure abstractions, suggesting Maeterlinck's influence. "Ces princesses," pointed out Adolphe Brisson, "sont proches parents des princesses de Maurice Maeterlinck; elles sont lointaines, vagues, et aptes à être parées de mille grâces, au gré de l'imagination de chacun."[12]

The symbolic character of the work, the haughty detachment felt in it—a detachment typical of the "superman" artist D'Annunzio—had little attraction for the average reader, indifferent to the perfection of style and the musical rhythm of D'Annunzio's prose. In Brisson's opinion the work "ne renferme pas de ces peintures qui ont fait le succès du *Triomphe de la mort*"; therefore, some readers, not finding what they had hoped for, declared the book to be boring. Doubtless there was some misunderstanding concerning the author. After his first novels it was generally thought that the natural domain of his art was sensuality and morbid passion. Only few critics sensed that this was not D'Annunzio's true genre, as the author was primarily a master of style. François Carry wrote in this regard: "On peut regretter la première manière de M. d'Annunzio, plus humaine et pourtant plus accessible à la masse du public. Mais il est incontestable que sa dernière manière est une manifestation plus personnelle et plus franche de son talent, dont elle constitue, pour ainsi dire, l'aboutissement logique."[13]

After *Le Vergini delle rocce* the public expected *La Grazia* and *L'Annunciazione*, since, according to the general outline of the trilogy of the "Novels of the Lily," the same characters were to reappear in the two novels as in a "roman-fleuve." *La Grazia* was to be a tragic novel, the *punctum saliens* of the story (the death of Anatolia and the folly of Violante); *L'Annunciazione* the novel of happiness.[14] But from 1896 on, poetry and the theater absorbed the author, and the two novels never reached their finished form. They were announced as forthcoming several times in French journals and on book jackets, along with titles of other works which similarly were never composed. D'Annunzio enjoyed attracting the public's attention with sensational announcements, but always felt free to change his plans and to follow the inspiration of the moment. For example, in October 1892 he announced that he was working on a new novel entitled *La Nemica*, which Hérelle was to translate and publish in the *Revue des Deux Mondes*. Later *La Nemica* was to be a play; but it was never finished. A scene from it, found in manuscript, was published in 1938 by the review *Dante* (Paris) in its May–June issue. In June 1896 Maurice Muret spoke with enthusiasm of a book on Sardinia to be published by D'Annunzio—a book of lyrical exaltation, descriptions, and impressions. But it was never printed. On January 27, 1899, the *Journal* made the announcement that Treves would soon publish no less than five new novels by D'Annunzio: *La Grazia, L'Annunciazione, Il Fuoco, Il Dittatore, Il Trionfo della vita*. "A côté de cela," the announcement said, "M. d'Annunzio met la dernière main à deux volumes de poésie, un volume de critique littéraire et un volume de nouvelles."[15] In October 1903 *La Presse* (Paris) announced *La Grazia* as finished and ready for publication in the *Revue des Deux Mondes*.

Of these works only *Il Fuoco* was destined to be published; after *Le Vergini* D'Annunzio devoted most of his efforts to its composition. The book was to be a part of a new trilogy—that of the "Novels of the Pomegranate" or of esthetic pleasure, in which the author meant to express the triumph of art. According to *Le Gaulois*, December 22, 1900, the trilogy of the "Pomegranate" would also show the difference between the Germanic and the Latin character. However, *La Vittoria dell'uomo* (which D'Annunzio also called *Il Dittatore*) and *Il Trionfo della vita* (which were to continue the story begun in *Il Fuoco*) were never written. *Il Fuoco* was finished in February 1900, and by that time a good part of the translation had already been completed, for Hérelle was working on it while D'Annunzio wrote the novel. In fact the book appeared in Italy in March 1900, and the following May the *Revue de Paris* began the serialization of it. Brunetière had hoped to have *Il Fuoco* for the *Revue des Deux Mondes*, and when he learned that D'Annunzio had committed the novel to the rival journal he complained strongly against the author. "... Si j'ai tout de suite accepté de publier les trois Romans du Lys," he wrote to Hérelle, "c'est que je désirais vivement l'attacher uniquement à la *Revue des Deux Mondes*. ... C'est à vous, cher Monsieur, pour le moment que je fais ces doléances me réservant d'en entretenir d'Annunzio quand nous aurons réglé l'affaire des *Vierges aux rochers*."[16]

Il Fuoco was the work into which D'Annunzio put all of his art and all of his stylistic virtuosity in an effort to attain perfection and beauty. The particular artistic qualities of the novel, such as harmony and color, presented delicate problems for the translator—problems entailing a strange verbal alchemy. There was in the work something untranslatable owing partly to the strongly Italian character of the expression. Eduardo Scarfoglio, who had seen a few pages of the manuscript, said to D'Annunzio: "Our dear Hérelle has his work cut out for him."[17] He was not mistaken. Hérelle found the novel too long, cumbersome, slow moving, and sometimes obscure. In translating he often had to confine himself to literal exactness, renouncing the special rhythmical qualities of the original. The first part of *Il Fuoco*, for instance, contained a long speech by Stelio Effrena meant to give an example of his genius. This speech—all lyrical eloquence, full of luxuriant images and musical rhythm—became stilted and artificial in translation, where the verbal wealth and the ornate style lost their original luster. Hérelle suggested lightening the speech which, placed so early in the story, would spoil the beauty of the work. D'Annunzio agreed and was prepared to make the necessary change when the problem of translation complicated matters and resulted in a quarrel between author and translator. As the proofs began to come off the press, Hérelle corrected them and sent them to D'Annunzio for approval. The latter, often dissatisfied with the translation, made additional changes, and instead of returning the proofs to the translator for final revision (especially on the changes made) sent them directly to the *Revue de Paris,* requesting Ganderax to make no further alterations. D'Annunzio expected thus to have the last word on the translation. But his corrections were often inappropriate from the linguistic point of view, and he could not bring himself to admit that he might be wrong. "... Je suis le seul responsable de mon art," he wrote to Ganderax, "et je veux bien être jugé avec tous mes défauts, que je cultive, comme vous savez, passionnément."[18]

Hérelle, on the other hand, felt the responsibility for the translation he signed, and claimed for himself the right to give the final approval. He complained energetically about D'Annunzio's sending the proofs directly to the *Revue de Paris* instead of returning them to him. In his opinion D'Annunzio's corrections were not always acceptable; they were even occasionally laughable. Ganderax agreed. The barbarisms, awkward phrases, and improprieties of expression proposed by the author made the French text seem like a schoolboy's translation. D'Annunzio in turn maintained that Hérelle's translation was false to his meaning, and pointed out a number of phrases rendered into French in a rather banal manner. His overly-refined artistic taste permitted him to see clearly the failing of the translation. What he demanded was not absurd, it was simply impossible to achieve. In this quarrel author and translator appealed to Ganderax and through him exchanged uncomplimentary remarks. In a letter to Ganderax, D'Annunzio wrote: "Je vous ai dit déjà que, dans la première livraison il y a des choses détestables qui *danno la pelle d'oca*" (give one goose flesh).[19] And Hérelle, answering through Ganderax, said: "S'il arrive que mes traductions lui donnent *la peau d'oie,* certaines de ses corrections donneraient la chair de poule à un Malgache de l'Exposition" (would make a Madagascan's flesh creep).[20]

However, the misunderstanding was settled and the work was finished. D'Annunzio later wrote Hérelle in a more conciliatory tone admitting that, in a general way, the translation was more than satisfactory: "Je trouve admirable le fond de votre oeuvre et je suis peiné de quelques détails qui la ternissent."[21] Although unduly exacting in matters of translation D'Annunzio invariably showed a deep and sincere affection for his collaborator even in the most critical moments of their relationship.

When the first installment of *Le Feu* appeared in the *Revue de Paris*, May 1, 1900, a press campaign was organized against the novel. The author was sharply rebuked for having basely exploited his relations with Eleonora Duse and for having revealed the most intimate details of their love affair. D'Annunzio, while indifferent to criticism within the artistic domain, became furious when it pried into his personal life. The censure against *Le Feu* was in his opinion unfair and malicious. "Comment," he wrote to Ganderax, "on a pu si lourdement et si cruellement méconnaître en France un livre où j'ai tracé avec tant de ferveur les lignes de la plus noble figure féminine qui soit dans le roman moderne? Connaissez-vous une créature plus douce, plus héroïque et plus déchirante?"[22] He expected that, in this deliberate and noisy outcry against his novel, an honest voice would come to his defense. He thought at first of Marcel Prévost who in the past had been sympathetic toward him. But, alas, Marcel Prévost was himself at the head of the hostile campaign. In *Le Figaro*, May 20, 1900, he published under the title "Secret sentimental" a sort of homily of virtuous indignation against D'Annunzio, flaying the latter's conduct toward Eleonora Duse. Since Duse was as yet unaware of the content of the book, Prévost's article, revealing the unfortunate role she played in the novel and the humiliating references to her beauty, shocked her deeply. She was at the time living with D'Annunzio at the famous Capponcina, and to keep their passion unmarred by misunderstanding the author had always cautiously hidden the manuscript from her. Art was for him the absolute and he would never have sacrificed a work of beauty for love. Although he always denied it, Foscarina was without doubt Eleonora Duse whose portrayal in the novel so crushed her that she would gladly have broken off with the author forever if she had been able to do so. D'Annunzio attempted to soothe her, but despite his efforts their life continued thereafter in a tense and stormy atmosphere.

Ever more irritated by the press campaign against *Le Feu*, the author

wrote to Romain Rolland (whom he had met in 1897) bitterly com-
plaining that both in France and Italy the very spirit of his book had
been stupidly misunderstood. Since there was no immediate reaction
from Rolland, a week later he wrote him a second time, explicitly asking him to come to his defense in the Paris press:

> Vous savez qu'en France on m'attaque bassement, au sujet du *Feu*. On
> veut voir dans la Foscarina une femme admirable que nous connaissons
> et que j'aime de toute mon âme. On veut voir dans un livre d'invention
> pure une sorte de biographie! Et on méconnaît l'essence véritable de ce
> livre, qui n'est qu'une célébration et une exaltation des plus hauts senti-
> ments humains, un acte de reconnaissance vers une âme héroîque et
> seule. ... Je voulais vous demander si vous seriez disposé à prendre
> ma défense, à écrire un article qui pourrait—en partie—être une *inter-
> vista*. ... Si vous étiez disposé à m'aider, je pourrais au moins vous
> envoyer des notes. ...[23]

D'Annunzio's contradiction was evident. On the one hand he stated
that *Le Feu* was a purely fictional work containing nothing biographical; on the other, he maintained that the novel was "un acte de reconnaissance vers une âme héroïque et seule." Rolland, as a result, found
himself in a somewhat embarrassing situation. He could not, contrary
to all the evidence, deny D'Annunzio's intention of evoking Eleonora
Duse under the mask of Foscarina. He replied that he would be willing
to write an article doing justice to the artistic merit of the work, but
that he would not be able to conceal the biographical character of the
story. To deny that Foscarina was not Eleonora Duse regrettably portrayed in her declining beauty would have been asking too much, and
Rolland was not inclined to assert in the press that *Le Feu* did not concern Eleonora Duse at all; the more so since his friendship with the
actress did not allow him to hide the truth. To Rolland's limited offer
D'Annunzio remained silent. He undertook himself the task of defending the purity of his work, and in two articles in *Le Figaro* (May 22
and 31, 1900) he asserted that all of the episodes of *Le Feu* were
purely fictional and that the book, even if it were to be viewed as drawn
from real life, was but the glorification of the highest expression of
human generosity. He emphatically rejected Prévost's accusation and
asked that he read the novel again. D'Annunzio's assertion that the
book contained nothing offensive about Eleonora Duse astonished and
amused the literary world. D'Annunzio's admirers were irritated by

the harassment to which he was being subjected; they considered it impertinent to pry into the author's private life and to judge the book on that basis. His accusers, on the other hand, held that had not Marcel Prévost reproached his bad taste he would have continued in that vein with supreme indifference.

The controversy, far from damaging the success of the book, increased the number of readers. *Le Feu,* in the eyes of most literary critics, was the sign of unabated fecundity and extraordinary creativity. Through this novel—one of passion and style, experience and symbols —D'Annunzio was returning to the world of reality. The "Novels of the Pomegranate" were meant to be a compromise between the trilogy of the "Rose" and the trilogy (not completed) of the "Lily." Less voluptuous than the first and less symbolic and obscure than the second, *Le Feu* is close to life by virtue of its human drama; it is removed from it through its metaphysical flights. The mysterious symbolism of *Le Vergini delle rocce* and the extreme sensuality of the three novels of the "Rose" are attenuated and fused in *Il Fuoco* where all the elements vanish into richly colored and luxurious decorations. "Nulle part," wrote Adolphe Brisson, "M. d'Annunzio n'a déployé une si surprenante virtuosité. ... La poésie coule de lui comme l'eau d'une fontaine. C'est une onde intarissable. Elle nous grise, à travers l'excellente traduction de M. Hérelle. Jugez ce qui doit être dans l'original. L'Auteur du *Feu* joue avec les syllabes de la langue écrite et parle comme Wagner avec les notes, comme Titien avec les tons et les valeurs. Il en tire des symphonies étrangement compliquées."[24] *Il Fuoco* is in no way a novel in the true sense. It lacks action; the plot is insignificant; and the story drags on with no dramatic interest, filling some five hundred pages with interminable sentimental and philosophical conversations between a sort of Don Juan artist and a withered comedian—without a single turn of events. All this would be enough to bore the reader to death. Instead, by a strange miracle, one is immediately captivated by the work. "Gabriele d'Annunzio," said Brisson, "vous agace, vous irrite, vous exaspère et, tour à tour, vous ravit; il est odieux et vous désarme. Il exite chez le lecteur tous les sentiments—excepté l'indifférence."[25]

On literary grounds critics had nothing to reproach in the author. But, although sympathetic, they could not overlook the indifference and cruelty with which he recounted his love secrets with the most celebrated and gifted actress of the time. As an artist he was often contrasted to French writers who had not been able to free themselves from traditional conventions. In the *Mercure de France* of April 2, 1901, we read of *Le Feu*:

> Gabriele d'Annunzio a du génie et c'est justement pour cela qu'il embête un peu le lecteur français très habitué aux conventions littéraires françaises. Qu'est-ce que le feu? Voici, au sens ordinaire du mot l'histoire du feu: tout ce qui brûle, consume et purifie. L'art, l'expression de la beauté. ... Chaque fois qu'un artiste français fabrique de l'amour, on peut être sûr que ce n'est pas ardent et ça ne brûlera personne; c'est de la mécanique et presque toujours une sorte de technicité obscène qui se voile, cérémonieusement, de phrases singulièrement savantes. ... Nous sommes très vieux depuis quelque temps, chez nous, et l'amour sincère, tout nu, armé de sa jeune flèche, n'est pas un attrait suffisant. Gabriele d'Annunzio sans consulter le goût momentané, s'imagine que le devoir du poète et du romancier est de faire luire le feu sacré très haut. ... D'Annunzio a surtout oublié le vilain. Il a outrepassé son humanité de romancier pour arriver à la divinité de son art. ... On devrait bien, à tous les carrefours des lettres françaises, allumer et brandir de pareilles torches.[26]

5. The Last Novel: *Forse che sì forse che no*

AFTER *Il Fuoco* D'Annunzio produced no new novels for about ten years even though at least two were announced as forthcoming. The *Gil Blas,* October 12, 1905, reported that the author was about to publish a novel which would completely upset the conception critics had had of him so far. "Le nouveau roman s'appelle *Amarante;* il célébrera la beauté de la vie moderne et traitera d'un cas tragique de la chronique parisienne: le tourbillon de la mort. M. d'Annunzio, qui la connaît, se dit que le bruit fait autour de son divorce sera, sans nul doute, une belle réclame de librairie." And in *L'Éclair,* November 29, another reference was made to the work, reporting D'Annunzio's words: "Je veux donner le frisson de la mort aux lecteurs. ... Il faudra fermer les yeux pour lire le volume." In a letter to Hérelle, dated February 1906, D'Annunzio mentioned *Amaranta* and another novel entitled *La Madre folle* which he was hoping to finish that year and which, he felt, would be his best work. But these never went beyond the planning stage.

In 1909 a volume of D'Annunzio's earliest short stories, *Terre vierge,* was published in French translation (Paris: Juven). Some of these pieces had already appeared in French journals and had later been reprinted in *Episcopo et Cie* (1895). But since *Terre vierge* was D'Annunzio's first prose work, it seemed significant to present it to the French readers in its entirety in order to show the author's sensual and picturesque lyricism in its most sincere and natural form. The critics' reaction was favorable. In reviewing the volume in the *Annales politiques et littéraires,* Gaston Rageot went so far as to reprint one of the stories—*Totò*—which he considered to have a particular charm. "Je m'empresse donc à déclarer," he wrote, "*Terre vierge* est un livre qui ne saurait inspirer que de l'enthousiasme, d'abord, parce qu'il est beau, et, ensuite, parce qu'il révèle un aspect tout nouveau du talent ou du génie ... de l'illustre disciple de Carducci."[1] This new aspect was undoubtedly that of a D'Annunzio unvarnished, less stilted, more natural, without the stylistic luxuriance which marked the prose of his novels. Rageot concluded that, in his opinion, D'Annunzio's prose never attained so high a degree of perfection as in some of his short stories. However, D'Annunzio never cared for his earliest works; he showed dissatisfaction even with the trilogy of the "Novels of the Rose" which had brought him wide popularity.

In 1910 finally his last great novel *Forse che sì forse che no* was published. One of the secrets of D'Annunzio's success was the element of surprise; in each novel he proceeded in an entirely unsuspected direction. In contrasting him with French writers, Gaston Rageot remarked that the latter seldom surprise the reader. "C'est tout le contraire avec un écrivain tel que d'Annunzio, qui possède tant de dons, et qui les gouverne de façon si imprévue. Il nous fait si souvent passer—nous Français—de l'extrême enthousiasme au pire agacement que nous ne savons jamais—en ouvrant son dernier livre—de quel coeur nous allons l'aimer, si nous le bénirons ou le maudirons."[2] D'Annunzio himself had pretentiously pointed out to Hérelle in 1896: "Je suis une force vivante et féconde. Je suis sûr de pouvoir étonner le public pour plusieurs années encore. Ma faculté de métamorphose est prodigieuse. ... Je donnerai toujours non ce qui est attendu, mais ce qui est inattendu; et je réussirai toujours à troubler, à irriter ou à entraîner une partie de la foule."[3]

Forse che sì forse che no is a novel of heroism and passion, and it reveals a new facet of the author's art. His previous works had some elements in common, namely, extreme individualism and sensuality, although their treatment and form markedly distinguished one from another. In the new novel the tone and atmosphere are completely modified. Having known good and evil, having experienced joys and disappointments, voluptuousness and disgust, sin and depravity in their most poignant, most cruel and most inebriating forms, he was far from becoming prey to morbidity, bitterness, or irony. His book revealed vibrant new impulsions which raised him far above his former narrow aspirations. He discovered now the beauty of the human will in action. The artist-superman in him progressed toward a new world lying beyond the domain of pure art—the world of heroic endeavors. In his novel, in fact, he directed the life of the protagonist toward heroic efforts. Women, love, and art no longer hinder the realization of the virile dreams of the superman, but prod him instead to heroic and superhuman achievements.

The novel was not translated by Hérelle, but by Nathalie de Goloubeff, a Russian beauty whom the poet had met in 1908 in Rome. D'Annunzio called this new conquest (she was living in Paris estranged from her wealthy husband) Donatella Cross, and this was the name she used as translator of the work. The relations between Hérelle and D'Annunzio had become strained in 1905 during the translation of the play *La Figlia di Iorio;* thereafter their collaboration had slackened, ceasing completely in 1913. The text of Donatella's translation was revised by the French writer Charles Müller. D'Annunzio, regretting that he had to use another translator, dedicated the work to Hérelle with these words: "To Georges Hérelle, this book, saddened for not having received from him a second life." The reasons for the change in translator were other than purely literary as D'Annunzio himself readily admitted: "Je veux aussi vous expliquer toute cette histoire de la traduction: histoire de femme, hélas! comme vous pensez."[4]

Forse che sì forse che no echoes, to a certain extent, as do all of D'Annunzio's previous novels, one of his own experiences, this time a particularly tumultuous and passionate one—a summer (that of 1909) of erotic frenzy with Donatella. In fact his first thought had been to entitle it *Vertigine,* which would have been more appropriate to the content of the book than the enigmatic *Forse che sì forse che no.* But he discarded "Vertigine" because the Coty company had vulgarized this word by using it as a label for one of its perfumes. At the last moment D'Annunzio wanted to change even the title *Forse che sì forse che no* when it was jokingly pointed out to him that the rhythm of these words vaguely recalled a Neapolitan popular song—*Funiculì, Funiculà*. But his Italian publisher, Treves, having sent out the announcements on the book, did not allow any change. The French translation began appearing in *La Grande Revue*, January 10, 1910, under the title *Peut-être que oui peut-être que non* without the name of the translator. It was published in book form the same year by Calmann-Lévy with the original title and the name of Donatella Cross.

The French public, accustomed to Hérelle's translations, immediately noticed the difference in the quality of the work. Hérelle, despite strong opposition from D'Annunzio, had always treated the text with a certain freedom, thus giving his renditions a marked French flavor which largely concealed the foreign origin of the works. In *Forse che sì forse che no*, on the contrary, D'Annunzio's own idea of translation was strictly followed, i.e., literality. In his opinion, a work in translation should not become part of the national literature of the country receiving it, but it must retain its original imprint even at the cost of violating the fundamental structure of the language. He urged Donatella to translate literally: "... La traduction littérale est ce qui altère le moins la vigueur du texte"; and he pointed out that the phrase "... elle sentait battre son coeur avec force" was not so effective as the original Italian which read literally: "... elle sentait battre la force de son coeur."[5] The result of his theory on translation was that the readers found the prose of *Forse che sì forse che no* cumbersome and even obscure. D'Annunzio himself had to admit this later.

Nevertheless the novel met with success. Gaston Rageot devoted to it a highly admirative article in the *Annales politiques et littéraires*, July 3, 1910; Ricciotto Canudo remarked in the *Mercure de France* that D'Annunzio had reached such mastery in exposition and psychological analysis that "tout ce qu'il observe jaillit pour nous avec une évidence réelle et poignante, nous étonne, nous émeut."[6] And he called the work "un incomparable poème en prose de notre modernité, le premier poème de l'aviation, que d'Annunzio consacre au triomphe de l'héroïsme latin."[7] Jean Dornis wrote in the *Revue des Deux Mondes* that the publication of *Forse che sì forse che no* was a great revelation: "Les coeurs sincères s'émurent, s'interrogèrent, s'exaltèrent."[8] Paul Hervieu expressed this eloquent judgment in a letter to the author: "... J'admire cette oeuvre qui est plus qu'un roman, plus qu'un poème, qui est autre chose que tout, qui est un monstre prodigieux et resplendissant. Il hante avec ses gigantesques ailes, avec ses multiples têtes, qui ont une même âme subtile et farouche, caressante, intolérable, souveraine."[9]

In 1911 D'Annunzio had planned to write another novel— *L'Homme qui a volé la Joconde*—promised to publisher Pierre Lafitte, editor of *L'Excelsior*. But the outbreak of war between Italy and Turkey in Libya prompted him to compose instead his *Canzoni della gesta d'Oltremare*, so that Lafitte waited in vain for the promised book. Furthermore, the stand taken by *L'Excelsior* concerning the conflict in Libya seemed to D'Annunzio to be italophobic; this was an additional reason for him to abandon the idea of *L'Homme qui a volé la Joconde*. The same year, however, Lafitte published an unauthorized selection of D'Annunzio's short stories under the title *Les Lions rouges* with illustrations by Lobel-Riche. This edition was later taken out of circulation, while a French version of *Il Libro delle vergini* (D'Annunzio's second collection of short stories) was published by Tallandier (Paris). The publication of this early work, of which only a careful selection of pieces had thus far appeared in French translation, clearly indicated that the public preferred the sensuality of D'Annunzio's early production to the subtle art of his later works.

In September 1910 the author asked Hérelle to translate, for the *Revue des Deux Mondes,* his *Vita di Colā di Rienzo,* a biography which was part of a larger work he planned to write under the general title *Vita di uomini illustri.* But Hérelle, now busy with the translation of other Italian writers such as Serao, Deledda, and Fogazzaro, had to decline. D'Annunzio reiterated the invitation a month later, reproachfully: "Je regrette que vous soyez si occupé à donner votre style et votre langue si pure à trois écrivains qui écrivent en patois."[10] The last works translated by Hérelle were a volume of selected poems published in 1912, and *Laus Vitae* (first book of D'Annunzio's major poetic work), both of which will be discussed later. The outbreak of the First World War changed all of the author's literary projects. The translation of his works into French was interrupted for several years, and when it was resumed D'Annunzio's new interpreter did not follow in the footsteps of Hérelle, whose method, although successful with the French readers, was often disapproved by the author. But apart from D'Annunzio's feelings on the matter, it seems pertinent at this point to review briefly the critics' opinions of Hérelle's work. In the beginning the most eminent men of letters expressed great admiration, and the Prix Langlois which the French Academy bestowed upon him for the translation of *Les Vierges aux rochers* appeared to be well deserved. Melchior de Vogüé wrote him on this occasion: "L'Académie a bien jugé; le mérite de vos traductions apparaissait à tous."[11] Hérelle enjoyed for many years an incontestable reputation as D'Annunzio's translator, and his work was considered to have achieved perfection in this respect. But what is "perfection" in translation? On this point there was no general agreement. On the one hand, Hérelle was praised for having gallicized Gabriele D'Annunzio through his excellent "adaptations"; on the other, he was lauded for his faithfulness to the Italian text and his literal rendering. In the *Journal des débats* for May 16, 1895, Édouard Rod emphasized that Hérelle translated freely, and that as a result the French public was not enjoying the real D'Annunzio but a D'Annunzio "revu, abrégé et atténué par M. Hérelle." Gaston Deschamps maintained in 1906 that Hérelle's great merit lay in his successful "adaptation" of the original: "Traduire à la façon d'Hérelle," he said, "c'est véritablement récrire, c'est faire oeuvre d'artiste."[12] Brunetière praised Hérelle for the same reason, that is, for his valuable collaboration in the delicate task of "adaptation."[13] René Doumic wrote that Hérelle's translations were "si fidèles et en même temps d'une allure si libre, écrites dans une langue simple, imagée,"[14] which also suggested the idea of "adaptation," for D'Annunzio's language was far from being simple and, whenever it became so in French, one must assume that Hérelle did not follow the Italian text literally.

Maurice Muret, on the contrary, spoke of Hérelle's "perfect translations" and asserted that the latter "se borne en général à traduire littéralement, à suivre comme mot à mot le texte italien."[15] And Paul Souday in 1912 maintained that Hérelle's merit consisted in having remained "également éloigné de l'infidélité à l'original et de la fidélité littérale qui conduit trop souvent à traduire une page éloquente dans un patois de cuistre."[16] And he returned to the subject in 1928, pointing to Hérelle's translations as "impeccable."[17]

But praise, whether justified or not, was accompanied by blame. Some critics showed a great deal of dissatisfaction with Hérelle's work. In 1898 Ernest Tissot accused him of having betrayed the original, and he stressed that to translate is not "trahir ou adapter."[18] Jacques Boulenger wrote in *Le Temps*, June 16, 1933, that *Il Piacere* was translated into mediocre French; and Pierre Lièvre in an article in the *Mercure de France*, August 15, 1935, went so far as to propose a new translation of D'Annunzio's novels.

The lack of consensus shown by these judgments often reflects differences in taste rather than an objective evaluation of Hérelle's work. It is unquestionable that the clear-thinking translator strove to remove the traces of foreign origin in D'Annunzio's novels; and the question arises as to whether his method did justice to the author. Most French critics found Hérelle's method legitimate, perhaps the only valid one. D'Annunzio, however, relentlessly opposed any attempts to obliterate the distinctive marks of his own style. Twice he quarreled with the translator—once during the translation of *Il Fuoco* and again during that of the play *La Figlia di Iorio*. It appeared at times that no one was less D'Annunzian than D'Annunzio's French translator. Hérelle's modest tone, his intrinsic need for clarity, his fear of altering the distinctive mold of his own language, led him to deflate somewhat D'Annunzio's prose. And in Hérelle's French D'Annunzio often felt that his works were being banalized. His aristocratic style with such careful selection of words, variety of tones, musical inversions, and alliterations, which gave so much luster to his prose, seemed to him to be completely impaired and impoverished in the French version, even when it was extremely close to the original in every detail. When Hérelle rendered the phrase "Gocce di pioggia, rare, cadevano" (*Il Fuoco*) by the French "Des gouttes de pluie, clairsemées, tombaient," D'Annunzio objected strongly. Why not translate: "Des gouttes de pluie, rares, tombaient?" he argued. The word "clairsemées," though musical, did not, in his opinion, convey the desired artistic effect which lay in the long "a" of "rares," as a sort of emphasized note. This instance illustrates clearly the delicate ground on which they were treading. D'Annunzio could not be made to understand that the musical quality of his style, the rhythmical movement of his expression could not be entirely preserved in French. Nor could he be convinced that whatever the original lost in brilliance and verbal wealth it gained in clarity. If the author and the translator, in their combined efforts to reduce to a minimum the inevitable damage done to a work in translation, were not always in agreement, it is perhaps due to the fact that behind their controversy was the conflict between two different linguistic patterns—the French and the Italian.

However, to state that Hérelle completely gallicized D'Annunzio, bringing his prose down to the level of the average reader, is definitely an exaggeration. D'Annunzio is ever present in the French text, with his qualities and defects, his verbal exuberance, his refinements, and resplendent imagery. Certainly some of his stylistic peculiarities, distinctly felt in the original, and the frequent archaisms have been lost in the attenuated form of the French translation; the general tone strikes a lower key, since the musicality of the Italian phrase was often diluted in the effort to achieve French clarity. While the content of the translations is always exact, they give nevertheless a D'Annunzio perceptibly divested of his usual tinsel.

No other Italian writer translated by Hérelle ever questioned the quality of his work. Never did Matilde Serao or Antonio Fogazzaro or Grazia Deledda ask to look over his translations; never did any of them show the concern for their writings that D'Annunzio showed for his, and Serao even explicitly requested that Hérelle correct the improprieties of the original. It was D'Annunzio alone who, boasting about the uniqueness of his style, made Hérelle's task so difficult. Always exacting in the extreme concerning the French translations, he was completely indifferent toward the translation of his works into other languages, leaving all of the responsibility in the hands of the translator and showing no interest whatever in the matter. It was only France and the cultivated French public that haunted him. It was the literary glory which the French capital bestowed upon the chosen few that he strove to win. "Ah! mon cher ami," he wrote to Hérelle in 1892, "la France reste bien le pays le plus intellectuel du monde."[19]

6 Other Prose Works

BETWEEN 1912 and 1916 D'Annunzio had written three more prose works—*La Contemplazione della morte, La Leda senza cigno,* and *Il Notturno*—which, by their nature, could well form a new trilogy. They are not novels (except for one part of *La Leda senza cigno*) but books of introspection, symbolic fancy, remembrances. The first work, *La Contemplazione della morte,* was composed in 1912 at Arcachon. It could be called, said D'Annunzio, "the agony of a new St. Francis." The work was inspired by the life and character of a saintly aged peasant of the Landes—Adolphe Bermond—a sort of spiritual friend of the poet, whose long agony and death he had piously witnessed. The passing of the poet Giovanni Pascoli, which occurred at about the same time, added a new and deeper emotion to this sad experience. These two events threw D'Annunzio into a long period of meditation on the mystery of life and death. The vision of the two men haunted him. He brooded on the fatality of human destiny, and from his reflections sprang the moving pages of *La Contemplazione della morte*, first canto of a prose poem devoted to the Unknown.

La Ledā senza cigno, also composed at Arcachon, in 1913, might be called a second canto. The content of the work is a tale of the Landes, written with magnificence of colors and rhythm. Its significance, however, does not lie in external events, which are almost non-existent, but in the atmosphere of incantation created by the suggestiveness of the narration. The effort of the author to go beyond the limit of the visible and to evoke states of mind which elude rational analysis give the tale a marked spiritual dimension. In 1916 he added a "Licenza," twice as long as the story and serving as a dedication of *La Leda senza cigno* to the beautiful Chiaroviso—Madame Marcel Boulenger—a close friend in the happy Parisian days. It was also a farewell and for this reason was attached to the end of the tale. The "Licenza" is an impressionistic diary, a recording of happy and sad memories. Confined to darkness and immobility by an eye wound suffered in the war and the necessary bandaging, the poet recalls lyrically his past in Paris and especially the tragic hours of the German invasion during the early weeks of the First World War—the heroic image of France in those moments of mortal danger. But the evocation assumes the form of an evanescent dream; reality becomes impalpable, pure sensation in a melancholic twilight.

From the same immobility and darkness came also the pathetic pages of *Il Notturno*—the third canto and unquestionably the best of the trilogy. This work also is a sort of impressionistic journal like the "Licenza" but in a gloomier and more nocturnal tone. It is a sequence of dreams, visions, hallucinations, sensations which seem to spring from a "twilight zone," from the obscure regions of the author's subconscious. Being on the whole a series of lyrical fragments, it lacks the structural coherence of a narration. The only element of unity is the nocturnal atmosphere dominated by shadows—the shadow of death, the shadow of the invisible, the shadow of the night. Before the unseeing eyes of the wounded poet, the first years of war unfold with the heroic and mourned dead, bodies in decomposition, and specters. However, the funereal tone of the evocation is often broken by the intrusion of a sensual love for life. Thus *Il Notturno,* as a critic put it, is not the book of war—the true contemplation of death—but the journal of a sensual man confined to darkness. Written shortly before the "Licenza," the work remained unpublished until the fall of 1921.

Immediately after the First World War the task undertaken by Hérelle in 1892 was resumed by another admirer of D'Annunzio— André Doderet, author of several novels, a poet, and known as an excellent stylist. As D'Annunzio's translator, Doderet did not acquire the widespread reputation enjoyed by Hérelle; when he began his work the literary interest in the Italian author was already well over in France. However, although his role in the D'Annunzian "legend" was not as conspicuous as that of his predecessor, it was no less important and certainly deserves more recognition than is usually accorded it. Doderet had felt a strong attraction for D'Annunzio since his reading of *L'Intrus* in his early youth. It was in fact this reading that aroused in him a keen interest in the Italian language. In 1910 he was introduced to the poet at the home of a friend; but this casual meeting did not lead to any close association. Doderet had just published his first novel and since D'Annunzio had feigned an interest in it, he promptly sent him a copy on the following day. Two days later the poet reciprocated with an autographed copy of *Forse che sì forse che no.* This gift so pleased Doderet that he showed it to all of his friends. He saw D'Annunzio again, four years later, at the Champs-Élysées during the first days of the war. The poet was seated and one of his greyhounds lay at his feet; but Doderet, timid by nature, dared not approach him. At the end of the war he learned from Marcel Boulenger, who was returning from a visit with D'Annunzio in Venice, that the poet had resumed his literary activity and was looking for a French translator. "Par suite de quelle hardiesse inattendue osai-je me proposer?" wrote Doderet.[1] But at the suggestion of Boulenger he translated a few pages of *La Leda senza cigno,* which Boulenger himself forwarded to the poet. Upon receiving these samples D'Annunzio answered with a telegram reading: "Les essais de Doderet sont excellents. Envoyez-moi son adresse."[2] The address was sent immediately, but Doderet waited in vain to hear anything more. However, with the encouragement of Boulenger he began slowly to translate *La Leda* without waiting any longer. Customarily the poet's long silences were followed by urgent telegraphic requests and one had to be prepared to cope with his whims. D'Annunzio had, meanwhile, occupied Fiume and had more than enough to claim his time and thoughts. But Doderet encountered so many difficulties in the Italian text that in June 1920 he decided to join the poet in Fiume in order to discuss with him his first "essais de traduction." Doderet's literary taste was much closer to that of the author than was Hérelle's. Their collaboration, therefore, was a perfectly harmonious one. D'Annunzio showed complete confidence and never questioned the work of his new translator for whom he soon developed a personal affection. He found Doderet's translations to be more accurate, more faithful, more concerned with the musicality of his prose than Hérelle's. In D'Annunzio's mind, their closeness to the original rendered them more artistic, even if the French readers generally found them not completely conforming to their taste or to the nature of their language. Doderet was in fact more inclined than Hérelle to *dannunzieggiare*.

Doderet's arrival in Fiume was warmly welcomed. He was immediately settled in a room directly connected with D'Annunzio's apartment, and when the poet was free of his daily duties Doderet would read to him the translation in progress: "Le poète suivait attentivement sur le texte, la tête penchée. ... De temps en temps, il m'arrêtait pour changer un mot, accélérer ou ralentir le rythme d'une phrase."[3] *La Léda sans cygne* was completed and revised during the early part of the following year at D'Annunzio's new residence on Lake Garda. The first tome, containing the tale proper, was published in the *Revue des Deux Mondes* from August 15 to September 15, 1921; the "Licenza" was serialized with the title *Envoi à la France* in the *Revue hebdomadaire* beginning on October 8, and both parts were published together by Calmann-Lévy the following year. *La Leda senza cigno* had already appeared in Italy in 1916, and Giovanni Papini had given it an uncomplimentary review in the *Mercure de France,* March 17, 1917, leveling his attacks not only against the literary qualities of the work but also against the author, with deliberate intention of undermining D'Annunzio's role in Italy's intervention in the war. Papini's article received a quick answer from Henri de Régnier in the *Mercure de France*; Régnier protested the unfair criticism: "Mon silence," he wrote, "pourrait laisser supposer une approbation tacite au jugement porté sur le poète que j'aime et que j'admire aussi bien en son oeuvre d'écrivain qu'en son héroïsme de soldat."[4] Théodore de Wyzewa présenté a highly sympathetic analysis of the work in the *Revue des Deux Mondes,* March 15, 1917, objecting mildly only to the length of the

"Licenza."[5] The French translation, on the contrary, was received very favorably. The preference of the French public went especially to the *Envoi à la France,* which contained a moving evocation of the dramatic and crucial event—the invasion of France and the French victory on the Marne. Maurice Barrès warmly thanked the poet in *L'Écho de Paris*[6] for the *Envoi* published with "cette épigraphe émouvante: 'France, France, sans toi le monde serait seul.'" No one had spoken of these tragic hours of the First World War with such depth of feeling as did D'Annunzio: "Quel Français," wrote Jean Dornis, "l'a fait plus ardemment, plus pathétiquement, plus patriotiquement?"[7]

The translation of *Il Notturno* required about four months of intensive work. Doderet, installed in D'Annunzio's luxurious residence on Lake Garda, toiled under the author's direct supervision. After the translation of *La Leda senza cigno,* he felt less uncomfortable with the new work, having acquired greater familiarity with the poet's style and imagery, yet the task was not altogether easy. D'Annunzio, in fact, at Doderet's first visit in Fiume, had mentioned to him *Il Notturno,* still unknown to the public, but he had stressed the necessity of translating *La Leda* "avant d'aborder le *Nocturne* qui est mon oeuvre capitale en prose."[8] The translation was completed early in December 1921, to the full satisfaction of the poet, and the happy occasion called for an impromptu celebration. But the planned publication in the *Revue des Deux Mondes* angered both author and translator, owing to the bowdlerization to which the translation was subjected in order to cater to the taste of the general reading public. The *Notturno* had appeared in Italy in December 1921, and in February 1, 1922, the *Revue des Deux Mondes* began to serialize the French version. But after the second installment (February 15) the publication was stopped by Doderet, who found the corrections and deletions to be damaging to the integrity of the work. D'Annunzio's bitter reaction to the editorial "mutilation" is found in a telegram to Doderet: "... Veuillez communiquer ma volonté à Monsieur le Directeur. Je peux me passer de tous les honneurs et rester le mutilé de guerre."[9] *Le Nocturne* appeared in book form at Calmann-Lévy's the same year, with the illustrations by Adolfo de Carolis already printed in the Italian edition.

With *Il Notturno* D'Annunzio returned to the literary scene after six years of silence. This return was something of a literary event. Critics believed at first that they were witnessing the emergence of a new artistic dimension; but some were disappointed, for *Il Notturno,* in their estimation, offered nothing new. The work appeared to be fragmentary and completely lacking in organic form. Girolomo Lazzeri wrote in the Mercure de France that the love of country D'Annunzio displayed in his book was merely a pretext for exalting his own vanity: "Le *Nocturne*," said Lazzeri, "est une pente de décadence artistique et reflète une impressionnante insensibilité morale et éthique, une pauvreté de puissance créatrice."[10] Benjamin Crémieux, on the contrary, asserted that the work foreshadowed "une troisième jeunesse aussi exubérante que la première."[11] André Doderet considered *Le Nocturne* to be the masterpiece of the trilogy.[12] René Gutman, in a physio-pathological study of the work, found it to be "une oeuvre organique, née de la douleur non métaphysique mais par une transformation immédiate de chaque sensation réelle."[13] G. de Pawlowski compared *Le Nocturne* to Pierre Mac-Orlan's *Malice*, both of which deal with the subconscious. D'Annunzio, in Pawlowski's opinion, "en est le prophète émerveillé," and Mac-Orlan "le prophète épouvanté." The remembrances of the past, arising from the poet's subconscious, formed, according to the critic, the most admirable and the most frightening "chaos que l'on ait jamais vu mis en livre."[14]

After *Le Nocturne* Doderet translated *La Contemplazione della morte* for the *Revue de Paris*. The work appeared in the issues for July 1 and 15, 1923, and was printed in book form by Calmann-Lévy in 1928. The publication of the Italian text in 1912 had aroused speculation on the possibility of a mystical turn in the author's life. It was suggested that D'Annunzio might have been moved by Barrès' conversion and wished to follow him. But D'Annunzio's mysticism and piety exuding from the book were too ambiguous to indicate conversion in the religious sense: he was not capable of any metamorphoses of this sort. His work, therefore, contributed nothing to the mystical revival of the time. Ricciotto Canudo pointed out in the *Mercure de France* that D'Annunzio had found inspiration in Maeterlinck, namely, in "l'oeuvre dite philosophique,"[15] but he questioned the timeliness of *La Contemplazione della morte:* the author should have put off the writing until "les portes d'or d'un mysticisme plus profond, plus pensif, plus nouveau, lui fussent ouvertes."[16] From the strictly literary point of view, critics found in the work the habitual rhetoric, the stylistic redundances, the pretentious display of the author's ego, which often irritate the reader. But these defects are soon outweighed by D'Annunzio's magic power. The solemnity of tone, the musicality of expression, wrote Edmond Jaloux, soon enchant the reader like a series of "formules magiques," and "... on oublie ce qu'il y a de factice dans cette prose cadencée et on se grise de l'atmosphère enchantée qu'elle dégage."[17]

In 1924 D'Annunzio published the first volume of another prose work—*Le Faville del maglio* (the second appeared in 1928)—containing loose pieces: art impressions, reflections, studies, autobiographical pages, and other passages which had not found a place in his other works. The title is indicative of the fragmentary nature of its content; the various parts belong to different periods. Of the first volume, subtitled *Il Venturiero senza ventura* and dedicated to the memory of Eleonora Duse, André Doderet translated into French one excerpt, "La Fleur du bronze," whose composition goes back to 1896. It appeared in the *Nouvelles littéraires*, August 16, 1924, with an article by Doderet himself in which the entire work is discussed. The second tome was never translated. In the *Mercure de France* of September 15, 1939, Marcel Coulon spoke of *Le Faville del maglio* as the masterpiece of D'Annunzio's prose; and so was it unanimously considered by critics. The last works of any importance in Doderet's translation were *Ritratto di Luisa Bàccara* (in French, *Portrait de Loyse Baccaris*), published by Kra (Paris) in 1925, and *Solus ad Solam*, published by Éditions Balzac (Paris) in 1944 after being serialized in the weekly *Gringoire*. (In the meantime he had translated the plays *Fedra* and *La Fiaccola sotto il moggio*, and several poems—all of which will be discussed in appropriate chapters—and many other prose pieces of less importance.) The *Ritratto di Luisa Bàccara*, written and published in 1920, is a short biographical work in the praises of the art and beauty of a Venetian musician who had joined the poet in Fiume in 1920 and who became his last official mistress. (The *New York Times* of March 5, 1921, reported that D'Annunzio married her on February 3 of that year.) *Solus ad Solam* is a sad diary recording impressionistically the feeling of the poet toward a beloved one—Amaranta—now stricken by insanity and taken away from him. The work, written in 1908, was published in Italian posthumously in 1939. Some of its pages were woven into *Forse che sì forse che no* composed immediately after.

In 1935 Treves published one of D'Annunzio's strangest books, *Cento e cento e cento pagine del libro segreto di Gabriele d'Annunzio tentato di morire*, a sort of confession in which the veil of fiction is pulled away and the author appears unmasked in the impudicity of his intimate life. The book was immediately banned by the Catholic Church, but this action only served to increase the curiosity of the reading public. From the literary point of view it offered nothing new, having the same stylistic qualities—richness of images, verbal exuberance, sumptuous colors—as his previous works. But the sincerity of the confession, the tone of pessimism and despair which underlies D'Annunzio's hedonism, made the *Cento e cento pagine* a revealing work. In its pages the real D'Annunzio is seen in the intimacy of his life. The singular role he played in the literature of his times, the reasons which prodded him to his artistic achievements, appear in a truer light and in the right proportions. In the *Cento e cento pagine* the sensual man, the war hero, and the man of letters are combined in a homogeneous and coherent character.

The work was received in France with much curiosity. A number of reviews analyzed and discussed it sympathetically. Its condemnation by the Church gave it wide publicity. In the *Mercure de France* Paul Guiton pointed out that this being "l'époque du nudisme universel, il serait naïf de s'étonner des scènes de dévêtement de d'Annunzio."[18] And Marcel Brion, in commenting on the qualities of the work, called D'Annunzio "le plus magnifique instrument d'expérience sensibles qu'ait connu notre époque," and he added: "l'épreuve tactile du monde, plus encore que colorée, fait de son oeuvre quelque chose d'inoubliable, d'inimitable."[19]

D'Annunzio's last prose work—*Le Dit du sourd et muet*—written in archaic French, was published in 1936. It had no literary interest, except for the strange linguistic mixture he used to compose it. This work will be discussed in another chapter.

These late writings failed to arouse much reaction. In Italy Croce's negative judgment on them was tacitly accepted. According to this judgment D'Annunzio's originality had ended with *Alcyone* and *La Figlia di Iorio;* the later works were simply a repetition of images and thoughts fully expressed previously. Most recent criticism, however, seems to prefer or at least to judge more sympathetically his late writings. *La Contemplazione della morte, La Leda senza cigno, Il Notturno, Le Faville del maglio, Le Cento e cento pagine del libro segreto* are considered more introspective and less sensual, more sincere and less purely decorative in their expression than his previous works. This increasing interest in the later D'Annunzio shows a tendency to revise Croce's condemnation. Some feel that D'Annunzio's later literary production is the expression of a new youth, more complete and true, and not the result of artistic exhaustion. It seems to spring from an inner crisis rather than creative weariness. The gradual change of his prose from artificial over-refinement to a more sincere expression, from physical sensuality to spirituality culminates in *Il Notturno*, where for the first time the author was forced to probe into the complicated labyrinth of his inner self. Cut off from contact with the outer world, self-expression was for him an impelling necessity and no longer a mere game of verbal technique. Thus the entire tone of his prose changes: his phrases become more subtle; his sentences, shorter with frequent use of elliptic forms suggestive of a more human self. In this process of purification, D'Annunzio's prose is not impoverished; it acquires more allusiveness and evocative power and a smoother and lighter movement. By D'Annunzio's own confession his prose had reached the finest and most complete form in his later works, with the departure from his sensual orgy and the withdrawal into the shady corners of the self, with the passage from materiality to spirituality.

The preference of the French public, however, remained attached to D'Annunzio's first novels—the trilogy of the "Rose." Gaston Rageot remarked in 1909 that the author's success in France was due to the poetic qualities of his works. "... Ne lisant guère les poètes," said Rageot, "nous aimons à retrouver la poésie dans le roman."[20] The "Novels of the Rose" had revealed a subtle and complicated art which captivated the readers by its ardent sensuality and an extraordinary power of expression. Of the two other trilogies, he added: "les *Vierges aux rochers* nous déconcerta par son symbolisme excessif," and "le *Feu* nous étonna par la naïveté et la grandiloquence avec lesquelles l'auteur s'y mettait en scène."[21] These two novels were appreciated only by the literati, although the latter enjoyed a broader favor for its human and tormented tone, for the passion and suffering portrayed in it. The sensuality of *Les Vierges aux rochers* was too subtle and too cerebral to interest the general reader, who sought in D'Annunzio the voluptuous "libertinage" of the senses. This novel, unlike the others, did not go beyond the first edition.[22]

Nonetheless, D'Annunzio's artistic conception was fully realized in *Les Vierges aux rochers* and in *Le Feu* where formal perfection represents the ultimate achievement for the author. It is in fact this formal perfection, this search for the rare and elegant expression, this delicate handling of the rhythm of his phrases which make D'Annunzio a master innovator. But this art was not for the appreciation of the average reader, and the author's popularity began to decline. His production, by detaching itself from life in order to express a lofty ideal of art, no longer had the magic appeal which had won the readers of 1895. And neither the brilliance of expression nor the perfection of form could save it from indifference. Those who in 1895 were charmed by *L'Enfant de volupté*, a few years later turned to new idols rising on the literary horizon.[23] D'Annunzio's "sweet poison" had prodigious but short-lived effects. His vogue did not last long enough to exert literary influences in France. D'Annunzio recognized in Pierre Louys the only D'Annunzian. In 1896 in answer to Hérelle's fear concerning a possible adverse reaction, D'Annunzio wrote: "Le succès de Louys est une preuve en ma faveur. Louys est un dannunzien; je sais qu'il est parmi mes plus ardents admirateurs. N'a-t-il pas triomphé à cause de certaines qualités dannunziennes? C'est un signe que mon poison—mon doux et amer poison—est dans le sang des lecteurs."[24] Pierre Louys had offered something new—what Remy de Gourmont called, in his book *Les Masques,* "le romanesque sexuel."[25] And this "romanesque" sensuality, expressed in a brilliant style, was the very essence of D'Annunzio's works. The *Annales politiques et littéraires* of May 12, 1907, reported a strange anecdote about D'Annunzio, in connection with a book by Camille Flammarion—*Forces naturelles inconnues.* The poet, according to the journal, was taking part in a séance at the home of his friend Clemente Origo in Florence when the spirit was asked for a literary judgment of his works. After emitting some rumbling sounds, the spirit flatly answered: "La littérature de d'Annunzio n'est toute entière que de la fumée, de la fumée qui sera vite dissipée."[26] The spirit may have been right, if this judgment is to be applied to D'Annunzio's novels. In these works there is a durable aspect—the artistic, the cult of love and beauty; but there is another—the sensual and amoral—which is characteristic of a decadent epoch, an epoch of instability, uncertainty, and skepticism.

The philosophical oneness of the world that romanticism had reached through its idealistic synthesis had been shattered by experimental science; but the narrowness of positivism could not satisfy the profound exigencies of the searching mind, and the bankruptcy of science had soon become inevitable. In this intellectual climate the Self, bereft of its necessary foundation, is faced by a world without values. Hence, there results: on the one hand, the haughty exaltation of the Ego, now the demiurge of all values which it creates and destroys to gratify its whims; on the other, the disheartening vision of a meaningless world. On the one hand, there is the extolling of the Ego and its aphrodisiac madness, the elevation of art to the absolute goal of life; on the other, a gloomy or ironical tone, a feeling of bitter resignation which takes form in a melancholy confession.

D'Annunzio represented the former aspect of decadence. His evolution reveals his constant search for absolute values. The voluptuous sensuality to which he yielded completely in his youth, the philosophy of the superman whose god is art, the heroic action as an escape or an altruistic sacrifice are the three steps of this evolution. The first was the easiest to grasp, since it was more concrete and human. The enthusiasm of his "Novels of the Rose" can be explained by the general atmosphere of the time marked by the absence of moral values and by indulgence in sensual pleasure as an escape from the bewildering and tormenting problems confronting human existence.

Paul Guiton in 1938 praised D'Annunzio "d'avoir liquidé la douleur romantique," although he appears as an epigonus of romanticism. For almost one and a half centuries writers and artists "ne juraient que par la douleur," emphasizing their personal suffering and comparing themselves to Sysiphus and Ugolino. Rousseau, Chateaubriand, Lamartine, Hugo, Vigny, and many others glorified themselves as being the most "malheureux des hommes." No one dared confess any happiness. Musset's line, "L'homme est un apprenti, la douleur est son maître," had become an indisputable truism. Finally D'Annunzio came to liberate everyone from this doom of self-inflicted suffering, "et nous eûmes licence de trouver que le monde était beau quelquefois."[27] In some pages of *Il Fuoco*, Stelio Effrena placed enjoyment above suffering, stating that only those who enjoyed more lived more. Whatever the ethical value of this statement, it brought in a new concepion of life, that is, what François Porché called "la mystique sensualiste d'un paganisme nouveau." As a novelist, said Porché, D'Annunzio "est à l'origine d'un certain romanesque lyrique, tout à l'opposé de l'école naturaliste. ... Il a créé une atmosphère d'enchantement ... détourné le XIXᵉ siècle finissant des spectacles amers, des étalages complaisants de la bassesse humaine. ... Il nous a induits en des rêveries fastueuses."[28]

Although he did not exert any lasting influence in France, his works served as a touchstone. His first novels called the attention of the critics to the relative merits of the various literary tendencies—naturalism, estheticism, the psychological school, and so forth—providing them, at the same time, with an opportunity to discuss and evaluate the positive and negative aspects of the literary influence of North European literature and to extol or reject the idea of a Latin renaissance. *Les Vierges aux rochers* was viewed in the light of the idealist reaction against positivism and of a certain antidemocratic trend in politics.[29] *Le Feu* astonished and charmed the cultivated reader for its unprecedented power of expression and lofty ideal of art. Henry de Montherlant expressed thus his indebtedness to *Le Feu*, which he read in 1915 at the age of nineteen: "... Ce livre, à la lettre, transforma ma façon d'écrire. ... Il m'apporta des éléments nouveaux: un style de vie, qui me posséda durant dix ans. Et un style d'écrivain."[30] If neither *Les Vierges aux rochers* nor *Le Feu* held the interest of a wide public, they offered, nevertheless, an unusual example of the highest artistic achievement in a period of deterioration in literary taste.

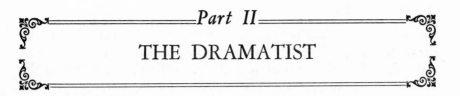

7. D'Annunzio's Debut as a Dramatist

IN AN ARTICLE on D'Annunzio's theater Jean Dornis wrote in 1904:

> On s'était habitué à considérer exclusivement M. d'Annunzio comme un romancier et un poète, quand une tournée de Mme Duse ... le présenta à ses admirateurs sous la figure d'un auteur dramatique. Et, aussi bien, il semble que cette dernière incarnation de son talent soit chère entre toutes à l'auteur de l'*Enfant de volupté*.[1]

The revelation of this new dimension of the author took place in June 1897, when Eleonora Duse presented at the Théâtre de la Renaissance *Il Sogno d'un mattino di primavera*—a one-act lyrical play which D'Annunzio had "improvised" for her. For many years thereafter his dramatic works created as much stir in France as had his novels. Some of his plays were presented in the Parisian theaters before they were even known in Italy. The circumstances bringing about the composition of *Il Sogno d'un mattino di primavera* were related by Count Giuseppe Primoli in a detailed article in the *Revue de Paris* of June 1, 1897. According to Primoli, Madame Duse, having been invited to appear at the Théâtre de la Renaissance, was reluctant to face the Parisian public with stock plays already performed by Sarah Bernhardt. It was at this time that she asked D'Annunzio to write a play for her—something special—for the occasion. "Pour faire honneur à la Reine des Poètes,[2] donnez-moi des rythmes et des images, improvisez-moi une oeuvre de poésie."[3] But there was not enough time for such an undertaking: "En une semaine! C'est une folie!" said D'Annunzio. "Alors faites-moi un rôle de folle," reiterated Eleonora Duse. Since the poet wanted her to accept the Paris engagement, he set to work: "Dans dix jours, vous aurez votre folie!" This "folie" was *Il Sogno d'un mattino di primavera*, written in less than two weeks. D'Annunzio immediately informed Hérelle of the work, asking him to translate the manuscript as soon as he received it. At the same time he made arrangements through Primoli to have the French translation published in the *Revue de Paris* of June 1.[4] The play in fact appeared in the review as planned, and on the 15th of June it was performed in Italian at the Théâtre de la Renaissance. The program for the evening included Goldoni's *La Locandiera*, which followed D'Annunzio's play. The author had announced to Hérelle that he would be in Paris for the occasion, but obviously he changed his plans, for no one reported his presence in the French capital.[5]

Il Sogno d'un mattino di primavera was clamorously applauded. Madame Duse accomplished a miracle of theatrical skill in the leading role of Isabella. Without the great actress the play would perhaps have failed, as it did later in Italy. But her first appearance in the French capital had so excited the curiosity of the public that D'Annunzio's play was judged on her performance rather than its own merits. After this presentation it was completely forgotten. The *Sogno* is a sort of Shakespearean drama. Isabella, like an impassionate Juliet, receives her lover—a new Romeo—secretly in her room. The two are discovered together, and the unfortunate lover is killed in her presence. She loses her mind as a result of the tragedy, but even in her aberration remains faithful to the memory of her lover. Attempts to cure her are of no avail. Her madness persists as her only escape from reality. The situation was not completely original, but the lyricism which D'Annunzio injected into it had an extraordinary power. Critics rightly remarked that "contrairement à l'esthétique du théâtre, qui est action, c'est-à-dire progrès d'une situation, ce *Songe* piétinait sur place."[6] In fact, the spectators do not see the events culminating in the murder of Isabella's lover and in her insanity. When the curtain is raised she is already mad and will remain so to the end of the play. The last lines of the drama leave her in exactly the same state of mind in which she was found at the beginning.

Despite these weaknesses, which are clearly perceptible on the stage, the play was not completely lacking in artistic beauty. "M. d'Annunzio," wrote Jean Dornis, "a des mots si merveilleux pour évoquer dans l'imagination de son lecteur les choses qu'il veut peindre et voit lui-même, que, la brochure en main, on respire vraiment avec lui l'odeur des roses."[7] The situation and plot were dramatic; the tenderness of the two lovers, the murder of the one and the suffering of the other, were portrayed with lyrical intensity; the atmosphere created by this evocation was highly suggestive. And particular note was taken of this new technique. François Carry wrote in *Le Correspondant*:

> Si vide que soit le contenu de ce drame, il faut reconnaître que l'auteur y déploie une puissance de lyrisme incomparable: c'est un mélange exquis d'harmonies, de couleurs, de transparences lumineuses, allié à des observations psychologiques d'une délicatesse et d'une ténuité merveilleuses. Les personnages du drame, comme ceux de Maeterlinck, parlent une langue mystérieuse qui éveille en nous les mêmes sentiments indéterminés que la musique.[8]

But *Il Sogno*, rather than being a real drama, was only the shadow and the lyrical evocation of a drama. Critics defined it as a "poème dialogué"—poetry rather than theater. Its merit consisted mainly in the lyrical description and not at all in dramatic action. "Plus que d'un drame véritable," observed Armand Caraccio, "il s'agit d'une nouvelle portée à la scène. La description, fort abondante, y prend volontiers la place de l'action sans que l'on soit choqué."[9] The play was monotonous and only Duse's talent rendered it tolerable to the Parisian audience. The poet himself realized that on the stage the drama was almost completely nonexistent. In fact, after seeing the first rehearsal of it in Rome a few days before Duse's departure for Paris, he wrote Hérelle: "J'ai assisté aux répétitions de ma pièce, avec un dégoût inexprimable. Je ne puis vous dire le choc violent qu'a reçu mon esprit en voyant si grossièrement réalisé mon pur rêve de poésie."[10] His disappointment, however, was to be attributed to the quality of the play rather than the staging of it.

Accustomed to the great success of his novels, D'Annunzio was not satisfied with the reception of his play in France. Drama critics praised only the Divine Duse, not *Il Sogno d'un mattino di primavera*. Someone suggested that D'Annunzio's drama was but a dilution of Maeterlinck and that the author seemed to be condemned to perpetual influences and to the production of "oeuvres réflexes."[11] Critics, nonetheless, agreed that the play, while poor for stage presentation, was excellent for reading because of its extraordinary lyricism. This judgment was repeated again and again about all of D'Annunzio's theatrical works.

The second play of D'Annunzio's to be staged was *La Città morta*, written before *Il Sogno*. In the order of composition this was his first play and it, too, was presented in France before being known in Italy.

La Città morta is a tragedy in five acts which took form in the poet's mind during a cruise through the Greek islands at the end of July 1895 aboard the yacht Fantasia in the company of Hérelle and other friends. The voyage gave him the opportunity of visiting the ruins of Mycenae, where his modern tragedy unfolds, with the past speaking to him through the remains of the city. In September 1895, upon returning from the cruise, D'Annunzio announced to Hérelle his plans for the composition of the tragedy: "Je crois avoir trouvé une matière précieuse. ... Ce sera le premier fruit de mon esprit fécondé par le soleil de Grèce."[12] He asked Sarah Bernhardt to play the lead in his drama at the Théâtre de la Renaissance, and she accepted enthusiastically. In October 1896 he informed Hérelle that the first two acts were already finished, and he urged him to begin the translation immediately. D'Annunzio at first had thought of writing the play in French, submitting the text to Hérelle for revision, and then presenting it as a French work. "Très souvent, en écrivant en italien, la phrase française me vient sous la plume et me semble plus efficace et—comment dire—plus parlée. ... Votre langue est plus fluide, plus légère, moins compassée."[13] But since time was pressing, he was unable to carry out his project as he had planned. However, he proposed that Hérelle translate the play for a fixed price and let him present it as a work originally written in French. D'Annunzio wanted to avoid the expression "translated from the Italian," which, in his opinion, seemed to put a barrier between the spectator and the play.[14]

Hérelle accepted the proposition without bargaining. The friendship between him and D'Annunzio had always been above any selfish interest. In their correspondence they never discussed matters of money. The work was finished in November 1896, and in sending Hérelle the last acts D'Annunzio urged him to hurry with the translation since Sarah Bernhardt was pressing him with telegrams. *La Ville morte* pleased the translator a great deal, and he complimented the author enthusiastically. The French version was completed toward the end of December, and the manuscript was immediately passed on to Sarah Bernhardt, who was waiting for it impatiently. She also was deeply impressed with the drama, and after reading it she sent D'Annunzio a telegram: "Ai lu votre tragédie. Admirable, admirable! Tout mon coeur reconnaissant."[15] This message filled the poet with joy. He felt in these words the sincere expression of the esthetic emotion produced by his play on the great actress, and he considered her favorable reaction as a good omen for its success. D'Annunzio had written the tragedy with Sarah Bernhardt in mind for the leading role. If we are to believe his words, he created the part of the blind protagonist, Anna, to suit Sarah Bernhardt's particular gestures, motions, attitudes, and general stage technique.[16]

Since previous engagements of the theater had prevented an earlier presentation, the play was performed on January 21, 1898. Bernhardt used every available means at the Théâtre de la Renaissance to provide a magnificent stage setting. She consulted the author himself in the various details of the decor so as to render fully his poetic vision.[17] A few days before the performance *La Ville morte* was published by Calmann-Lévy, and since the text did not bear the translator's name, the public believed, as D'Annunzio had foreseen, that the play had been written originally in French. In fact, Léon Blum in his *Au théâtre* declared that *La Ville morte* had been written in French and that the Italian text was a translation.[18] A similar error was committed by Guillaume Apollinaire in his *Théâtre italien* and by Angelo Sodini in his *Ariel armato*.[19]

The theatrical event drew D'Annunzio to France for the first time. He arrived in Paris in the company of Eduardo Scarfoglio, who had been one of the Argonauts on the cruise through the Greek islands. At the first performance of the play, intellectual and fashionable Paris was at the theater. Octave Mirbeau, Edmond Rostand, Jules Lemaître, Ferdinand Brunetière, and Melchior de Vogüé were among the spectators. *La Ville morte,* although generously applauded, had in general a mediocre success, and the reaction of the critics was not entirely favorable. It was only a "succès d'estime." However, the reception given the author was one of those which the French capital reserves for the "personnages dont elle s'est entichée."[20] For a week D'Annunzio was the idol of the mundane salons; he was overwhelmed by invitations and homage of all kinds. In the poet's apartment at the Mirabeau Hôtel, Hérelle noticed an array of books, flowers, and above all, letters: "Des centaines et peut-êtres des milliers de lettres, de tous les aspects, de tous les formats, enveloppes satinées et de papier bulle, feuillets parfumés et feuillets arrachés à un cahier d'écolier."[21] Finally, official homage. The Minister of Education gave a large reception in honor of the distinguished guest. The week in Paris was for D'Annunzio a personal triumph.

With *La Ville morte* the poet intended to restore Greek tragedy;

but he succeeded only in part. The dramatic action takes place in Mycenae, the very city of the Atridae, but the characters, though animated by the superhuman passions of the ancient demigods, are modern. Leonard, a young archeologist, has come to Mycenae to search among the ruins for the tombs of the Atridae. He is accompanied by his sister Blanche-Marie, his friend Alexandre, a sensitive and refined poet, and the latter's blind wife Anne. Alexandre soon falls in love with Blanche-Marie, a creature of charm and purity and, though she resists him at first, she finally yields to his passion. Anne senses what is happening and is ready to kill herself for the sake of the two lovers and for fear of the terrible loneliness awaiting her. Meanwhile, Leonard's heart is poisoned by the incestuous flame dormant in the Atridae's tomb, and he falls in love with his own sister. He reveals his terrible secret to Alexandre. But when he learns from Anne that Alexandre is his rival, his jealousy drives him to sacrifice Blanche-Marie, and he strangles her to free himself from his incestuous passion. Her death climaxes the tragedy.

The drama revolves around these two loves—one adulterous, the other incestuous. Both passions are fatal and criminal, and they possess a mysterious power against which the human will is helpless. The ruins that the protagonists touch in their archeological research mysteriously awaken the ancient passional furies in the soul of the modern characters. The denouement is logical. Only the murder of Blanche-Marie can purify and liberate her brother from his passion. This conclusion, of course, could not be easily grasped by the average spectator who was unable to understand why a brother should kill his sister just to free himself from an incestuous love. But for D'Annunzio, who considered events from a higher point of view, the catastrophe of La Ville morte was logical and ineluctable due to the superhuman nature of the main character—Leonard.

From the point of view of modern standards the tragedy seemed to be unreal—Blanche-Marie, a pure and noble creature, causing so much suffering; the tragic irony of her unsuspected death; Anne wishing to perish; Leonard murdering his sister to quench his impure flame—all presented more than one questionable point. Furthermore, the characters and passions were too lofty and uncommon to interest a modern audience. The power of ancient passions in modern characters was considered somewhat anachronistic. This lack of verisimilitude disappointed the public and irritated the critics.[22] D'Annunzio, however, claimed that he was pursuing a high artistic ideal which only the elite could appreciate. "Pour moi ..." he wrote to Hérelle, "la question théâtrale—dans le sens vulgaire actuel du mot—est secondaire. ... J'ai voulu écrire le drame tel que—selon mon idéal—il doit être et non tel qu'il pourrait plaire à la foule."[23] The idea of his tragedy was grandiose but not moving. In placing beauty as the supreme purpose of art, D'Annunzio achieved in his play an uncommon brilliance and originality; but his passionate cult of beauty put his work outside the concreteness of life into the regions of pure lyricism.[24] The psychology of the characters suffers from this unique artistic preoccupation. The drama is overcharged with lyrical effusions and loses in human truth, thus becoming artificial. D'Annunzio, prey to his unbridled cult of the Ego, constantly projects his own personality into his characters. According to Victor Hugo's definition, "génie lyrique" means to be one's self, whereas "génie dramatique" signifies to be the "other." D'Annunzio was never able to be other than himself, and this tendency was prejudicial to his dramatic works. Emile Faguet wrote of *La Ville morte:* "Comme drame, cela n'existe pas."[25] On stage the play was not living. There was in it a deliberate intent to submerge the dramatic action in a display of rare emotions and sensations pushed to the extreme without any moral restraint.

However, his attempt to revive the Greek tragedy was recognized as legitimate and of great merit, even by those who did not approve of *La Ville morte;* but, it was remarked, "il dépasse la mesure quand il prétend faire revivre l'esprit religieux et les rites dionysiaques qui ont donné naissance à la tragédie grecque."[26] Adverse critics attacked the tragedy on moral grounds. D'Annunzio was accused of defending incest; the ardent sensuality displayed by the author suggested, in the opinion of these critics, that he perhaps regretted the necessity of avoiding the consummation of the incestuous love. *L'Illustration* expressed the view that *La Ville morte* should have been composed in verse, since poetry, being the language of indefiniteness, would have been more suitable to D'Annunzio's play. The carnal passion of a man for his sister—the main theme of the drama—would have appeared less shocking if clothed in the language of poetry. According to the critic of *L'Illustration* the tragedy was a composite work which "ne plaira qu'aux adeptes de la petite école des esthètes anglo-français."[27]

Nevertheless, not all of the critics were completely hostile. Some found D'Annunzio's idea brilliant. Jules Lemaître, for example, discussed the qualities and the defects of *La Ville morte* with admirable impartiality. He judged D'Annunzio's idea as extremely interesting. "Il a voulu faire une tragédie dont les personnages fussent d'aujourd'hui, mais où la passion fût aussi entière et fatale que dans la tragédie antique."[28] Lemaître pointed out, however, that the characters in the play were simply juxtaposed rather than facing each other and that, as a result, the drama ended suddenly without a real conflict. He defined *La Ville morte* as a "lyrical poem":

> Elle vaut par la splendeur des discours, par la nouveauté fréquente des images, et par l'intensité de la rêverie. ... Ce qui est émouvant ici, ce n'est pas le drame lui-même, c'est la profonde sensibilité artistique de M. d'Annunzio. ... L'âme du poème c'est cet ardent néopaganisme du poète, dont la joie s'assombrit çà et là de mélancolie moderne et, malgré lui, chrétienne. Ce sont, assez souvent, des songeries du Nord qu'il habille de soleil, et cet Italien ressemble pas mal, quelquefois, à un Maeterlinck somptueux.[29]

The *Annales politiques et littéraires* called *La Ville morte* "un très beau poème," "un superbe roman à la Byron," and "un beau rayon de soleil italien qui tombe à point au milieu de notre brouillard!"[30] Jean Dornis praised in the tragedy "cette sensation d'apparitions hallucinantes, de richesses inouïes, de splendeurs terribles, révélées comme dans un songe surhumain."[31] Léon Blum spoke of "l'originalité et l'extrême beauté de l'oeuvre," of its "grave et forte simplicité," of its "noblesse dramatique," and "puissance lyrique."[32]

As for the originality of the play, opinions were divergent. In *Il Sogno d'un mattino di primavera* similarities with Maeterlinck's theater were vaguely pointed out; in *La Ville morte* some critics perceived not only the influence of Maeterlinck but that of Ibsen as well. As noted, Jules Lemaître found in the play "des songeries du Nord" and spoke of D'Annunzio as of "un Maeterlinck somptueux." Since the poet had intended to give symbolic meaning to his characters (Anne was Endurance; Blanche-Marie, Purity), critics found an added reason for pointing to the symbolist influence on him. Ernest Tissot, on the contrary, insisted on D'Annunzio's originality, and maintained that critics, by forcing the idea of derivation and taking the accessory for the essential, went so far as to consider *La Ville morte* as drawn from *Rosmerholm,* since both plays dealt with the moral influence exerted by the environment on the characters.[33] He stressed that D'Annunzio, as a poet, was indebted to Carducci; as a novelist, to French writers; as a dramatist, to ancient literature and to Shakespeare, but not to Ibsen. Jean Dornis considered D'Annunzio's dramatic production as being independent, that is, "une affirmation nouvelle de la nature très originale ... du romancier italien."[34] In any event, *La Ville morte* is a composite work in which it would not be difficult to detect the origin of the various elements. In this respect, critical judgments, even when conflicting, were not without foundation. What is unquestionably D'Annunzian in the play is the style and the ardent sensuality pervading all the elements of the dramatic fiction.

Despite the shortcomings of the tragedy, the extraordinary performance of Sarah Bernhardt saved it from complete doom. Like Eleonora Duse in *Il Sogno d'un māttino di primavera,* the French actress did wonders with her leading role in *La Ville morte.* The spectators were conquered more by the talent she displayed than by the play itself. "Jamais," wrote Jules Lemaître, "Mme Sarah Bernhardt n'a été plus belle que dans ce rôle de l'aveugle qui pressent, souffre, accepte, absout et se retranche de la vie par miséricorde autant que par désespérance."[35] Ernest Tissot said in *La Quinzaine* that those who had seen Sarah Bernhardt in *La Ville morte* "ne sont pas loin d'estimer que cette tragédienne n'a peut-être jamais recontré de rôles qui convinssent mieux à sa nature exceptionnelle."[36] According to the *Annales du théâtre et de la musique* Sarah Bernhardt "a été subjuguée par la joie d'incarner un genre nouveau" and in the role of Anne she was able to display "toutes ses admirables qualités."[37] It seemed that the performance of *La Ville morte* benefited Sarah Bernhardt's reputation more than the author's. Rather than revealing a new dramatist it revealed a great actress whose talent had not as yet fully manifested itself.

D'Annunzio's play was presented again in 1933 at the Théâtre des Champs-Elysées, but without success. André Doderet wrote of it with little enthusiasm, noting among other things that the play was shown in a different light. In the past the center of the drama had been the blind Anne, interpreted by Sarah Bernhardt or Eleonora Duse. In the new production the role of Anne was overshadowed by that of Leonard, interpreted by Zacconi, thus giving the play a new emphasis.[38] However, whatever theatrical success *La Ville morte* had was always due to the presence and talent of great actresses and actors rather than to its own merits.

8. La Gloria, La Gioconda

AFTER this debut as a dramatist, D'Annunzio, inspired by Eleonora Duse, continued to write for the stage despite the meager success of his play and the hostility of the critics; from 1896 on his theatrical works overshadowed his novels. In 1897 he composed one more one-act drama, *Il Sogno d'un tramonto d'autunno*, another of a cycle of four plays conceived under the general heading *Sogni delle stagioni* and entitled, respectively, *Sogno d'un mattino di primaverā, Sogno d'un meriggio d'estate, Sogno d'un tramonto d'autunno*, and *Sogno d'una notte d'inverno*. Of the contemplated four, he finished only two. The *Sogno d'un tramonto d'autunno* was never staged in France, but it was translated by Hérelle and published in the *Revue de Paris* of February 15, 1899. It was performed for the first time in 1905 at the Teatro Rossini in Leghorn, where despite Duse's dramatic skill it was received coldly. Accustomed to the French realist theater and to the English and Scandinavian psychological plays, the Italian audience was not responsive to D'Annunzio's "dramatic poems" such as *I Sogni delle stāgioni*. The play was written in the same dialogued form and was set in a background similar to the preceding *Sogno d'un mattino di primavera*. Therefore, its structure seemed more suited to a lyrical poem or an operatic libretto than to a prose drama.

The Dogaressa Grandeniga, passionately in love with a young man, has poisoned her aged husband. But the lover soon turns from her to the young courtesan Pantèa, who is the incarnation of pure beauty. Grandeniga plots her death by fire on board a sailing vessel. But her vengeance goes beyond her plans, for the young man perishes in the flames with Pantèa. Grandeniga watches in horror the disaster she has caused. The subject is undoubtedly tragic and is expressed with lyrical intensity; Grandeniga's passion—the inner drama of a woman in her declining age—is penetratingly portrayed. But dramatic action is again completely lacking. The spectator waits in vain for something to happen in the midst of the narration. The play is uneventful. Neither Pantèa nor the young lover appear on the stage. The latter has not even a name. The setting is a palace hall and a gate, and the events are known only through narration. D'Annunzio's previous experience with the presentation of *Il Sogno d'un mattino di primavera* must have enlightened him concerning stage requirements, and for this reason perhaps he put off the theatrical performance of his play. In 1914 *Il Sogno d'un tramonto d'autunno* was set to music by Francesco Malipiero, and in this latter form it was better appreciated at least for its lyrical intensity, rendered more suggestive by the musical score. Henry Prunières, in fact, reviewed the work quite favorably in the *Mercure de France*. "L'impression de rêve et d'irréalité que d'Annunzio voulait déterminer dans l'esprit du spectateur," he said, "est renforcée par l'effet de la musique, tantôt vaporeuse et nostalgique comme la brume errante au matin sur les canaux, tantôt enflammée et d'une ardeur dévorante, comme les couchers de soleil embrasant les palais marmoréens, le ciel et l'onde en de fulgurantes incendies."[1]

In the course of 1898 D'Annunzio composed *La Gioconda* and *La Gloria,* two tragedies which aroused a great stir when first presented in Italian theaters. They were translated by Hérelle and published by Calmann-Lévy in 1903 in a volume entitled *Les Victoires mutilées* which included also *La Ville morte*[2] (*La Gioconda* had already appeared in the *Revue de Paris* of May 1, 1902). But before speaking of their fortune in France it would be of interest to have a glimpse at their reception in Italy, since the reaction of the Italian audience conditioned to some extent French opinion. The coldness met by the two *Sogni* in the theaters of north Italy prompted the author and the actors to try the public of the South. A tour was organized by Eleonora Duse and Ermete Zacconi (two names whose association was considered a great theatrical event) to begin with performances in Sicily. *La Gioconda* was presented at the Teatro Bellini in Palermo on April 15, 1899, and it was well received. *La Gloria,* on the contrary, had a quite different outcome. It was staged on the 27th of that month at the Teatro Mercadante in Naples, where it failed pitifully. The audience, unable to understand it, booed it. Despite Duse and Zacconi, who performed magnificently, it was a complete fiasco. As a result the play was dropped from the billing, whereas *La Gioconda* continued successfully on its tour northward. D'Annunzio had dedicated *La Gioconda* to Eleonora Duse "dalle belle mani"; to avenge himself against the Neopolitans, he dedicated *La Gloria* "to the dogs who booed it." The echoes of the colossal failure in Naples arrived in France through literary correspondence. In the *Mercure de France* (June 2, 1899) Luciano Zuccoli wrote: "On est arrivé, à Naples, jusqu'à se battre en duel pour ou contre la *Gloire,* et un étudiant a reçu un coup d'épée suffisamment incommode dans le flanc droit. Donner ou recevoir un coup d'épée pour une oeuvre qu'on ne considère pas comme digne de son attention, n'est-ce pas le *nec plus ultra* du don-quichottisme oiseux."[3]

The unsuccess of *La Gloria* cannot be ascribed exclusively to the deliberate hostility or incomprehension of the public; fully as contributory is the fact that D'Annunzio never felt the necessity to comply with the special requirements of the theater. In his plays he remained an incomparable artist as to details, but he never concerned himself sufficiently with the total effect. In addition, the theater needs action, precisely the element most lacking in his dramatic works. It must also be pointed out that in *La Gloria,* a political tragedy, the author did not clearly bring out his ideas, thus leaving the audience somewhat perplexed. D'Annunzio's dramatic art was a peculiar conception of his own. The actual events in his tragedies are narrated by the characters and not unfolded on stage; and although the narration is in admirable language, it fails to convey a direct impression of the facts.[4]

La Gloria was written by D'Annunzio after his political and parliamentary experience in 1897–98, and the ideas and tendencies expressed in it spring from his contact with Nietzsche's works. Its tone, in fact, is typically Nietzschean—the protagonist impelled by an indomitable will to power. The subject of the drama is the political rivalry between the tribune Ruggero Flamma, and Cesare Bronte, the old tyrant in control of the Parliament and the Army. Ruggero has just addressed the chamber and his vigorous speech has inflamed the people. But the dictator Bronte is far from being defeated. He counters Ruggero's poetic eloquence with impudence and brutal frankness. His corrupted wife, Comnena, whom the people have branded the "Empress of Trebizond," hates him and awaits her opportunity to strike at him. She is now attracted to Ruggero Flamma by the illusion of his genius and forcefulness. The mysterious death of Bronte clears the way for the tribune to found Ruggero's new political order. But Comnena soon masters him, and in her thirst for power she drags him through a series of bloody deeds. In her hand Ruggero Flamma is reduced to a powerless plaything. Aware of his downfall he attempts in vain to retrace his steps. The woman's hold on him is too strong to break, and he must proceed to his inevitable ruin. He has alienated the people, who demand his death, and he finally falls under the stiletto of his rapacious mistress.

The public found in the play a series of political innuendos and remained confused as to its ultimate meaning. Some of the characters seemed incoherent and therefore incomprehensible. As in all of D'Annunzio's plays, fatality dominates the dramatic action. This external force, to which man's destiny is subjected, obliterates the superhuman power the author meant to depict in his leading characters. In this respect Ruggero Flamma is disappointing. The young dictator fails to bear out the strong-willed character seen in the beginning of the drama. He is easily crushed by the woman's destructive power. This point of criticism was refuted by D'Annunzio in a letter to Hérelle in which he said that in Ruggero Flamma he did not intend to present a hero in the Carlylean sense but a false hero, capable of aspirations and not action.[5] It was in Comnena, with her beauty and ruthlessness, the author maintained, that he meant to portray the irresistible power, the symbol of Glory. But this did not convince the critics who felt that Comnena, rather than the symbol of Glory, seemed to be the symbol of Sterility. In fact, feminine beauty, which was necessary for the achievement of the artistic ideal in *La Città morta* and *La Gioconda*, becomes a destructive force in *La Gloria*. As for the dramatic action in the play, the critics remarked that "tout se passe dans l'imagination de l'écrivain,"[6] that events are known only "par ouï-dire,"[7] that the author did not realize that action was "un élément essentiel du drame."[8] D'Annunzio held that his tragedy was "toute intérieure" and that factual details were alien to his subject. However, *La Gloria* passed for a weak theatrical work, and the first negative impression did not completely change over the years.

D'Annunzio, who at first had complained about the reception of *La Gloria*, later realized that the critics and the public were not entirely wrong in their judgments. He recognized the necessity of complying more with theatrical exigencies. It was in this frame of mind that he later wrote his *Francesca da Rimini*, which will be discussed in another chapter.

Although Hérelle's opinion of *La Gloria* was very favorable,[9] the play was never presented in France. After its failure in Naples it disappeared from the Italian theater until 1927, when the Compagnia Drammatica added it to its repertoire. The play met with great success during the entire Fascist period, with critics seeing in Ruggero Flamma a prefiguration of Mussolini. Against the dilapidation, fraud, corruption, and shame of demagogic Rome, Ruggero leads a revolution and moves in to seize the capital. The situation had something in common with that in 1922. "... Accomplir une révolution sans destruction barbare," said Jean Dornis, "est un fait inouï, cependant Ruggero Flamma, figure pathétique de Mussolini, idéal type latin, a réalisé ce miracle."[10] But this revival of *La Gloria* did not obliterate previous negative judgments on its dramatic qualities.

La Gioconda, on the other hand, was sympathetically received by Italian and French critics alike. Henri Lyonnet in his *Le Théâtre en Italie* gave a detailed account of the Duse-Zacconi tour and had words of praise for the play, which "fit couler des torrents d'encre."[11] He attended its last performance in Milan (where the stage setting reflected the theatrical decor D'Annunzio had seen in Paris the previous year) and reported that the audience was particularly fascinated by the musical quality of *La Gioconda*. Léon Blum, in a penetrating study on *Les Victoires mutilées*, presented the play as "le plus beau drame qu'ait encore écrit M. d'Annunzio," pointing out "la pureté de conception," "l'unité pathétique," and "le bonheur de l'exécution." He concluded on a note of high admiration for D'Annunzio's plays, which had been judged so severely by the critics:

> ... Ce qui me séduit en M. d'Annunzio, ce qui me fait saluer en lui un vrai poète de théâtre, c'est que dans ses drames, la poésie n'est pas factice et rajoutée, appliquée après coup comme des broderies sur une étoffe. ... Elle participe à toute la vie de l'oeuvre, elle est l'oeuvre même. ... Malgré toutes leurs imperfections, les tragédies de M. d'Annunzio montrent cette rare union de l'auteur dramatique et du poète. C'est leur beauté propre; c'est pourquoi il faut admirer en elles une des oeuvres les plus hautes et les plus nobles qui aient été produites en ce temps.[12]

It is evident that Blum's judgment bears only upon the uncontested poetic qualities of D'Annunzio's dramas. But poetry alone was not sufficient to produce a good theatrical work, and the critics, who judged the plays by the impression they made on stage, were right in considering them to be beautiful poems rather than dramatic works.

D'Annunzio had first thought of having *La Gioconda* presented in Paris by Eleonora Duse, but this was not to be. The play was staged in France only on January 21, 1905, and on October 18, 1906, respectively, at the Théâtre de l'Oeuvre (by Lugné-Poë) and the Théâtre du Gymnase, where it was performed thirteen times during that season. Its success was satisfactory and superior to that in Italy. The leading feminine role was interpreted by Suzanne Desprès, the only actress, besides Duse, to portray it.

In *La Gioconda* as in *La Ville morte* the main theme is fatal love, but here the author particularly emphasizes the rights of Genius to sacrifice all other mortals to his superhuman ideals. The superman is an artist, the sculptor Lucio Settala who, caught between his burning passion for his model, Gioconda Dianti, and his loyalty to his wife, Silvia, vainly attempts suicide. During his convalescence Silvia surrounds him with tenderness in the hope of regaining his affection. Lucio seems for the moment to have overcome his passion for Gioconda. But it suddenly returns in spite of himself. Silvia, overwhelmed by jealousy, faces her rival in the artist's studio. She informs Gioconda untruthfully that Lucio has decided to dismiss her. Angered by Silvia's words Gioconda strikes at the statue in which Lucio has recreated her beauty. In the vain attempt to prevent the destruction of her husband's masterpiece as it toppled to the floor, Silvia's hands are irremediably crushed. But her sacrifice is to no avail. By the fourth act Art and Gioconda have reconquered Lucio Settala. Silvia's victory is "mutilated"; hence, the title given to the dramatic trilogy.

The critics who saw *La Gioconda* on stage on the whole voiced, in a milder tone, the opinion expressed by Faguet on *La Ville morte*. The play, they felt, lacked dramatic movement. "C'est surtout comme suite de poèmes que vaut *La Gioconda*," wrote Ferdinand Herold in the *Mercure de France*.[13] And similar remarks were made by Jean Thouvenin in the *Annales politiques et littéraires:* "La pièce nous a paru un peu lente, surchargée de développements littéraires qui, fort magnifiques en soi, retardent la marche de l'action." He recognized, however, that D'Annunzio had "de ravissantes trouvailles d'imagination," and that "son art subtil, profond, et la grâce infinie de son verbe vous tiennent sous le charme."[14] The play presented also a certain confusion from the ethical point of view. The justification of pleasure in the name of a high ideal of Art, the identification of feminine beauty with the artistic dream of the poet seemed inconsistent, for Lucio Settala's temple of Art had in some respects the character of a "garçonnière." Furthermore, since D'Annunzio's protagonists were exceptional types, one would have expected from them completely uncommon acts—the most shocking crimes or the most sublime self-sacrifices. But they did nothing above the ordinary. Lucio behaved like any unfaithful husband; Silvia's stratagem to estrange Gioconda from Lucio was no less commonplace. And although every act was clothed in rare images and colors, a certain poverty of invention was nevertheless perceptible.

For D'Annunzio's admirers, however, *La Gioconda* was the best play of the foreign theater and the most intelligible to the Parisian audience. After the performance of 1906 at the Théâtre du Gymnase, Camille Marbo wrote in the *Revue du mois* that *Lā Gioconda* was a powerful and rare spectacle: "Le merveilleux talent de Gabriele d'Annunzio sait évoquer en admirables phrases, souples, sonores, semées de mots éclatants comme des gemmes, les obscurs tréfonds de l'âme humaine, déchirée d'angoisses et de combats."[15] Léon Blum in an essay devoted to the performances of *Lā Gioconda* reiterated his previous judgment on the high qualities of the play, considering it "d'une très belle invention dramatique" and its central feminine character, Silvia Settala, "d'une conception ... racinienne." After Monime and Phèdre, he said, "aucune héroïne n'a montré plus de pureté, de complexité, d'intensité, dans l'amour et dans la souffrance."[16]

Critical opinion was divided according to the point of view—poetic or dramatic—from which the play was judged. The performances, however, were well received. In commemoration of its stage success, the art printers Perette et Cie reproduced for a large number of subscribers an engraving by Riccardo Canale—*Suzanne Desprès dans la Gioconda;*[17] and the journal *Comoedia* of March 23, 1910, could still rhapsodize on the performances of *La Gioconda* given by "l'ardente Suzanne Desprès."[18]

Over the years the play was staged several times in the French theater. On June 5, 1916, it was presented at the Théâtre Réjane on the occasion of an artistic festival; in December 1922 it was performed at the Champs-Élysées, and on the following January again at the Théâtre de l'Oeuvre, where it met a certain resistance. Critics felt that the play was artificial and that it contained "en puissance tout ce qu'il y avait d'exécrable dans Bataille."[19] Lugné-Poë defined this critical attitude "malveillance aggressive" and commented that the public, "qui n'est pas si bête, s'est répété jusqu'à la contagion que c'était un admirable spectacle."[20] The last revival at the Théâtre de l'Oeuvre took place on October 9, 1926, and finally the play was staged at the Casino Municipal in Nice on January 15, 1930, always with Suzanne Desprès in the leading role.

Armand Caraccio pointed out in 1940 "l'influence indéniable" of Péladan's *Initiation sentimentale* on D'Annunzio's *La Gioconda*; the meaning of both works is that "la passion pour l'art dépasse infiniment la passion pour la femme."[21] He also suggested a certain likeness between D'Annunzio and Bourget: "Imaginons un Paul Bourget qui serait artiste et qui ajouterait en épilogue à ce débat psychologique une pure échappée de poésie, et nous aurons, schématiquement, le dessin général de la *Gioconda*."[22]

9. A Theatrical Success: *La Figlia di Iorio*

La Gloria and *La Gioconda* were followed by several other plays which always met with questionable success. D'Annunzio's increasing interest in the theater is shown not only by the works he completed but also by the many dramatic projects he announced and never carried out for lack of time or inspiration. The *Journal* of January 27, 1899, reported that, according to the publisher Treves, D'Annunzio had already finished the following plays: "Le *Songe d'un jour d'été*, le *Songe d'une nuit d'hiver*, la *Tragédie de la folle*, le *Soleil*; une trilogie: *Alexandriade*, et trois mystères: *Perséphone, Adonis, Orphée*." Le *Soir* of May 5, 1901, announced that he had just completed a new play entitled *Les Enfants de la terre*, adding that, in order to avoid being reproached for lengthy speeches, the author had decided that each character should say no more than thirty words at one time. None of these works ever appeared. (In September 1901, however, D'Annunzio finished *Francesca da Rimini*, a tragedy in verse, which will be discussed in the next chapter.) But the announcements of forthcoming plays continued. *La Revue* of February 15, 1903, made reference to a tragedy entitled *Ludovico il Moro*, reporting that D'Annunzio was sojourning in Novara to study the setting for his drama. And Le *Soir* of March 10, 1904, spoke of a prose drama of which D'Annunzio refused to reveal the title declaring simply that it would be a realistic play which would revive some episodes of *L'Intrus* and Le *Triomphe de la mort*. According to the journal the characters would be men of action, political figures, and businessmen, in their struggles, passions, and sufferings. The author would depict the figure of a modern woman moving about in this turmoil. If these press announcements often disappointed the public, it was due to the fact that no one knew what was going on in the author's mind. He deliberately strove to surprise.

In 1904 he completed *La Figlia di Iorio*, a three-act pastoral drama in verse, presented at the Teatro Lirico in Milan (March 2) and published by Treves the same year. Hérelle prepared the translation immediately, and the play was performed in Paris by Suzanne Desprès at the Théâtre de l'Oeuvre on February 8, 1905, about two weeks after *La Gioconda*. It appeared in the *Illustration théâtrale* on the 19th of that month, and finally in book form at Calmann-Lévy's in the course of the year (edition with engraving by A. de Carolis).

The translation of *La Figlia di Iorio* strained the relations between author and translator. D'Annunzio expected that the play would be rendered in French with its original poetic qualities intact and, contrary to Hérelle's better judgment, he insisted, as always, on literal translation.[1] He felt that in Hérelle's version the "partie lyrique" was intolerable, since the poetic rhythm was completely broken.[2] In an effort to give the French text the same poetic movement as the Italian, he made the usual arbitrary inversions and used awkward forms to which the translator could not subscribe. Hérelle's striving to render the text clear and logical conflicted sharply with D'Annunzio's wish to leave everything as vague and indefinite as in a musical passage. Corrections were then followed by countercorrections which, instead of eliminating the imperfections, aggravated them. Before the author's stubbornness Hérelle proposed that a note be printed at the head of the translation explaining his position and thus limiting his responsibility.[3]

But time was pressing; Lugné-Poë was planning to present *La Fille de Iorio* before *La Gioconda* at the Théâtre de l'Oeuvre, and promising, if the play met with success, a profitable series of performances. This would have been quite an achievement, since the performances at the Théâtre de l'Oeuvre were in general attended by the elite. After much quibbling, both author and translator had finally to seek a quick compromise, although D'Annunzio's opposition to Hérelle's method was rather strong. "... Dans les parties lyriques la traduction est une trahison noire. ... Toute l'oeuvre est banalisée justement parce que francisée."[4]

The translation was to have appeared in the *Revue de Paris,* but to keep Ganderax from putting his fingers on the manuscript D'Annunzio had decided instead to give it to *L'Illustration théâtrale*. He agreed to make some changes suggested by Lugné-Poë, who feared that the public might discover some resemblances between the third act of the play and Sardou's *La Sorcière* (performed for the first time on December 15, 1903). To clarify the problem and prevent any possible accusation,

D'Annunzio wrote to Hérelle, underlining (for the dates) that *La Figlia di Iorio* was finished on August 29 and read by the cast early in September 1903. He pointed out the incommensurable difference between his work and Sardou's "venimeux ramassis." But since the two words, "sorcière" and "bûcher," appearing in both plays could give "à la stupidité du public une apparence de ressemblance," he informed Hérelle that he had replaced "sorcière" by "louve" and asked him to do the same in his copy, and to replace also "Au bûcher! au bûcher! la sorcière!" by "Au feu, aux flammes, à l'Enfer." "Puérilité," he said, "dont M. Lugné-Poë sera content."[5]

The presentations at the Théâtre de l'Oeuvre of D'Annunzio's two plays within a fortnight with Suzanne Desprès constituted an unusual artistic event. They fully revealed to the Parisian public the real nature of his dramatic talent. "L'événement d'art le plus marquant de la quinzaine," wrote Gabriel Trarieux, "est sans contredit les représentations de l'Oeuvre, qui nous a offert coup sur coup la *Gioconda*, la *Maison de Poupée*, *Phédre*, et la *Fille de Iorio*"—works in which "la beauté latine," "la pureté française," and "la force saxonne" found expression.[6]

For *La Figlia di Iorio* D'Annunzio drew inspiration from a painting by his friend Francesco Paolo Michetti bearing the same title. With this play he goes back to the rustic world of his Abruzzi already portrayed in *Novelle della Pescara*. His protagonists are fierce peasants whose violent passions are of singular brutality. The central character is a country prostitute, Mila di Codra—the daughter of the sorcerer Iorio—whose seductive charm stirs the sensual appetites of the peasants, bringing calamity to the families. The curtain rises on the festivities for the wedding of Aligi, the son of the rich Lazzaro di Rojo. But the sudden appearance of Mila, pursued by a band of rude harvesters, upsets the happy atmosphere. Aligi is carried away by her mysterious spell. He forsakes his wife of a few hours and goes to his sheep in the mountains where Mila joins him. They love each other and he refuses to return home. But the figure of Lazzaro looms at the entrance of the grotto and, overwhelmed by carnal desire, claims Mila, who fights him off. Aligi in despair strikes at his father's head with an axe and brutally kills him. He is judged and condemned to die. Mila, believed dead, suddenly appears and accuses herself for the crime, in order to save Aligi's life. She convinces him that he was bewitched by her when the murder occurred. The gullible Aligi believes and curses her. Mila, now happy to save his life, purified of all shame by her unselfish love, runs into the fire, shouting in exultation: "La fiamma è bella! La fiamma è bella!" The subject, with its pastoral and primitive background, has a mythical flavor. The theme of sensuality, incest, murder of kin, links *La Figlia di Iorio* to *La Città morta*. But the rapid sequence of events, the fusion of realistic and symbolic elements, the moral and psychological theme, give the play a more dramatic unity and a more pronounced physical structure than are found in his other theatrical works, where the entire drama seems to be dissolved into lyrical fragments.

The play was presented with great success in Italy by Eleonora Duse. Luciano Zuccoli, whose attitude toward D'Annunzio had been definitely hostile, this time had to admit, in the *Mercure de France,* that D'Annunzio had found "la forme la plus directe et la plus empoignante pour parler à un public jadis défiant," and the success of the play was "colossal et sincère."[7] Only a few esthetes in Italy were dissatisfied with the work. They were, in the main, those who, whenever D'Annunzio's plays lacked dramatic effect, claimed that the author was at his best as a great artist; this time, on the contrary, they expressed regret that he was catering to the taste of the masses.

In France *La Fille de Iorio* also met with great success, and to convey his gratitude for the enthusiastic reception of the play, D'Annunzio sent a telegram to Suzanne Desprès who had so movingly interpreted the role of Mila di Codra: "... C'est par votre effort personnel qu'un public lointain et raffiné a pu accepter une oeuvre de poésie primitive qui sent si fort le terroir; vous avez sans doute ranimé par votre souffle cette tragédie religieuse dépouillée de son rythme natif, c'est-à-dire, de sa vertu essentielle."[8] Despite the impairment of this "rythme natif," and this "vertu essentielle," which D'Annunzio felt in the translation, critics unanimously agreed that *La Fille de Iorio* was a great dramatic achievement. Ferdinand Herold remarked "une entente réelle des effets scéniques," somewhat lacking in D'Annunzio's previous plays. During the entire first act, the critic said, "ils succèdent les uns aux autres avec une éblouissante rapidité. ... Les dernières scènes du second acte sont d'une force réelle. Le dénouement de la tragédie est d'une puissante ingéniosité."[9] He pointed out picturesque and colorful details "qui amusent, qui charment, ou qui terrifient le spectateur," and finally "les couplets brillants," "les morceaux de bravoure," which D'Annunzio could not renounce. Ricciotto Canudo, in a detailed analysis, found the play to be "une tragédie véritable."[10] Jean Dornis wrote: "Ici, il n'y a qu'à s'incliner. On admire la maîtrise de l'artiste, la parfaite tenue de la tragédie d'une simplicité magnifique, d'une sobriété classique, admirable en inventions poétiques."[11]

The collective cry of fear, hate, and death pervading the play was considered to be of high dramatic effect. What weakened the drama to some extent was a certain philosophical indefiniteness. In *La Gioconda*, for example, the meaning was clear when Lucio Settala finally returned to Art. Here, on the contrary, the symbols remained, as a critic put it, "imprécis dans l'humanité," although the characters were placed in a definite environment.

The performances of *La Gioconda* and *La Fille de Iorio* permitted critics to formulate a general judgment on D'Annunzio's theater. The stage clearly demonstrated the qualities and defects which a simple reading of the plays only suggested. Léon Blum brilliantly characterized the poet's dramaturgy. D'Annunzio had striven to recreate modern tragedy. Had he reached his goal? Blum doubted it. He found in D'Annunzio "un grand poète, et un grand poète dramatique ... un homme qui sait choisir, dans la vie moderne, des thèmes tragiques"; but he added: "... Chez lui l'inspiration poétique et l'invention tragique, qui concordent esthétiquement, ne s'accordent pas chronologiquement. C'est ce que la lecture révélait déjà, et que la scène fait apparaître avec une clarté plus crue. Le poète et le tragique sont d'égale qualité, de même nature. Ils ne sont pas du même temps."[12]

La Fille de Iorio was considered in all respects superior to D'Annunzio's previous plays. It was simpler, more human, and more musical. It combined fine artistic qualities with depth of inspiration and a certain primitive Christian sense of life. Théodore de Wyzewa noticed in the play a new spirit—the spirit "qui animait les grands drames wagnériens," of which D'Annunzio "reprend la forme poétique et les procédés."[13] Some critics expressed regret that the poet did not treat more "Christian themes" which could certainly have transformed his individualistic world and enriched the substance of his art—not in external forms but in ethical meaning.

As happened with *La Gioconda*, critics tried to find resemblances between *La Fille de Iorio* and French plays. D'Annunzio's work was likened to Henri Bataille's *La Lépreuse*, which seemed to contain the same symbolism, that is, the power of a fatal love carrying human beings away from tradition and family toward an unknown happiness, toward the beyond. Benjamin Crémieux remarked, however, that although D'Annunzio always needed models, he always surpassed them. There was no doubt in his mind that the technical model of *La Fille de Iorio* was Bataille's work, but "De combien l'emporte en lyrisme, en pittoresque et en beauté formelle la *Figlia di Iorio* sur la *Lépreuse!"*[14]

10. Plays Never Presented in France: *Più che l'amore, La Nave, Francesca da Rimini*

AFTER *La Figlia di Iorio* D'Annunzio published *La Fiaccola sotto il moggio* in 1905, which was followed by *Più che l'amore* in 1907, *La Nave* in 1908 (both written in 1905), and *Fedra* in 1909. Since *Fedra* and *La Fiaccola sotto il moggio* were not translated until 1923 and 1927, respectively, they will be discussed in another chapter. The other two tragedies were never translated,[1] and the French public knew them only indirectly. Dorothy Knowles in 1934 mentions *Più che l'amore* as "inconnu en France."[2] This is not entirely correct, however, since several articles were devoted to the play in French journals at the time of its presentation and publication in Italy.

The drama, performed in Rome at the Teatro Costanzi on October 29, 1906, scandalized the public. Thus, after the failure of *La Gloria*, D'Annunzio experienced again "l'ivresse de la débâcle."[3] Critics strongly objected to the amoral character of Corrado Brando, the protagonist, though they had to recognize the beauty of expression in the work. *Più che l'amore* is a two-act play in prose and of Nietzchean inspiration, in which the hero incarnates the superman with his dream of greatness and his deep scorn for common morals. Corrado Brando is dominated by a passion for geographical discovery. He kills to obtain the necessary funds for his explorations on the African continent; he cynically seduces and forsakes a young woman in his desires to prove to himself his uncommon power. This lust for power reduces the ideology of the superman to its crudest expression. D'Annunzio's intent had been to surprise the public; but he shocked it instead. The heroic part in the tragedy was received coldly, and the passionate scenes did not succeed in enlivening the drama, not even episodically. The only interest held by the play was the passion for Africa, which D'Annunzio expressed more forcibly thirty years later in a work entitled *Teneo te Africa*.

Critical reaction was especially vehement against this Nietzschean obsession, from which springs the figure of Corrado Brando. Moreover, from the artistic point of view, the character of the protagonist seemed artificial. This superman, who finally kills himself, revealed the absurdity of his own personality and the inconsistency of his ideology. To defend Corrado Brando as a tragic and plausible character, D'Annunzio wrote a preface for his play, thereby arousing a bitter polemic.

French critics, while disapproving of the main character, showed themselves to be less severe than the Italians. In the *Mercure de France* (December 15, 1906, and April 1, 1907) Ricciotto Canudo devoted two articles to *Più che l'amore*, pointing out the major weaknesses of the tragedy and concluding that it was nonetheless "une oeuvre d'art d'une valeur très réelle." In addition to the beauty of its expression which reaches "ce degré d'abstraction esthétique que le poète avait rêvé en écrivant sa tragédie," it reveals in D'Annunzio a rare interpreter of "l'esprit tragique ancien."[4] Maurice Muret, in the *Journal des débats* (April 27, 1907), and Ernest Tissot in the *Revue bleue* (June 22, 1907) voiced the views expressed by the Italian critics concerning the personality of the protagonist; but they did not hesitate to admit that, although the figure of Corrado Brando was objectionable, the play could not be entirely condemned. *Più che l'amore* possessed artistic qualities which French critics, more impartial than the Italian in this instance, did not fail to recognize.

The failure of *Più che l'amore* was followed by the triumph of *La Nave,* presented at the Teatro Argentina in Rome on January 11, 1908. In this play, highly patriotic in character, D'Annunzio exalts Italian Irredentism. Though the dramatic action is placed in the sixteenth century, references to the political situation of the time were so clearly perceptible as to arouse violent reaction in the Austrian press. In the last act, the people shout to the protagonist Marco Gratico: "Free the Adriatic! Free our sea from the brigands!" At these words the audience burst into wild applause. D'Annunzio had touched upon a delicate problem, and the acclaim won by the play led to bitter exchanges between the members of the Triple Alliance.

La Nave is divided into a prologue and three episodes. It begins with the lyrical evocation of the birth and development of Venice. The setting is an island of the Venetian estuary where two rival families, the Gratici and the Faledri, representing the aspirations of two factions, fight for supremacy over the city. The latter are finally defeated and destroyed, but one of them escapes with his sister Basiliola. Marco and Sergio Gratico are in complete control. However, Basiliola returns, certain that she will win over the Gratici with her irresistible beauty. Marco is quickly conquered by her charm and forgets that she is an enemy. He is now dominated by the woman and takes vengeance against those who had once insulted her; he exiles his mother; he scorns the advice of the seer who reminds him of his high mission. But Basiliola betrays him for his brother, and as soon as Marco realizes her deceit he rises up against Sergio and kills him. The spell is broken, and the spirit of probity and conquest is awakened in him. Basiliola is punished by fire, and with her perish also the seeds of corruption which threaten the city. But the fratricide weighs on Marco and demands expiation. He seeks in heroic deeds, which extol human power, the atonement for his crime. Thus, accompanied by his bravest followers, he departs with his ship for the conquest of the world.

The play had already been discussed in France by Ricciotto Canudo in the *Mercure de France*[5] and by Jean Carrère in *Le Temps*[6] even before it was presented at the Teatro Argentina. But the echoes of the patriotic feelings aroused by the performance and the hostile reaction of Austria resounded loudly in the French press. The event was reported in detail by the *Journal des débats* (January 15 and 22, 1908) and by many other journals. However, these repercussions were political rather than artistic in character.

From the structural point of view the tragedy was found to be unsatisfactory. Théodore de Wyzewa remarked a "dédain fâcheux pour les règles éternelles de la vérité et de la vie théâtrales," as the play was a series of scenes "que l'on supposerait découpées, un peu au hasard, dans un drame dont nous ignorons l'intrigue essentielle."[7] Furthermore, the sadistic voluptuousness, cruelty, and thirst for blood permeating *La Nave*, even in the stage directions, could not pass unnoticed. Ernest Bovet pointed out as an example of extreme sadism a scene in which Basiliola, moistening with her saliva the points of the arrows, kills, for the pleasure of killing, the prisoners "qui râlent d'amour pour elle."[8] But these elements were overlooked by the public in view of the enthusiasm aroused by the theme, and the powerful expression given to the play. Jean Dornis said that in *La Nave* D'Annunzio "a pu remuer des passions dignes des tragiques grecs;"[9] Ricciotto Canudo wrote that *La Nave* "est sans doute la plus parfaite tragédie vraiment 'méditerranéenne' que le théâtre de nos jours ait produite."[10] The play was set to music in 1908 by Ildebrando Pizzetti, and again in 1918 by Italo Montemezzi.

Between November 1910 and January 1911, the *Revue de Paris* published the French translation of *Francesca da Rimini*, which passed almost unnoticed. Louis Schneider, in fact, in the *Annales politiques et littéraires* of May 14, 1911, referred to *Francesca da Rimini* as a play which "n'a jamais été traduite en français."[11] Evidently he had not seen its publication four months earlier.[12] In Italy the tragedy had met with brilliant success in December 1901 when first presented at the Teatro Costanzi in Rome. Its performance assumed the proportions of a national celebration. Luciano Zuccoli, who kept the readers of the *Mercure de France* abreast of literary events in Italy, had to admit that D'Annunzio "a touché de près la perfection littéraire et dramatique."[13]

The poet had sent the manuscript immediately to Hérelle for translation, but only in February 1903 did he receive the first act for revision. The task was extremely difficult and, despite Hérelle's experience and efforts, the French version was far from satisfactory to the author. "... Toute la vertu rythmique—si importante dans une oeuvre de poésie —est perdue. La tragédie est méconnaissable et elle paraît médiocre. Toute la couleur linguistique, qui en constitue un des plus grands mérites, a disparu."[14] D'Annunzio himself recognized the difficulties of rendering into French a work such as *Francesca da Rimini*, which by his own admission was so profoundly Italian that it was almost impossible to transpose into another language. He felt nevertheless that translating it into simple prose, with no regard for rhythmical qualities, would inflict upon the work "une violence trop cruelle."[15] Because of these difficulties, the laborious translation dragged on; unable to agree on some passages, author and translator decided to set it aside temporarily. Only in 1910 did D'Annunzio ask Hérelle for the manuscript in order to make a rapid revision for the forthcoming publication.

On passing into the hands of Louis Ganderax, the meticulous editor of the *Revue de Paris,* the tragedy was fatally destined for a series of pedantic corrections of the sort which D'Annunzio detested. Upon receiving the first proofs, "hérissés d'observations si pédantesques," D'Annunzio wrote to Hérelle: "Je ne croyais pas que depuis l'*Enfant de volupté,* notre bon directeur eût fait un tel progrès dans sa manie ... La puérile subtilité de ces notes dépasse toute limite."[16] To revise the third act the author had to consult *Bestiaires* and *Lapidaires,* collections of medieval farces and treatises on surgery. Citing the authority of the ancient texts, he strove to retain in the French translation the archaic forms used in the Italian original, which he considered necessary for the artistic effect. But this time D'Annunzio, who defined himself as "le plus consciencieux des pédants,"[17] clashed with another pedant, of a different species—Louis Ganderax—whose corrections exasperated him. "... J'aimerais mieux composer 99 autres tragédies," he wrote to Hérelle after skimming over some of the proofs; "un simple regard a suffi pour me rendre malade."[18] He wished to preserve the archaic flavor of the Italian text, whereas both Hérelle and Ganderax insisted on the necessity of eliminating any trace of archaism. Furthermore, D'Annunzio could not tolerate corrections made without his approval, and he did not hesitate to rebuke Ganderax for changing some words in the play. "Si j'avais commis une faute, vous pouvez la blâmer, vous ne pouvez pas la corriger. Mon oeuvre est sans doute blâmable, mais elle est inviolable."[19]

The source of the tragedy—the fifth canto of Dante's *Inferno*—was well known. The public, therefore, did not expect anything new concerning the subject matter. Many dramatists and composers had exploited the theme with varying success. D'Annunzio's play was one of a long series. In 1815 Silvio Pellico wrote his *Francesca da Rimini*—a first attempt at a romantic drama in Italy; George Henry Boker had a *Francesca da Rimini* performed in New York in 1855; Francis Marion Crawford composed a drama in 1902 with the same title—a work which critics considered the best of the dramatic literature of the time in America; in that year Stephen Philips also had a play presented in London, entitled *Paolo and Francesca,* which Théodore de Wyzewa likened to D'Annunzio's tragedy.[20] After D'Annunzio, G. A. Cesareo added to dramatic literature one more *Francesca da Rimini* in 1905 to rival D'Annunzio's play, which he did not like.[21] Besides these works several operas were composed on the subject by Saverio Mercadante, Casimir Gide, Antonio Cagnoni, Ambroise Thomas (presented in Paris in 1882), Emily Aramy (performed in Paris in 1912), and finally by Franco Leoni (performed also in Paris in 1914). Since the theme was not new, only a new form could revive the drama, and this was what D'Annunzio meant to accomplish. Critics noticed that the author made great efforts this time to comply with theatrical convention. In this respect his *Francesca da Rimini* marked a certain progress with respect to his previous plays. The tragedy was never performed in France, and the public knew it only through the printed text (Calmann-Lévy, 1913).

The French audience had apparently already seen too many *Francesca da Rimini*'s to care for another one.

This "poème de sang et de luxure," as D'Annunzio himself defined it, is constructed on the historical facts which had inspired Dante's fifth canto. Francesca's parents were forced for political reasons to have her marry Giovanni Malatesta, an ugly and cruel cripple. In order to persuade her to agree, they deceived her into believing that she was becoming the wife of Paolo Malatesta, Giovanni's brother, who had come to arrange the match, and with whom she had fallen in love. But in the second act Francesca realized, heartbroken, that she was the wife of the cripple. When some time later she saw Paolo again, her dormant passion overwhelmed her. She reminded him of the deceit of which she was the victim, and of the part he had played in it. Repentant, Paolo would now die in order to atone for his misdeed. In the third act Paolo and Francesca are reading the passionate story of Lancelot and Guinevere. The entire third act is a development of the Dantean episode. In the fourth act Francesca is confronted by her husband's suspicion and the advances of another of his brothers, Malatestino. Having been rejected, Malatestino accuses Paolo and Francesca, and with his connivance the husband weaves a deadly net. They are surprised by him and murdered.

Despite minor defects observed in the play, French critics were favorably impressed with it. The poet had displayed all the wealth of his talent, handling the feelings and graduating the dramatic emotion masterfully. Opinions on the high dramatic qualities of this work have concurred over the years. Even if some parts seem to be purely decorative, the delicate passion and the profound suffering portrayed in the drama attest to a rich psychological insight. *"Francesca de Rimini,"* wrote Armand Caraccio in 1940, "est aussi prenante du point de vue dramatique, et, du point de vue formel, aussi belle qu'un drame de Shakespeare."[22]

Francesca da Rimini was to be part of a trilogy—*I Malatesti*—comprising *Sigismondo* (never written), and *Parisina*, published in 1913. This latter play, set to music by Pietro Mascagni, was presented at the Teatro della Scala on December 15, 1913, under the direction of Mascagni himself. The work, of which the composer used to say jokingly that even the commas had been set to music, remained completely unknown to the French public. Although composed and set to music in France, the drama received no notice in the French press.[23]

During the decade preceding the First World War, D'Annunzio's dramatic projects constantly grew in number, and the press continued to announce new works—a comedy entitled *La Dame impitoyable* (*Le Temps*, February 1, 1908); a tragedy on a theme similar to that of *La Nave*, *La Battaglia di Legnano*, evoking the most heroic episode of Lombard history (*Le Figaro*, January 22, 1909); a dramatic trilogy to be presented in 1911 during the celebration of the founding of Rome (a tragedy dealing with origins of the Urbs, the other with the republican period, the third with the empire); an unidentified dramatic work for the Vaudeville, with Mme Simone in the leading role (*Le Figaro*, September 1, 1910); a drama entitled *La Rosa di Cipro* to be set to music by Ildebrando Pizzetti (*Comoedia*, May 20, 1911); a very modern drama, *Le Vaincu*, dealing with the true story of a young man disillusioned by life and ending in a colorless existence (*Gil Blas*, July 19, 1911); a tragedy tentatively entitled *La Hache*, with the leading role for Suzanne Desprès; and finally a historical novel—the last two works to be written in French—"la seule langue dont il se servira désormais" (*La Revue*, October 15, 1911).

Some of these projects were carried out under changed titles; others were abandoned. Between 1910 and 1914, however, D'Annunzio completed, besides *Parisina*, three theatrical projects in French—*Le Martyre de Saint Sébastien*, *La Pisanelle*, *Le Chèvrefeuille*—and a highly successful film script, written in 1913 for Itala-Film—*Cabiria*.

The motion picture made from the script was a sumptuous historical view of the third century before Christ. The production required over a year and cost the company more than a million lire. The film was seen for the first time in Rome in 1914 and created a stir in the motion picture world. For the complexity of the subject and the enormous technical problems which had to be overcome in the production, *Cabiria* was considered to be a landmark in the movie industry.[24] The action takes place at the time of the second Punic War. We follow the terrible adventures of the orphan Cabiria,[25] a maid of Sophonisba, through battles, conflagrations, volcanic eruptions, and encounters with pirates. At the end of the story the young woman is married to the man of her choice. Her story is intertwined more or less with that of Sophonisba; but what the author meant to do was to give a magnificent picture—historical, artistic, patriotic—of the period of struggle between Rome and Carthage. His picturesque imagination is given free play, but the drama per se had little value. D'Annunzio had defined *Cabiria* "un drame greco-romain-punique, dans le genre de *Quo Vadis.*"[26]

The film, with French captions written by D'Annunzio, was presented at the Vaudeville on November 25, 1915, and it had forty-seven projections before the year was over. The French public regarded *Cabiria* as an exaltation of the French-Italian alliance which had been sealed a few months earlier. André Antoine in his *Théâtre* lists the work as follows: "25 novembre. *Cabiria*, un grand film de Gabriele d'Annunzio, très belle oeuvre qui remporta le plus vif succès."[27] The *Annales du théâtre et de la musique* contained this comment: "Jamais film n'a ... groupé autant d'attraits, autant de personnages, n'a reconstitué d'aussi grandioses visions historiques, n'a servi de cadre à un sujet aussi poétique, aussi émouvant, aussi varié"; *Cabiria* was defined as "le plus extraordinaire, le plus énorme, le plus vraiment sensationnel" of all films.[28] The following year it was revived at the Vaudeville on November 22, showing continuously until the end of the year. D'Annunzio personally did not like the work and avoided seeing it at any time, although Porel, the director of the Vaudeville, said to him: "*Cabiria* est un vrai chef-d'oeuvre."[29]

11. The French Plays

D'ANNUNZIO's French plays are of peripheral importance in his career as a dramatist. They reveal no new aspect of his artistic talent and add nothing to his reputation. Critics, in fact, have seldom given much attention to these works. They were widely discussed at the time of their first theatrical production and either highly praised or mercilessly condemned; then, except for occasional references in general studies of the author, they were almost completely forgotten.

From the artistic point of view they perhaps deserved no more. However, if they do not offer much in artistic interest per se, they are important in the study of D'Annunzio's relations with French culture. Inspired by a deep affection for his "seconda patria," they show the extent to which the poet assimilated its language and culture.

D'Annunzio had already tried his wings in French in 1896, when he wrote a series of twelve sonnets—*Sonnets cisalpins*—which will be discussed in another chapter. But if these sonnets represented a timid effort in the poetic use of French, his plays stand out as ambitious and almost rash enterprises. The first of his three French theatrical works —and the one which created the stir in France—was *Le Martyre de Saint Sébastien*, a mystery play in five acts, composed between 1910 and 1911 in the solitude of Arcachon. A work of this sort in 1910 was, indeed, an unusual literary event, and only D'Annunzio's temerity could have conceived such a project. In his dedication to Maurice Barrès the poet wrote: "Aucun ne pourra, certes, comme vous, comprendre le singulier plaisir que me donnèrent ma hardiesse et un si haut danger." When asked the reason for writing a medieval play in old French, he said that "un esprit, pour toucher au fin fond d'une race, doit descendre au plus mystérieux de ses sanctuaires, celui de la langue."[1] And, eager to produce a work which would give him the right of citizenship in the "douce France des poètes," D'Annunzio had undertaken this difficult task in emulation of Brunetto Latini.

The idea of a work on the martyrdom of St. Sebastian had been growing in his mind for a long time.[2] In fact a *Martirio di San Sebastiano* was included in a list of literary projects which he had handed over to the Milanese publisher Treves in 1908. He had found in a verse of Veronica Gambara, an Italian poetess of the Renaissance, the theme to be developed in his "mystical tragedy"—"Celui qui m'aime plus me blesse."[3] The poet's interest in the legend of the saint was not, to be sure, of a religious nature; instead, he viewed the beautiful figure of the bleeding youth pierced by the arrows as a Christian transfiguration of the myth of Adonis. But perhaps he never would have written his French play if he had not found an unexpected inspiration in Ida Rubinstein, who at that time was appearing with brilliant success on the Parisian stage as Cleopatra or as Scheherazade. In her lithe and slender body, long straight limbs, and absolutely flat chest, D'Annunzio asserts that he saw the ideal interpreter of his saint.[4] He must, however, have had reasons more personal than the mere idea of the Russian ballerina as the "perfect interpreter." He wrote to Robert de Montesquiou: "Je viens de voir Cléopâtre, je ne domine pas mon trouble, que faire?" And Montesquiou quickly answered: "Un ouvrage capable de mettre en lumière, de façon exceptionnelle, les dons uniques d'une telle interprète."[5] Since Ida Rubinstein had no knowledge of Italian, the poet had an added incentive for trying his wings once more in the French language.

There already existed two mystery plays on the life and martyrdom of St. Sebastian, one dating from the fifteenth and one from the sixteenth century.[6] D'Annunzio, guided by Gustave Cohen, examined at the Bibliothèque Nationale the two plays and other sources such as the *Golden Legend* and the *Acta Sanctorum*. However, he utilized his medieval sources only in part. An aging and bearded St. Sebastian, as was portrayed by medieval tales and mosaics, would not have served his purpose. The poet's mind was dominated by the image of the agile ephebus he admired in Renaissance paintings. His saint, therefore, would be modeled on a living exemplar—Ida Rubinstein.[7] He took his historical data by preference from the *Golden Legend,* making changes and additions of his own, borrowed from the earlier mystery plays their form and rhythm, eliminating the grotesque medieval elements, and composed an intensely lyrical work of a lofty and sustained tone.

The *Martyre* is divided into a prologue and five "mansions"—"La cour des lys,"' "La chambre magique," "Le concile des faux dieux," "Le laurier blessé," "Le paradis"—which appear as loosely connected episodes. As a result, the play lacks real dramatic crescendo and unity, and has the fragmentary character of the medieval compositions of the sort. Moreover, D'Annunzio crystallized the various elements in the immobility of lyric presentation, thereby failing to give the story even the little action it had in the *Golden Legend*.

In order to carry out his work in the verse form of the mystery plays, the poet had to engage in serious research. He made a thorough study of the medieval texts, and acquired complete mastery of the archaic phraseology with surprising rapidity. He created an artificial and stilted language characterized by a certain affected refinement peculiar to himself; archaic and modern expressions are brought together with such delicate musical taste as to result in an unusual orchestration of notes and rhythms. "C'est à la fois la langue de l'épopée galante du Moyen Age, la langue de Montaigne ou d'Amyot, la langue de Gautier ou de Banville, tandis que les emplois et les enchaînements de rythme rappellent tour à tour la façon des chansons de geste et des Mystères, les procédés des Parnassiens ou des récents poètes symboliques."[8] D'Annunzio's style, however, remains modern, despite the numerous archaisms.

The elite was not at all displeased with his linguistic artifice. Gabriel Trarieux hailed in D'Annunzio's play "des dons qui eussent fait rugir de joie le grand Flaubert de la *Tentation de Saint Antoine.*"[9] The poet had suggested the atmosphere of the mystery plays quite effectively. The day after the first performance, Léon Blum wrote: "Les lettres françaises comptent un grand poète de plus";[10] and expressed astonishment at the fact that a foreigner had been able to compose a dramatic poem with such mastery of the resources of vocabulary and rhythm. Gustave Cohen expressed himself in similar terms: "Gabriele d'Annunzio possède un prodigieux don verbal. Son vocabulaire français n'est pas moins riche que son vocabulaire italien." Cohen's praise extended to the artistic qualities of D'Annunzio's work as well: "Il offre à la France une oeuvre magnifique," in which the Christian and pagan spirit, the Italian and the French genius are intimately and profoundly fused.[11] *L'Illustration* referred to *Le Martyre de Saint Sébastien* as "... Cet admirable drame mystique," in which the Italian poet had overcome, with surprising mastery, all the difficulties of "une langue purement et noblement française."[12] Maurice Barrès wrote later: "C'est inimaginable ce qu'un mystère comme le *Saint Sébastien* ... suppose de civilisations amalgamées et d'imagination poussées à leurs limites."[13]

There were, nevertheless, many disparagers of the poet and his play. Jean Marnold said in the *Mercure de France*: "M. d'Annunzio ... se figura écrire en français parce qu'il employait les mots de notre dictionnaire, et de cette illusion s'ensuivit un verbiage informe, inane, incompréhensible même à la lecture."[14] Henri Ghéon attacked D'Annunzio in the *Nouvelle Revue française* by saying that French taste "si mesuré, si fin ... se refuse à prendre leçons de latinisme de M. Gabriele d'Annunzio."[15] And François de Nion, in *L'Echo de Paris*, went so far as to reproach him for errors in syntax. That Nion had called him "le troubadour qui a lu Ibsen" did not bother the poet in the least. But the criticism of his style infuriated him. These strictures, however, were not completely objective. D'Annunzio's French was perceptibly archaic and studied; but in order to create the atmosphere of the mystery plays, as the poet intended, it was imperative to use the language characteristic of the medieval religious theater. And this was considered to be nothing more than a stupid anachronism.

D'Annunzio's play was set to music (for solo voices, chorus, and orchestra) by Claude Debussy. Poet and composer worked together feverishly to translate into images and music the Christian myth of the Archer of God. To some critics the collaboration of Italy's foremost poet and France's great composer indicated complete ignorance of their respective talents. "Rien n'est plus éloigné du panache flamboyant et tonitruant propre à notre hôte," wrote Jean Marnold, "que la sensibilité délicate et profonde d'un Debussy."[16] Pasteur Vallery-Radot said that Debussy, having an aversion for pomposity, "n'était pas sensible au verbe prestigieux de l'animateur dont le perpétuel lyrisme l'agaçait."[17] And Léon Vallas later spoke of Debussy "entraîné par l'art de d'Annunzio très loin de son goût personnel."[18] But other critics maintained that Debussy was completely captivated by the subject of *Saint Sébastien*, which was the most suited to his esthetics. "Il écrivit cette admirable partition," wrote Jacques Durand, "dans l'exaltation."[19] Henry Malherbe quotes the composer as saying: "… le sujet du *Martyre* m'a séduit surtout par ce mélange de vie intense et de foi chrétienne."[20] D'Annunzio's *Libro segreto*[21] extols Debussy's spontaneous acceptance of collaboration in the project, and the happy circumstance is also confirmed by correspondence between composer and poet.[22] The score for the play was written in great haste and completed in less than two months, between January and March 1911. The task imposed an enormous physical and mental strain, and there were moments when Debussy was on the point of admitting failure. He felt that he should have had more time to penetrate the subject matter and dissolve it into music. But Gabriel Astruc, director of the Théâtre du Châtelet, and Ida Rubenstein were waiting impatiently; the opening date had already been set, the press had publicized the coming performance of the play, and the Parisian public awaited with great interest the theatrical event which was to reveal D'Annunzio as a French poet, set to music by Claude Debussy. On March 9, 1911, the play was read to the principals in the cast, and on May 22 it was performed at the Théâtre du Châtelet with a sumptuous stage setting by Léon Bakst.

Unfortunately, the presentation left the general public noticeably disappointed. The play met with strong adverse criticism from the Catholic press, whose attacks helped discredit it, at least for the moment. Monseigneur Amette, Archbishop of Paris, knowing the pagan tendencies of D'Annunzio's and Debussy's art, had publicly condemned *Saint Sébastien*, even before the opening performance, on the basis of reports from Catholic observers. The poet and the composer found it necessary to defend themselves in an open letter in which they declared: "Nous affirmons—sur notre foi et sur la foi de tous ceux qui connaissent le *Martyre de Saint Sébastien*—que cette oeuvre, profondément religieuse, est la glorification lyrique non seulement de l'athlète du

Christ mais de tout l'héroïsme chrétien."[23] But their defense failed to sway either Protestant or Catholic critics, to whom the figure of the saint seemed to be completely profaned by the sensual atmosphere of blood and perfume created around him. It was looked upon as unforgivable sacrilege that D'Annunzio, the author of *Il Piacere*, should have written a religious play. Henri Ghéon vehemently criticized the poet not only on religious but also on artistic grounds, affirming that the play was a blasphemy against art, since art selects, sacrifices, and respects, all of which D'Annunzio had failed to do.[24]

The equivocal religious nature of the play is unmistakable. In *Saint Sébastien* there is such a strange amalgamation of pagan myth and Christian legend that the martyr is often confused with Adonis.[25] In the third "mansion"[26] especially the poet gives a clear glimpse of the resemblances between Sebastian, beloved by Emperor Diocletian, and Adonis, cherished by Aphrodite. Of Sebastian one sees only his narcissistic beauty enveloped in languorous and voluptuous ecstasy, which the atmosphere of tortures and the fragrance of blossoms tinge with sadistic sensualism. The dramatic tone of certain passages recalls vaguely Oscar Wilde's *Salomé*. The figure of the saint seemed to be profaned not only by the poetry but also by the music, which became more suggestive at the very moment when the poet's inspiration, freeing itself from empty rhetorical forms, assumed an ambiguous mystical tone which was nothing but the exaltation of the senses. The Christian spirit which the work was to express is thus paganized and sacrificed to the idea of physical beauty, which dominates the play. Some critics maintained, in defense of D'Annunzio, that his intention had been to contrast the Christian spirit of Sebastian, destined to triumph, with the declining paganism of the Diocletian age. But, rather than a contrast between the Christian and the pagan worlds, D'Annunzio's play was meant to be a synthesis. The Renaissance painters had already offered this synthesis when, concerned with reviving the esthetic principle of paganism in a new Christian art, they fused the spirituality of the saint with the beautiful physical form of Adonis. In Sodoma's *San Sebastiano* (Florence, Galleria degli Uffizi), what stands out most prominently is not the mystical ecstasy of the martyr but his physical beauty pervaded by a certain sensual abandon. Similar characteristics are found in Antonio del Pollaiolo's painting (London, National Gallery), in which D'Annunzio claims to have found inspiration. The poet proceeded in the very spirit of Renaissance esthetics, and it is in this spirit that he insistently magnifies and deifies, through the words of the emperor, the soldiers, and the women, the physical beauty of the saint. Diocletian, unable to convince Sebastian to disavow his Christian faith, commands that he be killed gently, under a shower of blossoms, "... car il est beau!"[27] It was quite understandable that the *Martyre de Saint Sébastien*, which would undoubtedly have been approved by any Renaissance churchman, should infuriate the Archbishop of Paris in 1911. Sebastian did not die under the blossoms and was subsequently riddled by the arrows of his archers. His death seemed the transfiguration of the god D'Annunzio had sung of in a sonnet of the *Intermezzo* —"La morte del dio":

> Così moriva il Giovine, in un grande
> mistero di dolore e di bellezza
> quale già finsero il mio Sogno e l'Arte.

The reason for the failure of the play, however, is not to be sought in the anathemas of the Church, but mainly in certain defects of the work itself and in technical errors in the production. The complexity of the themes and thoughts, the intricacy and subtlety of images, and the excessive verbosity slowed the development of the dramatic action and made the play difficult to follow. Moreover, the author's deliberate use of archaisms and the poor pronunciation of Ida Rubinstein resulted in complete obscurity of language in certain passages. Finally, the vast and complicated stage setting so engulfed the play that only a confused echo of words and music reached the spectators. D'Annunzio's high-sounding verse was lost amid the resplendent scenery. The public, before this enchanted forest of decoration, images, and music soon felt utterly bored.

The poet's attempt to revive the medieval mystery play and arouse feelings of tenderness or emotion of a mystical nature was smothered by his inveterate and outworn sensualism, from which he could not free himself even when dealing with a religious theme. The primitive religious fervor of the main characters, cast against such a decadent background, appeared as a ridiculous anachronism. The refinement of D'Annunzio's style, the languid tone of the music, the rhythm of the dance, and the splendor of the decorations clearly expressed his stylized and empty estheticism. The play, lacking in real religious emotion and psychological interest, dissolved into pure spectacle and music. Its mysticism was purely decorative. This explains why D'Annunzio sought the collaboration of a composer of an evanescent sensibility and of a dancer such as Ida Rubinstein. The erudite use of archaic French was particularly suited to a decorative work as an ingredient capable of rendering the matter more delicately palatable. From the strictly theatrical point of view, the same general observations made by critics concerning nearly all of D'Annunzio's plays applied also to *Saint Sébastien*. D'Annunzio was more of a lyric than a dramatic poet. His plays lacked the agility of movement and the sobriety of form necessary for dramatic action. On the stage they were stagnant. "A la lecture seulement," wrote Léon Blum of *Saint Sébastien*, "on goûtera pleinement cette beauté rythmique de l'oeuvre, on apréciera tout ce dont M. d'Annunzio vient d'enrichir le répertoire lyrique français.[28] Debussy himself seemed to enjoy the play much more when it appeared in print, some time after the theatrical production. He wrote to D'Annunzio: "Quel beau livre! ... J'ai tout relu et avec une joie pure que ne venait plus contrarier la présence lourde, les voix contradictoires, le bruit faux que fait le théâtre autour d'une belle chose."[29]

The *Martyre de Saint Sébastien* was first published in the theatrical supplement of *L'Illustration*, May 27, 1911, and about a month later was printed in book form by Calmann-Lévy. The volume carried the dedication to Maurice Barrès: "... Ce poème composé dans le pays de Montaigne et de la forte résine, je vous le dédie parce que vous avez trouvé vos cadences les plus mélodieuses à Pise, à Sienne, à Parme, dans le sépulcre de Ravenne, dans les jardins de Lombardie."[30] Barrès, knowing in advance that the work had been dedicated to him, did not wait for the volume to appear, and in a letter of May 31 expressed his gratitude to the poet: "Je rêve de ce livre encore inconnu auquel vous me liez pour ma gloire. ... Il n'est pas de décoration de Toison d'or ni de Jarretière qu'un roi puisse donner et qui équivaille à ce qu'il vous plaît de faire, cher et grand poète, pour votre reconnaissant admirateur."[31]

After the production of 1911, various attempts to revive *Saint Sébastien* failed for a number of reasons.[32] The first presentation had revealed the excessive heaviness of the poem, which the music, in its subordinate role, did little to relieve. The poet and the composer planned a revision whereby the poem would be shortened and the role of the music enlarged. This revision, which would perhaps have changed the mystery play into an opera, was never made. In the summer of 1922 *Saint Sébastien* was produced in its original form at L'Opéra, and was again received with extreme coolness. Long and boring, the play seemed to be more the martyrdom of the spectators than of St. Sebastian. "Si le *Martyre* ne durait qu'une heure, ce serait acceptable," wrote Boris de Schloezer, "mais il est pénible de respirer cinq heures durant cette atmosphère de paradis artificiel au goût parisien de 1911."[33] Jean Marnold acridly expressed again, and with more emphasis, the same views as in 1911: "Cette brève partition ... est une des choses les moins musicalement intéressantes. ... La tragédie qu'elle accompagne ... s'atteste d'une insanité toujours plus évidemment peu commune."[34] In 1926 the play was produced at La Scala. Despite the ban on it by the Archbishop of Milan, the theater was packed. Toscanini directed the orchestra, and the performance was received with wild enthusiasm. This seemed to be the long-delayed vindication of D'Annunzio and Debussy.

In 1941 the fortune of *Saint Sébastien* began suddenly to change in France. Thirty years after its first performance, the public finally discovered the music which, having failed in the theater, triumphed decisively in concert halls.[35] In 1911 the poet had said: "Quelle que soit l'opinion de la critique et du public sur mon poème, je suis assuré que chacun reconnaîtra dans la partition de Claude Debussy la plus divine source d'émotion."[36] But how could the music and the poem be considered separately? Since they constitute an inseparable whole, the play was to be revived in its integrity. It is perhaps in this spirit that, in the winter of 1957, *Saint Sébastien* was finally brought back to the stage of L'Opéra. In the new presentation the poem underwent judicious cutting (the score was left intact), its sensualism was attenuated, its erudite developments eliminated. The play lasted only two hours as compared to the five hours it required in 1911 at the Théâtre du Châtelet. Furthermore, the entire atmosphere of the work changed. The performance, without medieval costumes, in a stage setting somewhat similar to the Folies Bergère, obliterated most of its religious significance.

The *Martyre de Saint Sébastien* was followed in 1913 by another French play, *La Pisanelle ou la mort parfumée*, a three-act drama in verse.[37] This time, in addition to writing in French, the poet chose French knights, the Lusignans, as the heroes of his play, and the island of Cyprus, dominated by the French, as the setting for the dramatic action. The Parisian public was pleased by this new tribute to the French language and history. "La nouvelle oeuvre de M. Gabriele d'Annunzio," wrote Edmond Stoullig, "peut être considérée comme un éclatant hommage à notre littérature."[38] Although D'Annunzio called it a comedy, La Pisanelle is more of a romantic drama, in which shrieks, blood, and dances create an atmosphere both horrifying and voluptuous. The story is presented as a series of picturesque scenes in which the caustic and coarse spirit of the fabliaux is blended with the pathos of medieval romance. The protagonist is a harlot, native of Pisa, who bewitches the young and romantic king of Cyprus. The queen mother, in order to get rid of the adventuress, secretly lures her to court, and, after offering her drink, invites her to dance. While the girl dances before the admiring court, a shower of blossoms falls upon her until she succumbs under the weight of the petals. When the king arrives, it is too late.

The diffuseness noticed in Saint Sébastien is even more pronounced in La Pisanelle, where cumbersome details, especially seafaring terms and images, unduly burden the development of the drama. The play also contains the same pompous glorification of lust and blood which is found in La Nave and Il Sogno d'un tramonto d'autunno, and all the usual lust-laden clichés, calculated to raise every motif to ecstatic heights. What is significant is not the death of the protagonist but the manner in which she dies—under a shower of flowers. D'Annunzio's estheticism is now aggravated by cold and verbose erudition and by an immorality to which he vainly tries to give a tragic sense. An effeminate St. Sebastian who perishes at the hands of his archers and enjoys the sight of his own blood and a Pisanelle voluptuously smothered under a shower of blossoms express a sensualism too decadent to be dramatic.

The French of the play is even more artificial than that of Saint Sébastien, and at times it is more obscure. D'Annunzio had already acquired a close familiarity with medieval and Renaissance writers, and from their works he had derived a strange language compounded of Latinisms, Italianisms, lofty expressions and idiotisms, archaic and modern forms—the whole resulting in a bizarre linguistic potpourri conspicuous for its inconsistency. The completion of the play in March 1913 was announced by D'Annunzio in these words: "I have just completed the composition of forty-five hundred verses in a language so learned that only consummate philologists will be able to judge it."[39] And he boasted to Hérelle that the work was "le résultat d'une recherche de douze ans," adding: "Naturellement la langue est un peu archaïque, et certaines tournures sont hardies mais toujours appuyées sur un texte illustre."[40] Jean Schlumberger called the French of the play "le plus étrange, le plus indigeste, le plus barbare galimiatias qu'on puisse concevoir."[41] But, by a strange contrast of opinions, the linguistic effort was generously praised by other critics. Jean Thouvenin said of D'Annunzio: "Il se meut à l'aise dans le vocabulaire suranné et compliqué du treizième siècle. Il a la force de Ronsard, la grâce de Clément Marot, la robuste et plantureuse ironie de Rabelais."[42] The French of the play, however, is not always comprehensible.

La Pisanelle, also written for Ida Rubinstein, was produced at the Théâtre du Châtelet in June 1913, with music by Ildebrando Pizzetti. It met with no success. The stage setting, however, was a rare spectacle, perhaps unique in its magnificence. Léon Bakst applied all his artistic talent to give, with pompous and colorful scenery, a sumptuous picture of the Latin Middle East in the period following the Crusades. Meyerhold, one of the most skillful stage directors of the Petrograd Theater, was expressly summoned to Paris for the occasion. But the error committed in the production of *Saint Sébastien* two years earlier was repeated—the play was overwhelmed by the huge décor. After the opening night this was in part corrected, but the first unfavorable impression remained. Paul Souday attributed the failure of the play exclusively to the stage setting, which was, according to him, that of the Russian ballet. "Ce ne fut pas," he said, "la représentation de la pièce de d'Annunzio, mais l'assassinat."[43] However, this was not the sole reason for the failure. There are in *La Pisanelle,* in addition to the obscurity of the language, the same defects prevalent in all of D'Annunzio's plays: diffuseness, verbosity, excessive lyricism, slow action. There is a prologue of about thirty pages, and the rest of the play hides " ... autant de ficelles qu'il en faut pour entortiller le public."[44] Louis Chardon wrote in *L'Action française:* "Ces quatre actes distillent un ennui morne. Le dialogue est phraséologique, déclamatoire, niais et prétentieux."[45] Edmond Sée, on the contrary, was more circumspect in his judgment, not finding the play "du dernier détestable." He was impressed, if not with the drama in itself, at least with "la pureté des attitudes, les admirables groupements des personnages, les décors, les jeux de lumières," and considered the play "un spectacle éminemment artiste."[46] Jules Bois enthusiastically praised Ida Rubinstein for her excellent performance: "... Elle est l'âme ... de ce somptueux et très artiste essai théâtral."[47] In his *Le Théâtre,* André Antoine entered under the date of June 12, 1913: "La *Pisanelle* de Gabriele d'Annunzio. Splendide mise en scène venue de Russie et succès qui rappelle celui du *Martyre de Saint Sébastien*."[48]

Some of the critics who disliked *La Pisanelle* leveled their attacks not only at the play and D'Annunzio's French, but also at Ida Rubinstein's foreign accent. The actress' charm, it was maintained, vanished the moment she opened her mouth to speak. The atmosphere of the performance of *La Pisanelle* at the Théâtre du Châtelet was strangely exotic. The author and the composer were Italians; the set designer and the stage director, Russians; the others involved in the presentation were Germans, Hungarians, Poles; the leading interpreter was a Jewess from the Petrograd Theater. Altogether the mixture was anything but Parisian. If one adds to the exoticism of the play that of the language and the accent of Ida Rubinstein, the babel appears complete. René Doumic noted: "C'est un mélange de brutalité et de préciosité. Disons tout simplement que c'est une invasion de la barbarie."[49]

The criticism of the play, however, did not affect the poet's reputation in France. D'Annunzio remains, pointed out Doumic, "... après comme avant, un très grand écrivain."[50] And Michel Georges-Michel wrote in his *Gens de théâtre*:

> Tandis qu'on répétait sur la scène du Châtelet la *Pisanelle,* le glorieux et doux nom du poète voltigeait sur toutes les lèvres, ses oeuvres étaient dans toutes les mains. ... Dans Paris, toutes les brunes gardaient sous leurs bras l'*Enfant de volupté*, l'*Intrus*, le *Triomphe de la mort*. ... Les blondes portaient dans leurs mains pâles tous les "Romans du lys" et les flamboyantes rousses serraient sur leur sein dur les "Romans de la grenade." ... Tous les regards étaient tournés vers Arcachon, où il avait conçu son oeuvre nouvelle.[51]

Immediately after its production, *La Pisanelle* was published in the *Revue de Paris* (June 15, July 1 and 15, 1913), and in the same year it appeared in Italy, in a verse translation by Ettore Janni. Its book publication in France was delayed until 1941. D'Annunzio wished to write a preface for the volume (perhaps an erudite essay such as the one Manzoni wrote for his *Adelchi*) and, finding neither the time nor the inspiration, kept postponing it. Finally, in the solitude of his Vittoriale, he composed the long-delayed preface, which is said to have been about five hundred manuscript pages in length. Thus the publisher was faced with the dilemma of printing the preface separately or in a volume together with the play. What eventually happened to this unusual foreword is not known. The play, which had been in type at Calmann-Lévy's since 1913, was published in 1941 without the preface and with a changed subtitle: ... *ou le jeu de la rose et de la mort.* The moment for publication was ill-chosen, and the volume passed almost unnoticed. There was only one review article, "Un Revenant: Gabriele d'Annunzio," by André Bellessort in the weekly, *La Voix française,* of September 12, 1941, in which the poet and the play were sharply censured.[52]

The theatrical failure of *Saint Sébastien* and *La Pisanelle* did not disturb D'Annunzio in the least. At the end of 1913 a new French drama of his entitled *Le Chèvrefeuille* (a three-act tragedy in prose) was produced on the Parisian stage. The play had been sketched out in Italian and translated into French by I. de Casa-Fuerte at Arcachon.[53] *Le Chèvrefeuille* was presented and published without the translator's name, and the critics erroneously concluded that D'Annunzio had written it originally in French. The Italian text was published with the title *Il Ferro.* In the French version, revised by the poet, the names of the characters are changed. Although *Le Chèvrefeuille* and *Il Ferro* are collected in the various editions of D'Annunzio's works as two distinct plays, they involve no substantial differences. The French translation follows the Italian original so literally that D'Annunzio's stylistic acrobatics are often clearly perceptible. The French of the play, however, is definitely more consistent and uniform than that of the two previous works.

Le Chèvrefeuille is a gloomy drama of passion. Although its title reminds one of Marie de France's lay, the theme echoes Aeschylus, Shakepeare, and Bourget. The protagonist is an enigmatic girl (Aude) who finds herself in a situation similar to that of Electra, Hamlet, or André Cornélis. She is haunted by the mysterious death of her father. She senses that he was murdered, suspects the complicity of her mother, and seeks vengeance. The murderer is the man (Pierre Dagon) who married her widowed mother. Pressed by the girl's implacable hatred, he admits his crime. The mother attempts to reconcile the two enemies, but, when she learns that Dagon is the lover of her son's wife, she is overcome by jealousy and, grabbing the dagger from her daughter's hand, strikes at the "monstre": "Je l'ai tué pour venger le mort et protéger le vivant."

The plot unfolds in an atmosphere of mystery and terror, strange visions, hate, and jealousy. Artistically it offers nothing new. It repeats psychological attitudes and motifs of earlier works by D'Annunzio, such as *Lā Fiaccola sotto il moggio, La Gloria, Più che l'amore,* and so forth. The poet seems somehow unable to free himself of his outworn dramatic clichés. Aude, sensing the crime and invoking vengeance, resembles Gigliola in *La Fiaccola sotto il moggio.* Pierre Dagon is meant to be a superman, but he lacks the strong qualities of a superior character and appears therefore as a failure, just as was Corrado Brando in *Più che l'amore.* Dagon's death repeats that of Ruggero Flamma in *La gloria,* a death with little or no pathos. In *Le Chèvrefeuille* D'Annunzio's tendency to evoke the invisible behind the visible and to suggest mysterious secrets behind the uttered words is reminiscent especially of *Fedra* and *Forse che sì forse che no.* Although carefully planned in its structure and close to traditional tragedy in its mood, the play contains puzzling obscurities which seem intentional.

Le *Chèvrefeuille* was produced at the Théâtre de la Porte Saint-Martin in December 1913, and was published in the *Revue de Paris* of June 15, July 1 and 15, 1914.[54] Despite its obscurities and incongruities it had a greater theatrical success than *Saint Sébastien* and *La Pisanelle.* D'Annunzio, however, was not well satisfied with the reception of the play and, after the first presentations, he asked the director of the theater to discontinue the performances planned for the season: "N'en faites rien, je vous en prie. ... Il faut respecter les arrêts du Destin, notamment quand il s'agit d'une pièce, comme la mienne, hérissée de fatalités plus ou moins antiques."[55]

Critics hastened to admit that *Le Chèvrefeuille* deserved praise, for it was by no means sheer spectacle. Henri Ghéon, who had previously been an adverse critic of D'Annunzio, wrote of the new play: "... Et d'abord c'est un drame. Dépouillez-le des nuances fleuries qui l'enguirlandent, il ne se réduit pas au néant, il peut toucher, il peut charmer. ... Le *Chèvrefeuille* vaut dix fois, vaut cent fois et le *Martyre de Saint Sébastien* et la *Pisanelle.* ... Il a une certaine force dramatique."[56] René Doumic, who had attended the first performance of *La Pisanelle,* said now: "... On a su gré à M. d'Annunzio d'en avoir si tôt effacé jusqu'au souvenir et d'avoir tenu à prendre une de ces revanches comme prennent les vrais poètes."[57] The pure esthetes praised, as usual, the sumptuousness of his style and the magnificence of his images. Someone remarked that never before had D'Annunzio shown his real stature as a French poet. Yet *Le Chèvrefeuille* fell short of a complete success because of its verbal excesses and the complexity of its images. "... Les choses belles abondent," observed Alphonse Séché, "mais elles sont voilées par l'obscurité que le poète semble avoir laissé planer à dessein, sur la tragédie." In his opinion D'Annunzio's French was too stilted, too archaic, and totally "dénué de simplicité."[58] Jean Thouvenin echoed the same feeling: D'Annunzio's ideas "... se dissimulent sous un flux de mots magnifiques et rares qui déconcertent un peu le spectateur."[59] This stylistic speciousness undoubtedly appealed to the select few who were more interested in florid declamations than in dramatic action. In *Le Chèvrefeuille* only the stylistic splendor is D'Annunzian; all else echos other dramatists. "En présence du *Chèvrefeuille*," pointed out Henri Ghéon, "nous disons aux moments les plus pathétiques: voilà Eschyle, voilà Ibsen, voilà Shakespeare. Et nous ne disons: voilà d'Annunzio, qu'à propos d'une belle phrase ou d'une image fastueuse."[60]

12. After the First World War: *Fedra, La Fiaccola sotto il moggio*

WITH the outbreak of the First World War, D'Annunzio's dramatic production came to an end. In 1923, however, with the translation of *Fedra* by André Doderet there was revived interest in some of D'Annunzio's plays which had not as yet been presented in France. *Fedra* was inspired by the poet's passion for Donatella, who had just entered his life. In announcing the completion of the work on February 3, 1909, D'Annunzio wrote: "Je dois cette oeuvre si noble et si sévère, ce poème flamboyant de feu solaire et résonnant de musique marine, ô Donatella, à ton amour."[1] The play was also dedicated to her under the name of "Thalassia," and the text was to be preceded by a Sapphic ode "A Thalassia,"[2] which he never wrote. A contributing factor in his idea of a "new" interpretation of the Phaedra theme seems to have been some fragments of a musical score that the young composer Ildebrando Pizzetti was planning for Euripides' *Hippolytus*.[3] The play was composed in a musical vein; the poet declared that during the entire composition a beautiful "Variation de Beethoven sur un thème de Diabelli" resounded in his mind.[4]

The leading role of *Fedra* in Italian was deceitfully promised to Donatella who also hoped to interpret the play in French. In the spring of 1909 the poet negotiated with Jacques Rouché, the director of the Théâtre des Arts, for the presentation of *Fedra* in Paris. Donatella labored to translate the work into French in the vain hope of realizing her artistic ambitions under the aegis of her lover. But none of these projects materialized, and all her efforts proved completely futile.

Fedra was produced in Milan at the Teatro Lirico on April 10, 1909, and at the Teatro della Scala on March 15, 1915 (this time with the music of Pizzetti), but it did not obtain either the dramatic success of *La Figlia di Iorio* or the triumph of *La Nave,* although it contained the most violent and passionate verses of D'Annunzio's theater. The only interest the work seemed to have for the critics was a perceptible tendency in D'Annunzio's art toward introspection, toward the somber recesses of life. *Fedra* was considered as marking the beginning of the poet's transition from the "solar" to the "nocturnal" inspiration, from Panic inebriation to the allurement of the shadows, without however a loss of his inveterate sensuality.

Fedra, like *Francesca da Rimini,* revolves around a well-known theme, already treated by Euripides, Seneca, Racine, Pradon, Gilbert, Edmond Smith, Swinburne, and others. It was therefore the object of much curiosity in France. French critics, who knew the play only through reviews in the press, were anxious to see whether D'Annunzio's work revealed any new and unsuspected dimension of the dramatic theme. It seemed unlikely that the author would fail to leave upon it his personal imprint, even though with Racine's play it was generally assumed that the drama of Phaedra had received unsurpassed and unsurpassable poetic expression. D'Annunzio's *Fedra* is an erotic-lyric poem. Being a visionary rather than an analyst of souls, the poet made of his tragedy an epic of the madness of love. His heroine is another Pasiphaë, portrayed in her primitive and violent instincts. In Euripides' tragedy the central figure is Hippolytus—the chaste devotee of Artemis, the tamer of horses, and the hunter; in Racine's play the dominant character is the melancholy and remorseful Phaedra. In the Greek tragedy, conducted by external powers, Phaedra is only an indirect means of destruction, a vanishing appearance (she dies in the middle of the play), whereas in Racine she is the entire tragedy. Aphrodite, offended by Hippolytus' scorn for love, devises his destruction. The unfortunate wife of Theseus, stricken by the goddess with an incestuous passion, scornfully rejected by her loved one, hangs herself leaving beside her body an accusing tablet. Hippolytus' death resulting from Phaedra's false accusation represents Aphrodite's victory over Artemis, the goddess of chastity. D'Annunzio's play comes closer to this ancient model through the vigor of his characters; but in his work both acquire equal prominence and are portrayed with the same power of emotion. His Phaedra is no longer Euripides' suffering and doleful blond answering to the solicitations of her zealous "nourrice" with austere and noble maxims of wisdom; she is not Racine's delicate, passionate, and revengeful creature. D'Annunzio's Phaedra is the lustful woman who epitomizes the grim fatality of the whole of Hellas—the fatality of sex and blood. He portrays in her a celestial and infernal madness. In Phaedra's veins flows the fiery blood of her mother; she loves and desires violently and relentlessly. Her folly does not grow gradually; it explodes immediately before us, and proceeds fatally to inescapable death. Like a furious captive, she shouts her suffering throughout her sumptuous palace. Theseus is believed dead, and his alleged death fans the flames of passion in the miserable woman. But Theseus' victory and imminent return are suddenly announced by a messenger, who brings with him three gifts for Hippolytus sent by Adrastus, the king of the Argives—a silver vase, a wild horse, and a royal virgin. The news of Theseus' arrival prostrates Phaedra. But suddenly aroused by anger, she savagely kills the captive destined for Hippolytus. The young man runs to her help, too late. He violently reproaches his step-mother for the murder of the woman. Now Hippolytus, exhausted by the effort to tame his horse, falls asleep; and Phaedra, carried away by her passion, ardently embraces the young athlete, who awakens and rejects her. She offers her love and her power, and he insults her. She asks him to put her to death, and he refuses. She then accuses him of having raped her. Theseus curses his son and invokes his death from the gods. The horse sent as a present by Adrastus will be the instrument of Theseus' vengeance. Hippolytus is killed and his body lies on the shore. Phaedra arrives and proclaims his innocence. She is pierced by Artemis' invisible arrows and falls, thus descending to Hades with her beloved.

Hippolytus' death extinguished the great and somber flames that burnt her flesh, and a pale light envelops Phaedra. She had come to confess Hippolytus' innocence, but is not, as in Racine's tragedy, a criminal who accuses herself or grovels in defeat and humiliation. She was never ashamed of her incestuous passion. She has been able to free herself of it by causing the death of Hippolytus, whom Aphrodite had used against her. After the holocaust, she is great and free, and she no longer fears Theseus. She did not commit the crime to avenge her rejection. As in *La Città morta*, where Leonard kills his sister to free himself of an incestuous love, Phaedra has Hippolytus killed in order to subdue Aphrodite. She can thus celebrate the victory of her own law over celestial laws. She makes her terrible confession with the joy of a goddess, for no one and nothing can now hurt her. She recalls her atrocious suffering, which purified her, and, pale, almost incorporeal, she invokes the chaste goddess dear to the dead—Artemis—for the ineluctable vengeance, and, pierced by the deadly arrows, she falls on Hippolytus' body, smiling at the stars. She feels worthy of her loved one. Expiation more than death restores purity, and her expiation is but an apotheosis beyond good and evil, as in *La Città morta*. The goddess' bow means for her life through death.

This death is undoubtedly more beautiful and dramatically effective than the suicide imagined by Euripides and Racine. D'Annunzio's Phaedra is most desperately tormented, most violent and haughty. Her audacity and impiety are sublime. She would have killed Aphrodite and Artemis, if she could. She is a vertiginous creature. She defies men and gods; and struck by celestial wrath descends triumphantly to Hades, renewing her imprecation against the hostile deity who tortured her, but whom she finally conquered. D'Annunzio's new vision of the drama is a series of violent deaths—the captive's, Hippolytus', Phaedra's. Racine had introduced Aricie to arouse Phaedra's jealousy, but in his play jealousy only talks; in D'Annunzio's it kills. For the first time the figure of the heroine is lifted above ordinary humanity. D'Annunzio made of her a demigoddess torn by sensual desire, sick with passion, implacable and fierce. A similar type of heroine, raised above common mortals, had already been portrayed by Swinburne in an episode of his tragedy *Atalanta in Calydon* (1865). In D'Annunzio's drama Euripides and Swinburne contribute to the portrayal of the character of Phaedra.

The Italian public was deeply moved at the performance of the play, as perhaps was the Athenian audience by the story of Hippolytus riding the deadly courser. But critics seemed to seek any possible pretext for disapproving the tragedy. They claimed that it was not dramatic from the theatrical point of view.[5]

D'Annunzio's *Phèdre* was performed, in the French translation by

D'Annunzio and his French translator Georges Hérelle (1895).
All photographs courtesy of Rizzoli Editore, Centro Documentazione.

Ida Rubinstein in *Le Martyre de Saint Sébastien.*

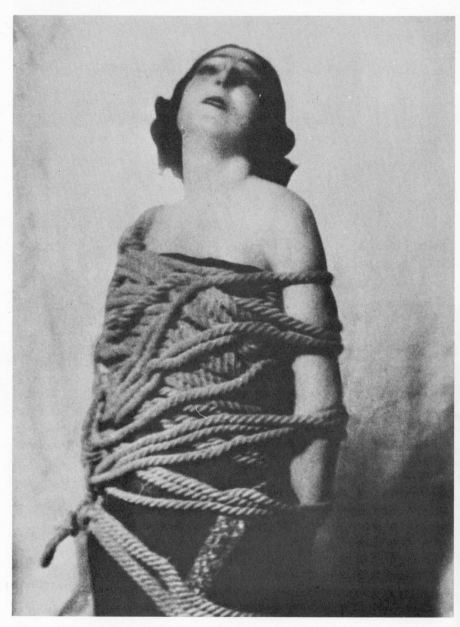

D'Annunzio arriving in Rome
from France (1915) to campaign for Italy's entry in the
First World War.

D'Annunzio at Fiume.

Il Comandante.

André Doderet, at the Théâtre de l'Opéra in June 1923 with music by Ildebrando Pizzetti and the stage setting by Léon Bakst. The play had five performances. The leading role was interpreted by Ida Rubinstein, who had just taken over the Opéra. It appeared in the *Revue de Paris* in the same year.[6] It was inevitable that French critics should compare D'Annunzio's play with Racine's; they took issue with the sensuality of D'Annunzio's work, with the excessive use of mythology, with the monotony of the elocution, and finally with the foreign accent of Ida Rubinstein and her dramatic pretensions. They even reproached her for having rented the Opéra and having thus disrupted the normal functioning of a national institution. These uncomplimentary remarks provoked a violent article by Louis Payen against the detractors of Ida Rubinstein.[7] Gabriel Marcel levelled a heavy attack against the play in the *Nouvelle Revue française*. Although he recognized in the work "les beautés lyriques qui éclatent à la lecture," he found all the rest completely detestable—"surcharge verbale," "fatras mythologique et métaphysique," and a revolting sensuality reminiscent of Wilde's *Salomé*. And he concluded: "Nous sommes bien ici sur un des chemins qui ramènent à la barbarie."[8]

Literary indignation, which had free play, was not always justified. The work was not without defects, but it was not completely lacking in beauty. The critics who objected to its excessive sensuality disregarded the emotional power of the drama and the extraordinary beauty in its plastic expression. It is unquestionable that Racine's Phaedra remains unsurpassed, since she is the most complex and the most complete. She is the whole of life—crime, remorse, purity; whereas D'Annunzio's heroine lacked this total humanity, being unidimensional, more elementary, and revealing only one trait of her personality, the most primitive, the most brutal one—her overwhelmingly sensual and deadly passion beyond good and evil.

D'Annunzio conceived his heroine as a physiological machine, a creature bereft of moral sensibility and lacking in profound psychological insight; she was a deadly creature, a splendid monster fatal to humanity. But these characteristics were not at all uninteresting, even if they showed a lamentable lack of morality, apart from the morality of the superman. Jean Dornis found D'Annunzio's *Phèdre* beautiful: "l'oeuvre dramatique la plus lyriquement belle du poète, ... la plus fourmillante de rares beautés." After the incomparable Racine, D'Annunzio was fully justified in treating the subject.[9]

In 1927 André Doderet submitted *Lā Torche sous le boisseau (La*

LIBRARY
EISENHOWER COLLEGE

Fiaccola sotto il moggio), which he had just translated, to the reading committee of La Comédie-Française, feeling that by virtue of its literary qualities the play deserved the honor of the French national theater. The tragedy was produced on December 7, 9, and 11, with great success. The Franco-Italian political situation in 1927 gave a particular meaning to the theatrical event, and the applause for the play went eventually beyond all expectations.

La Fiaccola sotto il moggio had been written immediately after *La Figlia di Iorio* in 1905. Critics had reproached D'Annunzio for neglecting dramatic action and for indulging in lyricism, and he answered with this tragedy of violence, in which he tried to comply more adequately with theatrical convention. The play, in four acts and in verse, was to be part of a trilogy in which *La Figlia di Iorio* appeared as the first drama, and *Il Dio Scacciato* (never written), as the third. The three tragedies were to give a poetic picture of the Abruzzi, where an archaic people with primitive emotions would give D'Annunzio the opportunity to revive the violent passions of the Greek tragic theater. *La Fiaccola sotto il moggio* (the title was taken from the Bible) was written in twenty-eight days and brought to the stage for the first time on March 27, 1905, at the Teatro Manzoni in Milan. The success of the presentation was open to question. The Italian audience, made up of the elite, warmly applauded the first and second acts, argued about the third, and received the fourth coldly, almost disapprovingly. The work remained almost unknown in France until 1927, although it was reviewed in the French press at the time of its publication in Italy. An article by G. Saint-Aubin in *La Revue* of May 1, 1905, gave a detailed analysis and reproduced two scenes from the play in the translation of Saint-Aubin himself, who pointed out differences between *La Fiaccola sotto il moggio* and *La Figlia di Iorio* which had just been performed at the Théâtre de l'Oeuvre.

In *La Torche sous le boisseau* the author had deliberately portrayed the drama in relentlessly dark and depressing colors. The entire plot is somber, recalling Ann Radcliffe's and Horace Walpole's terror novels. The setting is the old palace of Baron de Sangro in the Abruzzi —a gloomy house where a sinister silence reigns, broken only by a frightening noise resounding from time to time in the empty corridors. But more frightening than this noise are the bitter quarrels between two brothers, Bertrando and Tibaldo, who hate each other instinctively. They fight over the maid Angizia, a lustful and corrupted creature, whom Tibaldo finally marries. The woman thus suddenly rises from the position of servant to that of tyrannic mistress of the house. She seems to personify D'Annunzio's conception of the "éternel féminin" —a creature who is all flesh and whose mysterious power is an instrument of degradation and ruin. Tibaldo has two children by his previous marriage—Simonetto, a delicate boy dying of a mysterious sickness, and Gigliola, a pale and sad creature haunted by inscrutable thoughts. They have been told that their mother was accidentally killed when the heavy lid of a trunk fell down upon her head. But the strange circumstances of her death and the marriage of Tibaldo and Angizia a year later arouse suspicion that Donna Monica was deliberately murdered. Gigliola senses the truth and, like Electra in Sophocles' tragedy, is determined to uncover the facts and to seek vengeance. She questions her father to no avail. Angizia, fearful that the girl may win Tibaldo's confidence, watches every move. Finally she comes face to face with Gigliola whose accusing look drives Angizia to forget herself and to shout in defiance: "C'est vrai. C'est vrai. C'est moi. Je te le crie et je ne baisse pas les yeux. Me voici. Je t'ai répondu sans trembler. J'ai fait cela." Gigliola's father, torn by remorse, becomes aware of his degradation. In a violent scene Tibaldo tries to strangle Angizia, who, freeing herself from his grasp, threatens to call Bertrando. In the meantime Gigliola plans her revenge. She hides a stiletto and a sack full of snakes left in the garden by a snake charmer. She tells Simonetto, the new Orestes, the truth about their mother's death. The fatal hour is near and Gigliola is ready to strike. She plunges her hand into the sack, allows herself to be bitten by the snakes so that she may not survive her crime, and disappears in the darkness in search of her victim. A moment later she returns, livid and terrified; she has found Angizia already dead. Tibaldo has killed her prey. She falls on the floor—the snakes have brought the tragedy to an end.

The judgments expressed by critics at the time of its first presentation in Italy were generally confirmed later in France. One of the defects noticed in the play was that after the second act the emphasis is shifted from Gigliola to Tibaldo, and the only role she has in the vengeance is that of self-sacrifice. But the play on the whole, with its gloomy atmosphere, produced in the spectator an unforgettable shudder. Moreover, the poetic qualities of the work—the somber rhythm of the verse, the ardent and musical atmosphere pervading the tense dramatic action—were considered to be of an extraordinary beauty.[10] The lack of complete theatrical success in 1905 was attributed to the fact that the public was not yet used to the psychological depth and the musical atmosphere being brought to the theater. The play had, however, a "succès de librairie" due to its poetic qualities. *La Torche sous le boisseau* appeared in the *Petite illustration* of December 31, 1927, and it was published in volume by Calmann-Lévy the following year.

French critics showed themselves particularly benevolent toward the productions of the play; there was a concert of praise in the press. René Doumic defined *La Torche sous le boisseau* "une pièce pleine d'horreur sacrée."[11] Henry Bidou brought out in the *Journal des débats* the most salient characteristics of the play and likened it to Sophocles' theater.[12] André Antoine in *L'Information* spoke of "l'indiscutable succès" of the play and praised the performance and the magnificent stage setting.[13] In *Comoedia* Étienne Rey joined the chorus of acclaim of the entire press: "Il faut louer sans réserves la Comédie-Française d'avoir accueilli cette oeuvre violente et belle."[14] M. Nozière echoed in *L'Avenir* the same praise: "La Comédie-Française est honorée en montant la *Torche sous le boisseau*. Elle nous a permis de fêter le génie dramatique du poète Gabriele d'Annunzio."[15] Robert Kemp in *La Liberté* expressed admiration for the play and the emotion he felt at the performance: "Les paroles que ces êtres se lancent au visage ... sont dignes des Atrides. ... Vous frissonnez! ... Quel rythme ... quels sursauts, dans le mouvement de chaque scène! ... J'ai été ému. Je trouve cela beau ... !"[16] Gérard d'Houville (Marie de Régnier) praised the poet, his work, the Latin brotherhood: "Ce sont là de nobles soirées où, autour d'un grand nom, se resserre l'amitié latine de la France et de l'Italie."[17] Jean Prudhomme wrote in *Le Matin:* "Il n'est pas une minute d'apaisement au cours de ces quatre actes d'une angoisse comme passionnée. ... Le verbe incandescent de G. d'Annunzio, ... la puissance suggestive de ses images sont ponctués de cris, ... de plaintes, d'imprécations, de gémissements, de râles, à croire la scène ouverte sur un coin de l'enfer. Et l'on sort de ce spectacle, moulu, brisé, vaincu, tout près à se croire évadé d'un horrible cauchemar."[18] G. de Pawlowski in the *Journal* and Paul Ginisty in the *Petit Parisien* added their voices to the general approbation expressed by the public and the critics for the play. The echo of this is also found in the Italian press. The *Corriere della sera* of December 7 reported, "The reception by the public was extremely warm," and that at the end "the poet's name was acclaimed." Critics praised highly Doderet's translation for its "lucide fidélité,"[19] and for its "belle langue, sonore et ferme," which fully rendered "tout le lyrisme verbal du poète."[20] There were, however, those who did not agree with the choice made by the Comédie-Française, feeling that preference should have been given to other theatrical works by D'Annunzio—*La Fille de Iorio, La Gioconda, La Ville morte,* or *Francesca de Rimini.*[21] One of the difficulties which was evident at the performance of *La Torche sous le boisseau* was the fact that the play, entirely composed of paroxyms, required a relentlessly vehement presentation; whereas, in order to bring out the sumptuous verbal splendor of the play, the dramatic movement demanded a less violent pace. The actors, therefore, were confronted with the difficult task of finding a proper balance between the dramatic and the stylistic movement.

In her book *La Réaction idéaliste au théâtre depuis 1890,* Dorothy Knowles refers to *La Torche sous le boisseau* as a theatrical failure, a judgment which, in the light of the reactions registered above, seems rather strange. She cites from a note in *Le Cri* of December 1, 1927: "Qu'aucun auteur, s'il ne se nomme Gabriele d'Annunzio, ne se risque à porter à un directeur de théâtre une pièce pareille à la *Torche sous le boisseau.*"[22] On this authority she condemns the play, asserting that critics objected to the verbal exuberance, the apparent romanticism, the abuse of crime and terror, the exasperated atmosphere. No such criticisms appear in the articles here examined. Only Claude Berton expressed a pronounced dissatisfaction with the tragedy: "C'est une tragédie de l'Enfant de volupté qui a considéré le monde comme sa chose, pour son plaisir et sa domination."[23] On the whole the play enjoyed a better reception in France than it had had in Italy twenty-two years earlier.

13. Conclusion

D'ANNUNZIO's theater was viewed against the background of the reaction to naturalism. In fact, French critics, whenever they wished to define it, called it "théâtre idéaliste ou symboliste." Paul Flat, in his *Théâtre contemporain,* begins the first part of his study, "Le Théâtre idéaliste," with a chapter on D'Annunzio, followed by others on Maeterlinck, Edmond Schuré, and Joséphin Péladan, in which he analyzes the elements constituting the idealistic theater and the traits these authors had in common. D'Annunzio, according to Flat, "a bien mérité sa place parmi les Sculpteurs d'Idéal."[1]

Idealist art professed the cult of absolute, eternal values transcending the contingency of time and environment. Furthermore, it conceived of the human mind as the only reality and the creator of all visible manifestations. The world is but an appearance springing from and fashioned by our own creative imagination. Our inner life is thus the principle of the universe to which art furnishes the key. In D'Annunzio's theater, in fact, everything originates from his own conception of Beauty. For him Beauty is the only moving power—the absolute. And he looks upon it as a totality of effects—pictorial, musical, poetic —fused into an indissoluble whole. This idea of Beauty as the only animating force represents the original aspect of his theater and accounts for both the power and weakness of his plays. D'Annunzio's cult of absolute Beauty gives his dramatic works a suggestive and magic expression; but it creates a gap between art and life, leading him into the realm of pure lyricism.

D'Annunzio's idealistic tendencies are evident in all of his plays. In *Il Sogno d'un mattino di primavera* we are transported into the very atmosphere of symbolistic art which, in its reaction against the coarseness of naturalism, strove to create a world of illusion admitting only rare and delicate sentiments, controlled gestures and movements, and where violent passion was whispered in refined phrases. This first play echoed *Pelléas et Mélisānde*—not so much Maeterlinck's poetry as Debussy's music. This escape from reality into poetry and dream, achieved through the imaginative power, is one of the constant features of D'Annunzio's theater. "Son théâtre," wrote Henri de Régnier, "réalise certaines des visées chères aux jeunes esprits d'alors qui rêvaient de substituer aux pièces d'observation et aux pièces à thèse, des pièces à idées et à symboles, en des décors légendaires ou emblématiques."[2]

D'Annunzio was often reproached for making excessive use of symbolism and thus portraying nonexistent characters lacking in human verisimilitude. The accusation was not completely unfounded, for the poet sought inspiration constantly in the Supreme Idea. His characters were symbols. In *La Città morta*, Anna symbolized Resignation and Endurance; Bianca Maria was the symbol of Purity. In *La Gioconda* the real protagonist is the idea of Beauty—the animating force from which all action stems and toward which all things tend. The plot of *Francesca da Rimini,* observed Dorothy Knowles, "est un symbole signifiant que c'est toujours l'inconnu qu'aime la femme, c'est toujours lui qu'elle croit épouser."[3] *La Fiaccola sotto il moggio* is a symbolistic tragedy in which everything is dominated by Fate. The *Martyre de Saint Sébastien,* because of its mystical elevation and the neo-Christian movement from which it draws inspiration, is closer than any of D'Annunzio's other plays to the idealistic tradition. Gaston de Pawlowski observed that in *La Pisanelle* first place is reserved for ideas, not characters.[4]

While invariably admiring his lyrical power and brilliant form, French critics objected to the "symbolique-scandinave" taste (which had raged in France at the turn of the century) and to the lack of dramatic development and psychological insight. Armand Caraccio observed, in this respect, that D'Annunzio sought to arouse tragic emotions from physical mimicry, the material act, the violent gesture, which strikes the eyes, the senses of the spectator. Unable to work on the psychological level, he portrayed only the physical manifestations of passion.[5] This judgment was echoed by others: "Il cherche à fouiller l'âme, mais son art est encore plus celui d'un sculpteur de corps d'une incomparable beauté."[6]

D'Annunzio was mainly a lyric poet—a man who follows a dream rather than portraying characters in action. And his plays, in general, gave the impression of lyrical rather than dramatic works. The invasion of lyricism in the theater tends to crystallize the dramatic movement required by the stage presentation. Moreover, as a lyric poet, D'Annunzio was incapable of refraining from projecting himself, his incoercible ego, into his characters. "Au théâtre," wrote Léon Daudet, who had a strong literary antipathy for the poet, "... il importe de lâcher son ombre, opération dont notre Gabriele est ... radicalement incapable."[7]

Despite all the shortcomings of his theater, it was suggested that he was "le plus grand poète tragique des pays méditerranéens."[8] Sarah Bernhardt declared in 1908 that there were only two dramatic poets— Edmond Rostand and Gabriele D'Annunzio.[9] Pierre Brisson wrote in 1927 that D'Annunzio's plays "forment encore un monument lyrique d'une richesse admirable."[10] Although the influence of symbolism— particularly that of Maeterlinck—was undeniable, D'Annunzio's theater was considered unique in its originality and verbal power. "Par une mission providentielle," wrote Paul Flat, D'Annunzio "fut envoyé parmi nous pour réconcilier le Théâtre avec la Beauté."[11]

Critics in France did not fail to recognize the distinctiveness of D'Annunzio's theater, whatever his merit as a dramatist. A positive and fair appreciation was given by Léon Blum: "Sans doute, il n'a pas pleinement réussi dans sa conception propre de la tragédie. Mais ses qualités d'homme de théâtre n'en subsistent pas moins; elles sont précieuses; elles sont certaines."[12] And Ernest Tissot granted to the much discussed, censured, and exalted plays of D'Annunzio the right to survive by virtue of their rare and positive qualities. "A côté des philosophiques et nouvelles analyses dramatiques d'un Ibsen—des radieuses fantaisies lyriques d'un Edmond Rostand—des aventures sentimentales d'un Henri Lavedan, d'un Alfred Capus, d'un Paul Hervieu ... les tragédies de Gabriele d'Annunzio ont ... le droit d'exister." For they are "autres," and for this reason alone they deserve our sympathetic attention. D'Annunzio's theater is "une branche d'orchidées"; it has the exotic novelty, the supreme originality, "l'inconnu et l'inquiétant" of these flowers.[13]

Although far from traditional French taste in many respects, D'Annunzio's dramatic works aroused in general a positive reaction. They shocked and flattered French sensibility, serving as a touchstone for the discussions "sur les chances d'une tragédie moderne, sur la place de la poésie au théâtre, sur les droits respectifs de l'art et de la morale."[14]

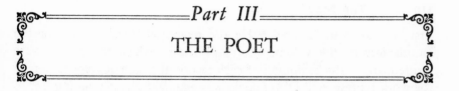

14. The Volume of *Poésies* (1912)

D'ANNUNZIO's poetic works had in France neither the success nor the diffusion of his novels and plays. If in Italy D'Annunzio was primarily the foremost poet of his times, in France he remained a novelist and a dramatist. Of his voluminous poetic production only a selected collection of poems was published in French translation, *Poésies* (Paris: Calmann-Lévy, 1912, 438 pages), and it does not include any of *Le Laudi*—the most outstanding of D'Annunzio's poetic achievements. This volume of selections, which Hérelle prepared with extreme care, is composed of poems from *Canto novo* (1881), *Intermezzo* (1883), *Isottèo* (1886), *La Chimera* (1885–88), *Elegie romane* (1887–91), *Poema paradisiaco* (1891–92), *Odi navali* (1892–93), and an appendix containing pieces from *Primo vere* (1878–80) and *In Memoriam* (1880) which are the earliest manifestations of his poetic talent. The whole represents, in its variety of meters and themes, the best of D'Annunzio's poetic collections composed before *Le Laudi*.

D'Annunzio agreed to the translation of his poems for the volume of *Poésies* with the same reluctance he had shown earlier about the translation of his short stories. The consummate artist of *Le Laudi, Il Fuoco,* and *La Figlia di Iorio* was extremely self-conscious about the works of his youth, considering them to be far below the standards of his now mature and highly sophisticated taste. "Je suis désolé," he wrote to Hérelle, "que vous ayez insisté pour publier les toutes premières poésies. Elles sont d'une intolérable fadeur, et je crois qu'elles gâtent le volume. Ces sonnets d'enfance à ma grand-mère, passables en vers, sont détestables dans la nudité de la traduction. Ils sont pleins de lieux communs, imprécis, stupides."[1] In some of the poems he even tried to modify certain phrases which in French became too commonplace and childish. The substance, however, could not be modified. At any rate, he insisted that Hérelle place the poems written at the age of sixteen or seventeen in an appendix, in order to avoid creating a poor first impression in the reader. He also requested Hérelle to put on the frontispiece of the volume the dates within which the poems were written, and at the beginning of each section the date of composition of the work represented. D'Annunzio was adamant about pointing out to the reader that these were works of his youth.

The only work he seemed to care about now was *Le Odi navali*—his first attempt at heroic poetry—and he would have liked Hérelle to translate it in its entirety. "En ce temps de résurrection guerrière elles prennent une nouvelle importance," he wrote to Hérelle.[2] The war in Libya (1911–12) had awakened in the poet strong patriotic feelings which inspired the composition of *Canzoni della gesta d'Oltremare* (*Laudi*, IV). He was now aspiring to heroic actions and was brought to love all that expressed force, courage, valor. The *Odi navali*, written twenty years earlier when D'Annunzio lived in the enervating atmosphere of the refined and decadent circles of the time, seemed to be an unexpected *tour de force;* and in 1912 this work assumed a new meaning in the mind of the poet-patriot.

Although long awaited, D'Annunzio's *Poésies* failed to arouse interest, despite Hérelle's efforts to reveal the poet to French readers. The failure was to be attributed partly to a change in literary taste. D'Annunzio's estheticism was at the time far removed from the main literary and political preoccupations of the public. The great D'Annunzian vogue had been over for at least a decade and it was impossible to revive. Patriotic lyricism and the exaltation of heroism and power were now more palatable than the sensuality and depressing atmosphere of the *Intermezzo* and the *Poema paradisiaco*. Furthermore, Hérelle's translation was by no means the most poetic. The translator of a poet must himself be endowed with poetic sensibility; he must be in close communion with the work he is transposing into another language. Hérelle was an intelligent and lucid scholar rather than a poet. Thus, it was hard for him to render D'Annunzio's lyricism into French without losing the most characteristic qualities of the original—its suggestive musicality.

This defect was immediately felt by critics. Ricciotto Canudo wrote in the *Mercure de France:* "M. Hérelle, qui est en effet un traducteur assez libre, mais excellent des romans de l'écrivain italien, est un piètre transpositeur de rythmes lyriques. On l'avait déjà remarqué pour la *Fille de Iorio,* dont toute la noblesse lyrique et rythmique a disparu dans sa transposition française."[3]

To these remarks Hérelle answered that D'Annunzio himself, so exacting in the matter of translation, had expressed satisfaction with the work.[4] The poet, in fact, had praised Hérelle many times especially in regard to the "excellent" rendering of the *Poema paradisiaco:* "La traduction est souvent très bonne et parfois même parfaite. De certaines poésies du *Poème paradisiaque,* très difficiles à traduire, comme par exemple la *Dame voilée,* vous avez fait de véritables merveilles. Dans l'*Isottèo* aussi vous avez fait des prodiges."[5] And he reiterated the praise in a subsequent letter: "Le *Poème paradisiaque* est votre chef-d'oeuvre. Votre traduction me ravit."[6]

Although the rendering of the lyrical rhythms of his poetry was extremely delicate, D'Annunzio showed himself to be more reasonable than he had been with the translation of his novels and plays, over which he had suffered long agonies. The verbal alchemy and the elusive subtleties that caused so much squabbling with Hérelle, especially during the translation of *Il Fuoco* and *La Figlia di Iorio,* did not now arouse his usual obsessive concern. Undoubtedly D'Annunzio realized the futility of expecting the impossible in the translation of his poetry. He had no illusion as to the quality of lyrical emotion that his verse could produce in a language other than his own. He declared to André Arneyvelde in 1913 that most of his works were untranslatable: "Mon oeuvre en vers, particulièrement, qui est une recherche constante de verbes et de rythmes, intraduisibles d'une langue à l'autre."[7]

This is unquestionably true. The main quality of D'Annunzio's poetry is in the rhythm and suggestiveness of its expression. And the musical nature of his verse is so deeply rooted in his native tongue that it cannot be reproduced in any other language without damage. D'Annunzio exploited superbly all the resources of the language— intellectual suggestion, rhythm, melody—in order to achieve the total esthetic effect he sought. A translation, however perfect, cannot preserve these qualities, which spring from the very nature of the original language, especially when the translator is not himself a poet. Therefore, D'Annunzio's verses, so melodious and suggestive in the Italian text, are somewhat badly impaired in translation. They lose the qualities characteristic of his art. The volume of *Poésies,* although prepared with great accuracy, fails to show the real measure of the poet. Here are a few examples taken at random:

> Non più dentro le grige iridi smorte
> lampo di giovinezza or mi sorride.
> La giovinezza mia barbara e forte
> in braccio de le femmine si uccide.

Dans le gris de mes prunelles éteintes ne sourit plus aucun éclair de
jeunesse. Ma jeunesse barbare et forte se tue entre les bras des femmes.

(*Intermezzo*, "Sed non satiatus")

La musica fluiva, nel sovrano
incanto di quel giorno moribondo,
con tal dolcezza che il mio cuore umano
non la sostenne. Ed un oblìo profondo
de la vita mi trasse in un lontano
mondo. Ah perchè di quel lontano mondo,
anima mia, non ti sovviene più?

La musique, dans le souverain enchantement de ce jour moribond, coulait
avec tant de douceur que mon coeur humain ne put la supporter. Et un
oubli profond de la vie m'entraîna dans un monde lointain. Ah, de ce
monde lointain, ô mon âme, pourquoi ne te souvient-il plus?

(*Poema paradisiaco*, "Romance de la femme voilée")

O Giovinezza, ahi me, la tua corona
su la mia fronte già quasi è sfiorita.
Premere sento il peso de la vita,
che fu sì lieve, su la fronte prona.

Ma l'anima nel cor si fa più buona,
come il frutto maturo. Umile e ardita,
sa piegarsi e resistere; ferita,
non geme; assai comprende, assai perdona.

Sur ton front, ô Jeunesse, ta couronne est déjà presque défleurie. Je sens
sur mon front qui se penche peser le poids de la vie, naguère si léger.

Mais mon âme se fait meilleure dans ma poitrine, comme le fruit mûr.
Humble et hardie, elle sait plier et résister; blessée, elle ne gémit pas;
elle comprend beaucoup, pardonne beaucoup.

(*Poema paradisiaco*, "O Giovinezza")

These passages need no detailed analysis to show the damage in
their translation. The version is unquestionably precise, almost literal,
but, unfortunately, unpoetic. The rhythm is broken, the tone is lowered,
the poetic feeling vanishes. Poetry has become prose. Even the lines
from "Romanza della donna velata," found by D'Annunzio himself to
be exceptionally well rendered into French, are far from transmitting
the qualities of the original. It is good prose. The difference between
a poetic and a prosaic translation of poetry becomes more evident when

one compares Hérelle's work with D'Annunzio's own rendering into Italian of Hugo's "Booz endormi." Following are some stanzas which clearly show how he remoulded the matter and how the brillance of images, harmony, and rhythm compare with the original:

> Pendant qu'il sommeillait, Ruth, une Moabite,
> S'était couchée aux pieds de Booz, le sein nu,
> Espérant on ne sait quel rayon inconnu
> Quand viendrait du réveil la lumière subite.
>
> Booz ne savait point qu'une femme était là,
> Et Ruth ne savait point ce que Dieu voulait d'elle.
> Un frais parfum sortait des touffes d'asphodèle;
> Les souffles de la nuit flottaient sur Galgala.
>
> L'ombre était nuptiale, auguste et solennelle;
> Les anges y volaient sans doute obscurément,
> Car on voyait passer dans la nuit, par moment,
> Quelque chose de bleu qui paraissait une aile.

D'Annunzio's rendering:

> Mentre Booz dormiva. Ruth, una moabita,
> s'era distesa ai piedi de 'l vecchio, nuda il seno,
> sperando un qualche ignoto raggio o ignoto baleno
> se venìa co 'l risveglio la luce de la vita.
>
> Ora Booz inconscio dormiva sotto i cieli;
> Ruth inconscia attendea, con pia serenità.
> Una fresca fragranza salìa da li asfodeli,
> e i soffi de la notte languìan su Galgalà.
>
> Era l'ombra solenne, augusta e nuziale.
> Volavan forse, innanzi a li occhi stupefatti
> de li umani, erranti angeli; però che in alto a tratti
> apparivano azzurri lembi simili ad ale.
>
> (*La Chimera*, "Booz addormentato")

Translation, of course, demands certain restraints, and creative talents are the least inclined to submit to these restraints. They are often carried away by their own imagination, thus losing sight of the original text. However, D'Annunzio seems to have succeeded in rendering the poem into his own language faithfully, without altering the subject matter or the general image in the original. Yet his translation bears his personal imprint; it is permeated by his own feelings. In its Italian version the poem appears as a new experience in a new expression. It becomes a poem which is parallel to the original. The true translator actualizes the subject matter by reliving and reexpressing it. This is the only way in which the translation of poetry can be poetic. It must be conceived as reinterpretation and reexpression of the theme. The view that a work of poetry is untranslatable in its intrinsic essence must be held true in this respect. A work of art is the personal expression of its author, and as such it cannot be reproduced or repeated. If the word is the expression of a particular feeling and is identified with the feeling itself, the substitution of words entails the substitution of feelings. Therefore, translation produces another work whose worth lies in the force and plenitude of the new expression.

The discussions which arose from Hérelle's translation of D'Annunzio's poems were the result of a basic misunderstanding bearing on the very nature of poetry. Paul Souday in an article on the *Poésies* protests the axiomatic contention that D'Annunzio's poetic works are untranslatable, but his argument cannot be accepted without scrutiny. "Ce qui ne peut passer dans la traduction," he writes, "c'est la sensation physique, le chatoiement et la sonorité des mots." But, he continues: "La beauté poétique réside avant tout dans la conception et dans le sentiment, dans l'éclat ou la délicatesse des images, dans l'ordre et le rythme de l'expression, laquelle ne dépend pas uniquement de la matière verbale. Une phrase n'est pas seulement un aggrégat d'harmonies lumineuses ou sonores: elle doit avoir un sens."[8]

However, it must be noted that meaning is not enough in a poem. If the artist does not give it breath and movement, it cannot come to life. And it is precisely these vital elements, which lie in the language, that translation, as it is commonly understood, cannot preserve. In D'Annunzio's poetry music occupies a vital place; his poems often become a play on images and melodies which have a value of their own in their suggestive power. The poet wrote in *Il Piacere:*

> Le vers est tout. Pour créer la beauté des rêves et dégager les essences des choses, aucun instrument d'art n'est plus subtil, plus acéré, plus multiforme, plus exact, plus obéissant, plus fidèle. Le vers est tout, le vers peut tout. Il peut rendre les mouvements les plus secrets de la sensibilité humaine et révéler par le son d'une syllabe les analogies les plus profondes.[9]

In translation the verse is destroyed. By changing the word order all the accords vanish, and in the case of D'Annunzio, particularly, the translated verse often becomes empty twaddle. In his prose, although the preoccupation with the rhythm of the phrase dominates over the content, the damage is less noticeable than in his poetry. Some French readers even maintained that D'Annunzio's novels gained in clarity, precision, and rapidity in the French translation. This is not true of his poems. On the other hand, if one is to believe the obsessive preoccupation of the poet to preserve the musical effect, the rhythm, and the melody of his phrases, it becomes clear that these were the poetic qualities to which he attached the greatest importance in his poetic creation. The notion that in order to translate a poem it is necessary to be a poet is particularly true in regard to D'Annunzio's works.

Paul Souday, however, is not of this opinion. He maintains that the translation always preserves "les idées, la sensibilité, voire la qualité générale et le mouvement du style."[10] But this must be accepted with reservation. For Souday "l'armature intellectuelle, le plan organique, l'essence purement humaine," have in a poem a primary importance. This consideration leads him to conclude that Hérelle's translation of D'Annunzio's poems is excellent. Undoubtedly the critic has in mind only one aspect of poetry—content, which in D'Annunzio very often has no importance whatever.

15. Before the Publication of *Poésies*

BEFORE 1912—the date of publication of *Poésies*—D'Annunzio's poetic talent had not been completely unknown in France. Excerpts of his rich poetic production had been frequently appearing in translation, either separately or in articles and essays devoted to the author. Vittorio Pica, who was the first to speak of D'Annunzio across the Alps, in his article on *L'Intermezzo* in the *Revue indépendante*, March 1887, had already given a short poem in translation—"O Faux de lune décroissante" (*Canto novo*, "Canto dell'ospite," vii). After the publication of the first novels, articles and essays using excerpts from D'Annunzio's poetic works were seen more and more frequently. The article by

Amédée Pigeon in the *Revue hebdomadaire,* June 4, 1893, carried four poems in the prose translation of Hérelle,[1] and four more appeared in the same periodical a few months later (January 4, 1894).[2] Melchior de Vogüé inserted four in his article on D'Annunzio in the *Revue des Deux Mondes,* January 1, 1894, and in the same review Jean Dornis published on February 1, 1898, an essay on D'Annunzio's poetry, giving some twenty poems in prose translation. In the *Quinzaine* for the following March, François Descôtes printed and discussed the poet's ode "Pour la mort de l'Amiral de Saint-Bon" (*Odi navali*) in the prose translation of Jacques Bourgeois. Simon Pacoret de Saint-Bon, born in Chambéry, was minister of the Italian Navy and one of the heroes in the war of 1866–67. His passing fired D'Annunzio's imagination and he exalted the hero, evoking his sickness and his serene resignation in the face of death with so deep an accent of Christian piety that François Descôtes was led to suspect a Christian inspiration in the most pagan poet of the time: "Il ne nous déplaît pas d'entendre une prière sur les lèvres de ceux dont le talent nous charme, mais parfois nous laisse inquiets et troublés en face des mystérieux problèmes dont la foi seule peut éclairer les profondeurs."[3] The rendering of the poem into French had no literary pretensions. It was done for pious reasons in a style which preserves the flavor of the Italian original and even its rhythm and inversions.

Two more pieces[4] appeared in the *Annales politiques et littéraires,* February 7, 1904, with a sympathetic study by Charles Dubois—"Gabriele d'Annunzio poète"—in which D'Annunzio's artistic qualities are penetratingly analyzed. "Ce parnassien," writes Dubois, "est un symboliste, qui pénètre dans le monde mystérieux des 'correspondances', où non seulement les parfums, les couleurs et les sons, mais où l'esprit et les choses se répondent, où un paysage est un état d'âme." Thus D'Annunzio's poetry, which was painting, becomes music; some of his poems were composed as symphonic pieces characterized by "indécision vaporeuse, évocations suggestives, sentiments vagues comme une émotion musicale."[5]

These and other pieces[6] had already given a first impression of the poet. Those who were familiar with his novels quickly noticed in his poetry some of the qualities and defects found in his prose—a brilliant form, morbid impressions and sensations, a vague anxiety, the search for over-refinement, and a complete lack of morality. It must be said that in D'Annunzio it is hard to draw a clear-cut line between prose and poetry. Some critics objected to the poet's ostentatious estheticism, his pomposity and magnificence of expression, the excess of colors, and the rare erudition. The abuse of erudition was considered especially to be a new and dangerous form of barbarity. They felt that in D'Annunzio there was more patchwork than real creation, and they refused to recognize that a writer, in composing his own works, cannot completely forget the masterpieces of the past which have become an integral part of his intellectual make-up, and that the sincerity of the artist consists in utilizing spontaneously all of his own intellectual resources. This accusation of excessive rhetoric, cerebralism, pomposity, and deafness to whatever is not cruel sensuality has been unfairly repeated for years by critics. But D'Annunzio's poetry does not lack real emotion; the musicality of his verse, which no one can deny, springs promptly and naturally from his poetic emotion and is in no way an empty sound.

However, despite these occasional criticisms, often inspired by moral reasons, everyone (even those who could not forgive his excessive sensuality) seemed to agree that D'Annunzio was a great artist. Paul Souday wrote in this regard:

> Ce qui ennoblit chez le poète les effusions voluptueuses et les pires égarements, c'est qu'il n'oublie jamais l'oeuvre à créer, la loi du labeur assidu, le devoir d'accroître le commun patrimoine de grandeur et de beauté. Ce païen sensuel dépasse l'épicurisme égoïste des médiocres; il brave parfois la morale établie et n'a pas du tout la notion du péché; mais il a une conscience et un idéal.[7]

If D'Annunzio's poetic works did not enjoy as great popularity as his novels, it is due not only to the difficulty of the translation, but also to the fact that his poetry revealed little which, to a greater or lesser extent, was not already in the novels. "—Vous aimez le romancier, nous disent les Italiens: —ah! si vous connaissiez le poète! Aussi bien, dans le romancier, que nous aurons comme d'abord, sentons-nous le poète qui survit heureusement."[8] And D'Annunzio remained in France almost exclusively linked to his novels and to his plays, which are the least original part of his literary production. For these works, in fact, he always borrowed ideas, psychology, attitudes, and techniques. On the other hand, his poetry, which fully reveals his creative power and originality, was known only by the elite who read Italian. The publication of *Poésies* gave the French public a more direct knowledge of the poet, but it did not constitute a significant revelation. The reviews of the work were scanty, and commercially the volume was a failure. It did not go beyond the first edition.

D'Annunzio had been aware of the difficulty of a poetic success in France, and after his brilliant introduction as a novelist there, he conceived the ambition to write poetry directly in French. His first attempts in this direction were made in 1894, when, as a linguistic exercise, he translated some of his own poems. "Je les ai traduites," he wrote to Hérelle, "pour me divertir et m'exercer. ... Vous n'aurez autre chose à faire que de corriger mes erreurs et de trouver, çà et là, quelques mots plus appropriés."[9] Hérelle claimed never to have received these translations. At the poet's death three of them were found in Paris in the collection of Gentili di Giuseppe, and were published in the May–June 1939 issue of *Dante* with the erroneous indication "Ébauches inédites de poèmes." Here is a specimen of D'Annunzio's rendering of his own verses into French:

> I nitidi mercanti alessandrini,
> profumati di cìnnamo e d'issopo,
> bevean sulla riviera di Canopo
> ne' calici de 'l loto i rosei vini.[10]

> Jadis les marchands alexandrins,
> parfumés de cinnamone et d'hysope,
> naviguant sur les rivières cruléennes buvaient
> des vins roses dans les calices de lotus.

In 1896, feeling more sure of himself in French, D'Annunzio began to aspire to poetic laurels in this language. Convinced that translations would never show Frenchmen the real dimensions of his poetic talent, he composed in French a series of twelve *Sonnets cisalpins*—classical in tone after the manner of Ronsard. He presented them with the humble dedication, "Le page craintif aux poètes de France." Eager to surprise Hérelle, he turned the manuscript over to Count Primoli, requesting him to submit it to Louis Ganderax, editor of the *Revue de Paris,* for immediate publication. Hérelle would indeed have been astonished to see these extraordinary poems in print, the more so since D'Annunzio had never mentioned any such project. But the plan failed. Ganderax, finding the tone and the form of the sonnets not completely suited to his pedantic taste, put the author off with the excuse that the *Revue* was unable to publish the *Sonnets cisalpins* for the time being because of previous commitments. D'Annunzio impatiently recalled his manuscript and later sent it directly to Hérelle, asking him to make any necessary corrections and to have it published, as a literary curiosity, in some other periodical.[11] He wished to see his sonnets in print, because he said: "J'ai promis à une de mes amies—qui voulait de moi des vers français—ces étrennes."[12] He was afraid, however, to expose himself to criticism by writing in a language of which he did not yet have complete mastery. After Ganderax's polite rejection he proceeded more cautiously. He urged Hérelle to show the sonnets secretly to Brunetière and, after learning his opinion, to have them printed, pretending to have received them "sans aucune mission," so that "plutôt qu'offerts, ils vous soient demandés."[13]

Hérelle's answer is not known, but can easily be inferred from the tone of a subsequent letter of D'Annunzio's: "Vous avez donc cru sérieusement que je voulais me 'naturaliser' poète français et, de plus, parnassien? Je plaisantais. J'ai composé ces sonnets par passe-temps. ... Je crois que je n'en écrirai pas d'autres."[14] Nevertheless, D'Annunzio insisted once more, although more mildly, on the publication of the sonnets, suggesting to Hérelle that they be printed as "étrennes de moi à vous ... afin que le page du premier sonnet paraisse aussi craintif que possible."[15] Despite his insistence, only two of the sonnets appeared, one in *Le Figaro* of January 3, and the other in *Le Gaulois* of May 27, 1897.[16] Perhaps because of Hérelle's excessive scrupulousness, the others remained unpublished until 1940, when the entire original manuscript was discovered and published by Guy Tosi in a special issue of *Études italiennes (1939–1940)* devoted to D'Annunzio.

The poet was not yet completely at ease with French. The *Sonnets cisalpins* lack the suppleness and rhythm of his Italian poems. One feels here and there a certain strain and affectation in the expression, due to insufficient mastery of the language. Some of them, however, are remarkably suggestive. "Le Page craintif," introducing the collection, possesses a singular grace:

> Sonnet, page de l'art que mon maître Pétrarque
> m'enseigna dans l'odeur des lauriers florentins
> où je rêvai longtemps de merveilleux destins
> épiant le fil d'or aux doigts blancs de la Parque,
>
> je veux que tout ton corps léger se courbe et s'arque
> comme une lèvre belle aux rires argentins
> pour offrir avec grâce à mes frères latins
> cet hommage en le règne où Ronsard est monarque
>
> .   .   .   .

The next three—"L'Hôte du roi," "Le Fils de Valentine," "Séjour d'honneur"—are devoted to the "anciennes relations entre la douce terre de France et le pays où le *si* résonne: Léonard hôte de François Ier, Charles d'Orléans et la Cour de Blois, Octavien de Saint-Gelais et la Cour d'Amboise où fleurit la jeunesse de François Ier,"[17] and reveal the poet's familiarity with the works of Charles d'Orléans (he quotes some well-known lines) and an unusual erudition which he attempts to enliven with verbal magic and occasional sensual images. The other compositions are on a variety of themes. They often echo a motif dear to the poet, now spurred by a new daemon—the idea of the superman. The desire to rise above himself, to conquer himself and others, to ascend to the heights of pure art is a theme recurring in nearly all these poems. Their form is characterized by that labored stylistic refinement typical of D'Annunzio—the choice of rare and musical words, the preference for archaisms, the use of sensual expressions. At times his French phrases seem to be a translation from his native tongue:

> Assises dans le sang du soleil moribond,
> près des noirs cygnes nés de l'ombre des carènes,
> plus d'une fois j'ai vu les divines Sirènes
> et j'ai miré mon rêve en leur regard profond.
>
> ("Les Donatrices")

The "soleil moribond" (sole moribondo), the "regard profond" (sguardo profondo), and the "j'ai miré" (mirai) are images and expressions whose transposition from Italian is clearly noticeable. Some of the sonnets have a marked Parnassian plasticity; images and words seem to be chiseled in marble:

> Le golfe était courbé comme une anse d'amphore.
> Le heurt du rostre dur, le heurt de mon pied franc
> firent lever des vols. Dans le ciel de safran,
> au sommet d'un rocher, je vis briller Phosphore.
>
> Le rocher haut et seul, comme un lampadophore,
> semblait porter l'étoile à son poing de titan.
> Outre-mer, outre-monts le message éclatant
> répandait la divine ivresse de l'Aurore.
>
> ("Le Flambeau")

D'Annunzio called Hérelle's attention especially to Sonnet X, "La Grenade," for a certain musical quality which, he said, "aurait beaucoup plu à Gustave Flaubert."[18] He also attempted to give his sonnets "une saveur latine" by using uncommon constructions which Ronsard and the other Renaissance poets would undoubtedly have approved. "Lisez ces sonnets," he said to Hérelle, "et n'oubliez pas en les lisant, qu'ils sont *cisalpins,* c'est-à-dire un peu italianisants en quelques tournures."[19] Following, perhaps, Ronsard's example, D'Annunzio even coined new words derived directly from Latin or Greek, as "léthales" for "fatales" (Sonnet VIII, line 12), "ripide" for "rapide" (Sonnet XII, line 13), "pharêtre" for "carquois" (Sonnet IX, line 10). As was to be expected, Hérelle replaced the words "léthal" and "ripide," which do not exist in French, with "fatal" and "rapide"; "pharêtre," however, was retained.

On the whole, the *Sonnets cisalpins,* although they offer no departure from the author's customary images, vocabulary, rhythm, and atmosphere, are far more than a simple exercise of a "page craintif" in French. They reveal a rare ability to handle Ronsard's poetic language.

16. *Le Laudi*

IN REVIEWING D'Annunzio's *Poésies,* translated by Hérelle, Paul Van Tieghem wrote in *La Revue du mois:* "Il reste au traducteur à faire connaître au grand public les plus importantes et les plus originales de ses poésies, les *Laudi.* ... Ce sera sans doute la tâche d'un autre grand volume."[1] After *Poésies* D'Annunzio did, in fact, hope to have *Le Laudi* published in French translation, beginning with *Laus Vitae* in a separate volume. But unfortunately nothing was done for the moment, and with the outbreak of the First World War all his literary projects were set aside.

Le Laudi is rightly considered to be the highest expression of modern Italian poetry. In its general design the work was to comprise seven books, each bearing the name of one of the seven Pleiades in the following order: Maia, Electra, Alcyone, Merope, Asterope, Taygeta, Celaeno. The poet, however, completed only the first three, between 1898 and 1904. The original sketch of this ambitious undertaking appeared in 1899 when he published a volume of lyrical poems with the resounding title *Laudi del Cielo, del Mare, della Terra e degli Eroi* (Praises of the Sky, the Sea, the Earth, and the Heroes). As the work expanded, these poems were appropriately distributed in the three books, published in 1903 and 1904. The work opens with two poems, "Alle Pleiadi e ai Fati" and "L'Annunzio," which serve as an introduction to the whole of *Le Laudi.* The first is the praise of Ulysses, the daring hero whose life is a constant search for knowledge, as portrayed in Dante's *Inferno* (although Dante would have disapproved of a superman who ignores his human duties toward his father, his wife, and his country). The second announces the return of the god Pan on earth—"The great Pan is not dead!" The two poems clearly indicate the pagan, pantheistic, and superhuman inspiration of the whole work by placing the son of Laertes above the Galilean, by opposing the ideal of the superman to Christian charity, and by proclaiming the advent of Pan as the moving force of nature. *Maia* or *Laus Vitae* is a hymn to modern life in its multiform, joyful, Dionysiac manifestations. In D'Annunzio's own words *Laus Vitae* is the poem of "total life," the true representation of soul and body, which appeared in Italy after the *Divine Comedy.* Over two-thirds of the work is the lyrical narration of a journey to Greece, highlighted by the poet's imaginary meeting with Ulysses—the first perfect type of superman—and ending in a cry of domination and destruction rising from the ancient battlefields. In the rest of the poem the author contrasts, to the ancient heroic ideal, the unheroic and debasing destruction of modern life, from which he seeks an escape in an ideal journey through the Sistine Chapel among Michelangelo's heroes. Although the lyrical effusions and the rhetorical developments overshadow the underlying design of the poem, the doctrinal thread can be followed through the tortuous unfolding of the symbolic narration. The name of Maia belongs to the same etymological family as "maius" (May) and symbolizes the power of growth, the ascending force of life. But the impulses of expansion are hindered by innumerable obstacles in nature. How to overcome them?—not certainly through Christian resignation and renunciation, which corroded the character of man and destroyed the joy of life, but through superhuman action, through heroic deeds, through the restoration of man according to the pagan concept of life. The future of mankind lies in its joyful activity, and *Laus Vitae* is a dithyramb to the beauty of a laborious and heroic life. Human progress is but the history of the efforts accomplished by heroic generations, in a world without God.

It is in the battlefields that civilization finds its strength and its luster. But this joyful pagan heroism has a moral and social dimension. It goes beyond egotistical interest: it is devoted to the service of the collectivity, to the betterment of mankind and civilization.[2] In *Electra* —the book of the heroes—the poet celebrates the great figures of modern history and the glories of Italian cities with magnificent oratory. The superhuman theme is even more pronounced than before, with a long ode dedicated to Nietzsche—"Per la morte d'un distruttore"— D'Annunzio's master of energy. *Alcyone* marks a moment of pause. After the superhuman effort of the two preceding books in which the poet, goaded by his Despot (Genius) and freed from the egotistical sensuality of his youth, had become the creator of energy, the prophet of humanity, he invokes his combative god for a rest so that he may enjoy the "divine summer" in the splendor of nature and recapture the freshness of his youth. *Alcyone* is the book of the senses, of nature, of the great Pan; it is the book of the summer, the ardent season—its beauty, its light, and the sadness of its vanishing into the fall. The work first appeared in 1904 in a volume with *Electra,* and in 1907 was published separately. It contains eighty-eight lyrical compositions in a variety of meters and themes in which culminate all of D'Annunzio's poetic experiences. Alcyone is considered to be the height of his poetry. In this idyllic pause the heroic themes are not completely absent; they are mingled with sensual ones, in the alternation of "solar" and "languid" tones characterizing the work. But D'Annunzio's love for nature, for all sense experiences, is now far removed from the naturalistic explosion of the joy of life as expressed in his youthful *Canto novo.* The external world has inner resonances; it is a pretext for the poet to listen to the mystery of the self. One feels a melancholy accent in the flowing of the season and an idealistic aspiration which rises above the pagan naturalism of *Canto novo.* The world of *Alcyone* is a mythical one in which all matter is volatilized and everything assumes an incorporeal form. Women are evanescent figures without flesh, impalpable creatures vanishing in the beautiful vision of the countryside. All seems to be dissolved into music and light.[3]

The publication of these three books of *Le Laudi* established D'Annunzio as Italy's foremost poet of his times. Even his harshest enemies had to surrender and recognize the great poetic talent of the "Immaginifico." In 1912, a number of patriotic poems—*Canzoni della gesta d'Oltremare*—inspired by the Italian-Turkish war in Libya (1911–12), were collected to form the fourth book of *Le Laudi*—*Merope;* and in the latest edition of the work (Mondadori, 1952) the fifth book—*Asterope*—made up of patriotic poems composed between 1914 and 1918, was included. Among these poems are a long ode exalting America's entry into the war, "All'America in Armi," and the *Ode pour la résurrection latine* and *Sur une image de la France croisée,* both written in French. But the true *Laudi* remain in the three first books; the last two belong to a different inspiration and were added to the work rather artificially. The sixth book—*Taygeta*—was to express the dream of the Hero, and the seventh—*Celaeno*—was to be *Laus Mortis. Le Laudi* in its whole constitutes now a volume of over one thousand pages of verse whose variety of themes, meters, and tones attests to an astonishing creative power and verbal virtuosity.

Of this vast and highly valued poetic work only excerpts appeared in France, mainly in periodicals, and nothing was published in book form until 1947 when *Laus Vitae,* which Hérelle translated in 1912–13 and which had been in type since that time at the Calmann-Lévy press, finally was printed. The reason for the long delay in the publication of the volume can be surmised. At first D'Annunzio seemed to be particularly eager to see the translation of *Laus Vitae* in print. He wrote to Hérelle in 1912: "Il me tarde de faire connaître ce poème aux esprits fraternels de France. Vous savez que je le considère comme mon oeuvre capitale."[4] And in 1913 he urged Hérelle again concerning the publication of the poem: "Vous le devez à une certaine 'élite' qui l'attend."[5] He seemed to be fairly satisfied with Hérelle's translation: "Je vois avec bonheur que le même esprit musical—du *Poème paradisiaque*—vous a guidé et inspiré."[6] D'Annunzio had requested the translator to preserve in the poem the "jumping pace" of the long phrases and the meter of each line in order to retain the vertiginous movement of the dithyramb, pointing out that the rhythm of *Laus Vitae* was totally of his own invention with some influence from the Pindaric prosody and the prosody of the Greek chorus. And he found the beginning of the poem to be perfect, even astonishing, in the French version:

O Vita, o Vita,	O Vie, ô Vie,
dono terribile del dio,	don terrible du dieu,
come una spada fedele,	(terrible) comme une épée fidèle,
come una ruggente face,	comme une torche rugissante,
come la Gorgóna,	comme la Gorgone,
come la centàurea veste;	comme la tunique du Centaure;

o vita, o vita,	ô Vie, ô Vie,
done d'oblìo,	don de l'oubli,
offerta agreste,	offrande agreste,
come un'acqua chiara,	comme une eau claire,
come una corona,	comme une couronne,
come un fiale, come il miele	comme une ruche, comme le miel
che la bocca separa	que la bouche sépare
dalla cera tenace;	de la cire tenace;
o Vita, o Vita,	ô Vie, ô Vie,
dono dell'Immortale	don de l'Immortel
alla mia sete crudele,	à ma soif cruelle,
alla mia fame vorace,	à ma faim vorace,
alla mia sete e alla mia fame	à ma soif et à ma faim
d'un giorno, non dirò io	d'un jour, ne dirai-je pas
tutta la tua bellezza?	toute ta beauté?

However, despite the pressure exerted by the poet for the publication of *Laus Vitae,* nothing was done. Guy Tosi maintains that the poem did not appear at the time because D'Annunzio neglected to give the authorization to print, requested several times by both publisher and translator.[7] But, although the poet often acted according to his changing moods, his failure to authorize the publication stems more from second thoughts concerning the quality of the translation than from "neglect." On the whole, he must have felt that the musical effect, which was for him an indispensable quality of poetry, was often impaired. Hérelle's preoccupation with precision destroyed the vaporous dream of the poet and the sense of vagueness which D'Annunzio considered an element of beauty: "... l'excès de précision gâte des choses que j'ai voulu indéterminées."[8] The outbreak of the war in 1914 turned his attention to other endeavors; he put aside his poetic laurels and began to aspire to the glory of the man of action, the hero, and *Laus Vitae* fell for the moment into oblivion. Perhaps D'Annunzio felt the times were not quite appropriate for such a book. The heroic atmosphere created by the war demanded completely different poems. In his *Canzoni della gesta d'Oltremare* (*Laudi,* IV) his excessive "esthetic pathos" and mannered lyricism, so characteristic of a large part of his poetry, had already disappeared, and his inspiration had taken a stronger and nobler tone. He had become the Tyrtaeus of the "Great Proletarian" in arms, reaching in these epic-lyric compositions the peak of his patriotic pathos. In this new aura *Laus Vitae* with its Dionysiac exaltation of life was far removed from the reality and the preoccupations of the moment. After the war Calmann-Lévy asked again for permission to print the poem, but again D'Annunzio refused on the grounds that the translation was unsatisfactory. In a letter to Doderet, dated August 13, 1921, he wrote:

> Je vous prie de dire à Gaston Calmann-Lévy que je ne peux autoriser la publication de *Laus Vitae,* ni dans une revue ni en volume, sans que je me sois d'abord prononcé sur le texte de la traduction. J'avais déjà fait observer à Hérelle, quand je lus le premier essai, qu'il avait le défaut coutumier des adoucissements et des à peu près. Or, *Laus Vitae* est une oeuvre capitale, et je désire qu'elle soit présentée sans déformations.[9]

As for the rest of *Le Laudi,* the earliest pieces appearing in French translation go back to 1900; but the difficulty of the task must have discouraged many a translator, since little was done to reveal D'Annunzio's highest poetic achievements to the French public. Scattered poems appeared here and there, but nothing substantial was published.[10]

After the *Canzoni della gesta d'Oltremare* the poet's lyre seemed to be broken. Nothing of note came from his pen. Thereafter the poems he composed from time to time are inspired by patriotic feelings and they extol heroism. These pieces, now collected in *Le Laudi,* Book V, are on the whole of no artistic significance. Echoes of his poetic works, especially those exalting patriotism, heroism, and Franco-Italian brotherhood are often found in French periodicals during the war. In the *Revue de Paris,* June 15, 1915, Gabriel Maugain comments upon the "Chanson à Hélène de France" (*Laudi,* IV) with great enthusiasm. Elena d'Orléans entered the royal family of Italy through her marriage to Amedeo, Duke of Aosta, cousin of the king. During the Italian-Turkish war she was an admirable example of devotion and self-sacrifice as a nurse and head of the Red Cross. In the fifty-four stanzas of his poem, filled with French national history and animated by his love for France, D'Annunzio praises Elena and her native country. Maugain inserts in his article the most touching passage in a prose translation. The same passage in a verse translation is found in a penetrating study on D'Annunzio by Jules Destrée. "Dans la 'Chanson à Hélène de France', qui fait fleurir un beau lys français dans la couronne des *Chanson d'Outre-Mer,*" writes Destrée, "il y a des vers fervents qui rapprochant Trente, Trieste et l'Alsace-Lorraine, dessinent le schéma de la guerre d'aujourd'hui."[11] The passage which the French liked to quote is deeply inspired and reflects D'Annunzio's sincere love for France. However, the translation impairs it badly and it is far from conveying the feeling of the original:

O douce France, ô soeur unique
Pour l'espérance muette qui s'incline
Sur les eaux claires de la Moselle,
Par la pieuse mémoire de Valentine,
Qui, fidèle à son deuil, voulut souffrir
Sans trève, l'épine aiguë au coeur;
Par les champs d'où la folle alouette
Bondit, en poussant ses appels, tandis que les peupliers de la Meuse
Frémissent, et que le sang crie dans les sillons,
France, reçois et conserve la joyeuse
Promesse, que te fait d'une vengeance
Plus grande cette chair ensanglantée.
Coupe pour nous avec la vieille faucille,
Un rameau du chêne de Lorraine
Sur la colline où Jeanne est en vedette,
Tresse, au rude rameau, la verveine
Sacrée, jadis, à nos pères, et envoie-la-nous.

The original follows:

O dolce Francia, o unica sorella,
per la muta speranza che s'inclina
su le chiare acque della tua Mosella,

per la memoria pia di Valentina
che, fedele al suo lutto, patir volle
senza tregua nel cor l'acuta spina,

pei campi onde l'allodola tua folle
balza chiamando, e i pioppi della Mosa
fremono, e il sangue grida nelle zolle,

Francia, ricevi e serba la gioiosa
promessa che ti fa, d'una vendetta
più grande, questa carne sanguinosa.

Taglia per noi con la tua vecchia accetta[12]
un ramo della quercia di Lorena,
sul colle ove Giovanna è alla vedetta,

intreccia al ramo rude la verbena
già sacra ai nostri padri, ed a noi manda.
Su le Statue velate il ciel balena.

In his excellent study Destrée quotes several passages from other poems, especially the "Chanson des Dardanelles" which had aroused a national controversy when *Canzoni della gesta d'Oltremare* was published in 1912. The poem is a direct invective against Austria which, as a member of the Triple Alliance, vetoed the decision of Italy to strike at the heart of the enemy—Turkey—by landing on the Dardanelles. The veto of the Austrian government, prompted by its hostility to a rapid victory by Italy, had stirred up the hate of the poet who flayed Austria and Germany with pungent irony. The Italian police immediately seized the *Canzoni della gesta d'Oltremāre* in order to avoid complications with the members of the Triple Alliance. The "Canzone dei Dardanelli" was reprinted afterward, but badly mutilated. This aroused public opinion against the Giolitti government not only in Italy but also in France where the poem was widely discussed and publicized.

After the First World War, French readers of D'Annunzio's poetry went back to his better poems, especially Book III of *Le Laudi*. When André Doderet became D'Annunzio's official translator, he undertook the translation of *Le Laudi*, mainly *Alcyone*, and he published several excerpts in periodicals; but he never collected his translations in a volume.[13] A substantial selection of twelve poems, translated by Henri Bédarida, and one by Guy Tosi, were published in a special issue of *Études italiennes (1939–1940)* devoted to D'Annunzio.[14] And in his book, *Doctrine et poésie dans Maia* (1943), J. Th. Paolantonacci quoted a large number of passages from Book I, in his own translation.

Most of these translations suffer from the same defect—they are unpoetic. In many instances the original is made banal and reduced to colorless prose. Some specimens follow:

> Settembre, andiamo. È tempo di migrare.
> Ora in terra d'Abruzzi i miei pastori
> lascian gli stazzi e vanno verso il mare:
> scendono all'Adriatico selvaggio
> che verde è come i pascoli dei monti.

> Septembre, viens avec moi. Il est temps de partir.
> A cette heure, sur la terre des Abruzzes, mes bergers

quittant leurs chalets, s'en vont à la mer:
ils descendent vers l'Adriatique sauvage
et verte à l'égal des pâturages de montagne.

(*Laudi*, III, "I Pastori")

The section in which this poem appears bears the heading "Dreams of remote lands," and the first line of the above stanza, "Settembre, andiamo," suggests, in its elliptic form, something vague, indefinite. The translation, "Septembre, viens avec moi," destroys the calculated vagueness of the expression by changing it to a phrase with a specific meaning. The drama of a remote land which underlies "andiamo" vanishes into the prosaic expression of "viens avec moi." Nor does "partir" render the suggestive vagueness of "migrare." The tendency to use the specific for the vague obliterates the poetic fancy. Furthermore, "stazzi" is improperly rendered by "chalets" since the Italian word means sheepfold and not hut. The difficulty of translation lies with the very nature of poetry. When the poem is not remolded by the poetic sensibility of the translator, the best one can expect from a translation is unpoetic correctness, unless semantic and phonetic closeness of the expression in the two languages permits the preservation of the poetic rhythm. The following is a passage from one of D'Annunzio's most anthologized poems—"La Pioggia nel pineto" (*Laudi*, III):

Taci. Su le soglie	Ne dis rien. Au seuil
del bosco non odo	de la forêt je n'entends point
parole che dici	les mots que tu dis,
umane; ma odo	simplement humains; mais j'entends
parole più nuove	les mots plus expressifs
che parlano gocciole e foglie	que disent les gouttes et les feuilles
lontane.	dans le lointain.
Ascolta. Piove	Ecoute. La pluie
dalle nuvole sparse.	tombe des éparses nuées.
Piove su le tamerici	Il pleut sur les tamaris
salmastre ed arse,	qu'ont brûlés le sel et le soleil;
piove sui pini	il pleut sur les pins
scagliosi ed irti,	écailleux, hérissés;
piove su i mirti	il pleut sur les myrtes
divini,	divins,
su le ginestre fulgenti	sur les genêts éclatants
di fiori accolti,	de fleurs serrées en grappes,
su i ginepri folti	sur les genévriers où se pressent

di coccole aulenti,	les baies odorantes;
piove su i nostri volti	il pleut sur nos visages
silvani,	de sylvains;
piove su le nostre mani	il pleut sur nos mains
ignude,	nues,
su i nostri vestimenti	sur nos vêtements
leggieri	légers,
su i freschi pensieri	sur les fraîches pensées
che l'anima schiude	qui naissent de notre âme
novella,	renouvelée,
su la favola bella	sur la fable belle
che ieri	dont hier
t'illuse, che oggi m'illude	tu t'enchantas et qui m'enchante aujourd'hui,
o Ermione.	Hermione.

The subject of the poem, which is the landscape of the pine grove in the rain, is here dissolved into musical rhythms. The material substance is volatilized, becoming pure descriptive music, a concert of rain drops on the pine trees. Each leaf is a note, each tree a delicate instrument vibrating in unison with the neighboring tree. And in the remainder of the poem, even the material substance of the poet is dissolved into the melodic concert. He becomes the voice of the leaves and the drops of rain; he identifies himself with them, is absorbed by nature and becomes the very feeling of things. It is futile to look for ideas in this poem, for it is simply music—melody and rhythm. And when this melody and rhythm are broken nothing is left of it. The translation presents the same defects noticed previously—the tendency to render the expression specific. Thus, the phrases "Ne dis rien" to render the indefinite "Taci," "simplement humains" with the unnecessary addition of the adverb, "mots plus expressifs," which is definitely prosaic (as are also "qu'ont brûlés le sel et le soleil" and "sur les fraîches pensées/qui naissent de notre âme ...") are expressions which mar the suggestiveness of the elliptic musical forms in the original.

The translators, however, deserve sympathy when dealing with a poem such as "L'Onda" (the wave) which is a piece of descriptive music, more so than "La Pioggia nel pineto":

Nella cala tranquilla	Dans la crique tranquille
scintilla,	scintille,
intesto di scaglia	brochée d'écailles
come l'antica	comme l'antique

lorica
del catafratto,
il Mare.
Sembra trascolorare.
S'argenta? s'oscura?
A un tratto
come colpo dismaglia
l'arme, la forza
del vento l'intacca.
Non dura.
Nasce l'onda fiacca,
sùbito s'ammorza.
Il vento rinforza.
Altra onda nasce,
si perde,
come agnello che pasce
pel verde:
un fiocco di spuma
che balza!

.   .   .   .   .   .

O sua favella!
Sciacqua, sciaborda,
scroscia, schiocca, schianta,
romba, ride, canta,
accorda, discorda,
tutte accoglie e fonde
le dissonanze acute
nelle sue volute
profonde. ...

lorique
du guerrier cataphracte,
la Mer.
On dirait une mue de couleur:
est-elle d'argent, est-elle de sable?
Soudain,
comme un coup rompt les mailles
de la cotte, la violence
du vent fait brèche.
Point ne dure.
La vague se lève paresseuse
pour mourir aussitôt.
Le vent souffle plus fort.
Une autre vague naît
et se perd,
tel un agneau qui paît
dans le vert:
flocon d'écume
qui bondit!

.   .   .   .   .   .

Et quelle voix!
Elle barbote, clapote
claque, craque, éclate
gronde, rit, chante,
accorde et désaccorde,
réunit et fond
toutes les dissonances aiguës
dans ses volutes
profondes. ...

The poem seems to capture the melody of the sea and is a masterpiece of its kind. It describes the wave—its formation in the quiet cove, its movement and character, the variety of its colors and sounds, the suppleness of its changing form. It is at first a sluggish one, then a capricious and playful one, and then another more animated, varied, powerful, swirling, tortuous, broken by the wind. The poem follows the rhythm, the lull of the wave in its sinuous and melodious evolution toward the shore, fusing visual, auditory, tactile, and olfactory sensations in a suggestively musical impression. The poet exploits particularly the phonetic resources of the word through alliterations, assonances, and the clash of sounds so as to reproduce by musical imitation the color, movement, and sound of the fanciful wave. But how can one render the melody of the original into another language? The difficulty of the translation is evident when dealing with such onomatopoeic forms as "sciacqua," "sciaborda," "scroscia," "schiocca," "schianta," "rotola," "romba," and the like, whose phonetic qualities are impossible to render into French. In fact, in the translation one hears a concert quite different from that of the original text.

If in general French readers preferred D'Annunzio's novels and plays to his poetry, there were, nevertheless, those who, knowing Italian, attached themselves almost exclusively to the poet. Marcel Coulon wrote in 1939:

> Grand admirateur de l'oeuvre de l'altissime écrivain, je préfère pourtant le poète au romancier et au dramaturge. C'est dans ses poèmes que son lyrisme, partout fervent, se trouve à l'état le plus pur—se trouve le mieux ordonné, le mieux composé, et, sans perdre de sa force, connaît vraiment la mesure.[15]

Coulon complains that D'Annunzio's poetic works have remained "a dead letter" in France, and he asserts that French poetry could have benefited from them. "Il est regrettable," he says, "non seulement pour l'agrément de nos muses mais pour leur profit, qu'une telle oeuvre lyrique soit restée chez nous lettre morte; que nous n'en ayons pas bénéficié davantage que nous fîmes de la poésie lyrique de Mistral. Puisse la lecture du poème que voici faire admettre que ce regret n'est pas vain!"[16] He presents his translation in verse of one of the most remarkable poems of Le Laudi, Book III—"La Morte del cervo." Coulon blames the existing translations—almost all of them in prose—for the lack of popularity in France of D'Annunzio's poetic works. He gives his own rendering of the poem to show that only the verse can do justice to the poet. The best translation in prose, however poetic, is never poetry. The translation, he maintains, must be rendered so as to produce a new poem as beautiful as the original. And this is precisely what Coulon had already tried to do first with another poem— "Undulna" (Book III)—published in L'Age nouveau, April 1939, then with "La Morte del cervo" from which is reproduced the following passage:

> Ritondo il capo avea, tutto di ricci
> folto come la vite di racimoli;
> e l'inclinava a mordicare i cimoli
> dei ramicelli, e teneri viticci

con la gran bocca usa alla vettovaglia
sanguinolenta, a tritar gli ossi, a bere
d'un fiato il vin fumoso nel cratère
ampio, sopra le mense di Tessaglia.

Des boucles encadraient la rondeur de sa tête,
Serrées comme sur la grappe sont les grains,
Et, la tête inclinée, il mordillait des brins
De ramée; il mâchait des feuilles tendrelettes
Avec la grande bouche à qui la chair convient
Sanglante, et qui les os broyés, se désaltère
En avalant d'un trait l'ample et profond cratère
Du vin fumant dans les banquets thessaliens.

Of course, Coulon's translation is poetic and far better than others
of the same poem. But when compared with the original, one feels
that little of D'Annunzio is left. The subject matter is the same; but
the order and movement of the poem have been altered. The translation, however poetic, gives the reader a different feeling. It is futile
to dwell on this question. In order to feel the power and the beauty of
D'Annunzio's best poems, they must be read in Italian, for no rendering—in prose or verse—can fully reveal their esthetic qualities.

17. Poetic Homage to D'Annunzio

ALTHOUGH D'Annunzio's poetry was not as popular as his novels and
plays in France, the ardent admirers of his poetic talent were nonetheless in large number there among the men of letters. The elite regarded
him as a great creator of images and myths and a brilliant evocator of
esthetic feelings. "Dans le domaine du vers," wrote François Porché,
"où il excella tout jeune, ... d'Annunzio possède le double don sans
lequel il n'est pas de grand poète: l'alliance de l'image neuve et de la
sonorité; il est plastique et musical."[1] Jules Lemaître called him "le
poète romantique de la Renaissance." Fernand Gregh tells him: "... La
poésie éternelle est fière de vous."[2] Robert de Flers writes, referring to
the poet's French works: "Gabriele d'Annunzio est un grand poète
français."[3] And Maurice Muret: "Je mets son oeuvre poétique sensible-
ment au-dessus de tout ce qui est sorti de sa plume. Il est, pour moi,
le poète des *Laudi*."[4] Marcel Brion said: "On lira toujours ses poèmes

pour l'étonnant jeu d'images et de mots qui en font la chair."[5] Louis Bertrand considers D'Annunzio "le dernier des grands inspirés" after Victor Hugo.[6]

His genius was occasionally celebrated by French poets who dedicated touching verses to him. The following sonnet by Jean Valderez appeared in the *Annales politiques et littéraires,* May 30, 1915:

GABRIELE D'ANNUNZIO

Tu naquis sur les flots, par une nuit lactée,
Comme un jeune alcyon dans un léger berceau,
Mouette qui se pose aux vergues du vaisseau,
Poète qui devait devenir un Tyrtée.

Ton coeur, pour ton pays, s'accorde à ta pensée,
Tel un archer qui veille à travers le créneau,
Et tu mets à ton doigt le symbolique anneau
Qui de l'Adriatique a fait ta fiancée ...

La houle, accompagnant ton sommeil enfantin,
Vibrait, comme aujourd'hui tout le monde latin
Qui, dans le même espoir, avec toi communie.

La lumière, la vague et le zéphyr de miel,
Comment n'aurait-il pas imprégné ton génie,
Puisque tes yeux n'ont vu que la mer et le ciel?

Alfred Droin, like D'Annunzio a war veteran, severely wounded, and like him favored by the Muses, dedicated to the poet this sonnet in the volume *Crêpe étoilé* (Paris: Fasquelle, 1917):

A GABRIELE D'ANNUNZIO

Il a chanté Vénus, ses sourires, ses ruses,
La couche sans sommeil des nouveaux épousés,
Les larmes des amants, les coussins écrasés:
Donnez-lui votre myrte et vos roses, ô Muses!

Il a chanté le Styx et ses rives confuses,
Il a chanté la mort et l'oubli des baisers;
Coupez donc le cyprès funèbre aux fruits bronzés,
Pour le fils du soleil, nourri dans les Abruzzes.

Tordez le chêne aussi, de vos pieuses mains,
Triomphante couronne aux citoyens romains,
Car son verbe enflammé ressuscite les Mille.

Mélodieuses soeurs, surtout n'oubliez pas
Que le héros latin mérite, comme Eschyle,
Le laurier teint de sang, salutaire des combats.

Henri de Régnier, a friend and admirer of D'Annunzio with whom he had much in common—especially a sincere devotion to art and beauty and the cult of pure form in artistic creation—dedicated to his Italian confrère the following:

A GABRIELE D'ANNUNZIO

La maison du poète est auprès de la mer,
La ville en est lointaine et la forêt voisine;
L'air qui l'entoure est plein d'une odeur de résine
Dont l'embaume le pin éternellement vert.

Son seuil hospitalier à mon pas s'est ouvert,
Mais le trident se dresse à sa porte marine;
La solitude sied à toute oeuvre divine
Et le vin de la gloire est noblement amer.

Salut, demeure, où vit, en face de la grève,
Volontaire exilé dans l'orgueil de son rêve,
Celui de qui le nom dit un avènement,

Fils illustre deux fois d'une double patrie
Et dont la fière main planta si fièrement
En notre sol de France un laurier d'Italie.

The sonnet appeared in the *Annales politiques et littéraires,* June 10, 1923, and the house mentioned in the poem is the Chalet Saint-Dominique in Arcachon, where the two spent friendly hours during Régnier's visits there.

The death of the poet inspired this extraordinary sonnet in Italian by André Pézard, a professor at the University of Lyons. This is a sonnet, wrote the author, "où j'ai voulu—bien gauchement—dire à la fois la passion que j'ai eue en ma folle jeunesse pour Gabriele d'Annunzio, et l'étonnement incroyable qu'il m'inspire encore, maintenant que mes goûts pourtant ont changé":[7]

ALLEGORIA

Io vidi scendere dalla montagna
(e nei crini n'aveva l'aspro odore)
una fanciulla fremente e grifagna,

pallida in viso di mortale ardore.
E mi parlò con voce che si lagna:
"Sparito è fra di voi il mio Signore:
non mi saluta più, nè m'accompagna
l'arcangelo soave e senza cuore.
Sono anni: un vino di fuoco e di miele
mi versò; bevvi; e forse non fui saggia,
ma non rinnego la dolce e crudele
fiamma che la memoria ancor m'irraggia.
Fui vostra Gioventù, gaia e selvaggia.
Sola me'n vo, chiamando Gabriele."

In his *Vingt ans d'amitié avec d'Annunzio* (p. 123), published post-humously, André Doderet recorded his shock and his grief when at 10 A.M. on March 1, 1938, his telephone rang and the voice of Paul Morand said: "La radio annonce la mort de d'Annunzio." Twenty years of close friendship, full of happy memories, could not remain silent in the spirit and the heart of the faithful Doderet who had so much enjoyed the affection of the poet. And he closes his book of remembrances with a long and touching poem, *A Gabriele d'Annunzio*, mourning, in a humble and sincere tone, his departed friend. Following are some excerpts of the poem:

Je ne vous ai connu qu'au soir de votre été,
Quand, sous les pins landais volontaire exilé,
Comme eux blessé, comme eux debout dans la souffrance,
Chanteur du bel Archer, pensif devant la Mort,
Vous donniez, enchâssant votre vitrail dans l'or,
　　Un nouveau Poète à la France.

.　　.　　.　　.　　.　　.　　.　　.　　.

Nous passons, ici-bas, selon nos destinées
Quelques riants matins et de sombres années.
Trop tard nous rencontrons, à la croix du chemin,
La compagne ou l'ami qui nous prend par la main,
Nous conduit vers son but ou marche vers le nôtre.
Et celui qui survit et qui cherche encor l'autre
Ne sait plus, remontant le chemin parcouru,
Qui des deux est vivant ou des deux disparu.

.　　.　　.　　.　　.　　.　　.　　.　　.

O Muse, pourquoi donc, au plus noir de l'allée,
T'ai-je surprise en pleurs et la face voilée?
Pour quelle ombre chérie cueilles-tu ce laurier?

Pour quel front de héros couronner, de poète?
Vers quel triomphateur, vers quelle sombre fête
Conduit cette voûte d'acier?

With D'Annunzio's poetic works appearing in French translation, some of his plays in verse should be mentioned in this connection. *La Fille de Iorio, Francesca da Rimini, La Torche sous le boisseau, Phèdre, Le Martyre de Saint Sébastien,* and *La Pisanelle* contributed greatly to the knowledge of his poetic talent in France, especially among the literati. However, his capital work, *Le Laudi,* where he gives the real measure of his creative power, still remains for a large part unknown in France even to men of letters.

18. Before the French "Exile"

D'ANNUNZIO'S private and public life aroused in France as much interest as his literary works. The publication of *L'Intrus* in 1892 drew attention not only to the artist but also to the man whose matchless personality constantly intrigued his readers. His activities and behavior became thereafter the object of both admiration and censure. His formal introduction to the French public came in 1893, when an autobiographical sketch, prepared at Hérelle's request, was inserted in a long article by Amédée Pigeon in the *Revue hebdomadaire* (June 24), and was reprinted in part in the *Revue de Paris* of December 16, 1894, as a footnote to the first installment of *L'Enfant de volupté*. In tracing his personal and cultural background, D'Annunzio conceived the idea of creating a legend about himself and deliberately stated that he was born on board the brig *Irène* in the Adriatic Sea in 1864. (He was born in Pescara on March 12, 1863.) This "nativité marine," he said, "a influé sur mon esprit. La mer est, en effet, ma passion la plus profonde."[1] This became the accepted version of his birth. In fact, Adolphe Brisson in the *Annales politiques et littéraires* stated that D'Annunzio was born "sur l'Adriatique, à bord d'un vaisseau marchand."[2]

Those who had read *L'Intrus, L'Enfant de volupté,* and *Le Triomphe de la mort* pictured D'Annunzio as a pagan of the Renaissance —a man of strong features and imperious bearing, standing amidst arms, gold, and purple as in a painting by Titian or a tale by Bandello or Guicciardini. But Gaston Deschamps, who had visited the poet in Milan in November 1895, found him more a man of letters than a condottiere despite "la jolie crânerie de ses moustaches retroussées à la Van Dyck," and likened him to Poliziano rather than Cesare Borgia. What struck Deschamps most forcibly was D'Annunzio's love for art and beauty, so strong and so sincere as to suggest the soul of a mystic dedicated entirely to his deity. This love was his religion, his morality,

139

and his strength. "D'autres," said Deschamps, "vivent pratiquement, commercialement, politiquement, joyeusement," D'Annunzio lives "artistement," forgetting everything else for a beautiful poem, for a beautiful painting, for a beautiful symphony, for a beautiful woman. His ideal seemed to be contained in Keats' verse: "A thing of beauty is a joy for ever."[3]

In 1897 D'Annunzio presented himself as a candidate for Parliament in the electoral college of Ortona (Abruzzi). He was duly elected and took his place among the right-wingers. His election was favorably received in France, and the suffrage which the people of Abruzzi gave to D'Annunzio—the poet, novelist, and esthete—was considered to be significant. Melchior de Vogüé, in an article devoted to the author's political success (*Le Figaro*, October 2, 1897), called the new member of the Chamber "le député de la Beauté." The case of a poet entering politics was not unique: one need only recall the names of Lamartine and Victor Hugo. But D'Annunzio's electoral victory gave the French press an opportunity to reopen the much debated question of whether poets can perform a useful function in government. It was pointed out that creative writers, being dreamers by virtue of their artistic nature, are often far removed from political reality. Vogüé remarked in this connection that Hugo's fervent admirers deliberately overlooked the insignificance of the speeches of this representative of the people, whose oratorical vacuity left Parliament completely unmoved. Likewise, Lamartine's eloquent discourses were greeted by scornful laughter in the Assembly for fifteen years; and if he finally had his hour of triumph as a political prophet, the usefulness of his activity in public affairs was, in Vogüé's view, still open to question. D'Annunzio had entered the world of politics without any definite ideological convictions. He was driven into this venture by an urgent need for new experiences which would broaden the scope of his literary work. The great figures of the Renaissance exercised an irresistible attraction for him. His turning to politics "n'a pas de quoi nous surprendre," wrote François Carry: "Le surhomme qui est en lui ne doit-il pas goûter toutes les émotions, s'initier à toutes les luttes, aspirer à toutes les grandeurs?"[4] For him politics was simply a means to achieve ends completely alien to political problems. As a result he had no political program. Nevertheless, he figured among the champions of conservative antisocialist principles, although, in reality, whatever belief he might have had was the logical outcome of his esthetic theories. He assumed, in fact, the strange role of the defender of Beauty, of the prophet of this new goddess who, in his opinion, was the sole principle of morality. In his electoral speeches there was not a word about general or local politics, not a promise, not an allusion to his opponents; there was instead a hymn to Beauty, to the Will, and to the secret Genius of the race. D'Annunzio spoke with lyrical loftiness of the nobility of agricultural labor (not without quoting Hesiod), the primitive Sabellian tribes, the festivals in ancient Latium, to an audience of two thousand Abruzzian peasants who, half bewildered, half charmed, allowed themselves to be swayed by the waves of his magnificent eloquence, and at the close of the speech applauded without having understood a word of it. The magician performed, with his extraordinary language, the miracle of Orpheus, who charmed and led the wild beasts with the sounds of his lyre.

But at Montecitorio the lyre of the poet-tribune did not produce a similar miracle. His eloquence fell on deaf ears, and the "député de la Beauté" found himself cut off from party politics and himself the only defender of his program. If his efforts to bring Beauty into Parliament failed, however, his attempt received words of praise from his French friends. "N'ayons pas la sottise," wrote Vogüé, "de railler le poète qui veut rapporter un peu de beauté dans les choses d'où elle est le plus bannie. S'il y réussissait, il serait notre bienfaiteur à tous."[5] His election was even taken seriously. "Il ne faudrait pas trop ridiculiser cette métamorphose politique de M. d'Annunzio," said François Carry, pointing out that the poet possessed "une fibre singulièrement énergique."[6]

The Italians, on the contrary, found the parliamentary mandate of "l'enfant de volupté" to be a mockery. D'Annunzio's program seemed to be the esthetic reform of Montecitorio, and they ridiculed him. A man of refined manners such as the author of the "Novels of the Rose" who had revealed himself as an extreme individualist was not the kind of political representative the Italian public was looking for. Moreover, until that time, D'Annunzio had remained completely aloof from political questions, only concerned with his esthetic ideal. How could he suddenly become a tribune?

In June 1897, when his *Sogno d'un mattino di primavera* was produced in France, the poet was planning, as mentioned elsewhere, to go to Paris for the occasion. In fact, he wrote to Hérelle: "La Duse part ce soir pour Paris. Je partirai, moi, entre le 25 et le 30." And he added:

"Je voudrais demeurer un peu à l'écart, à Paris; je voudrais ne pas trop me prodiguer, ne pas me vulgariser."[7] Romain Rolland said that D'Annunzio "hésita à partir, craignant les importuns qui l'attendaient."[8] In January 1898, however, he appeared in the French capital for the first time in order to attend the opening performance of *La Ville morte*. His personal success during his week in Paris, the homage he received from his many admirers, and the receptions given in his honor were mentioned earlier (see Part II). But the most amusing event of the week took place at a luncheon organized by Hérelle at the home of Gustave Dreyfus, a member of the Commission for Historical Monuments. There D'Annunzio was asked what he thought of his contemporary Antonio Fogazzaro. After a moment of seemingly deep reflection he answered, not without poise: "Fogazzaro? Il est de Vicence!"—a phrase which quickly made the rounds in the literary and fashionable circles of the capital. Romain Rolland reported that, during this Parisian visit, D'Annunzio yielded recklessly to all sorts of pleasure and that in a letter to an intimate friend he confided having made a wager on his ability to carry out certain erotic extravagances which would surely have impaired his health. Upon receiving the letter, said Rolland, the poet's friend and Eleonora Duse hurriedly boarded the train for Paris and within twenty-four hours took him away from the French capital.[9] His departure after a week of social triumphs brought these comments from the *Annales politiques et littéraires:*

> Le jeune poète ne se plaindra pas qu'il ne lui ait pas été fait ici un accueil hospitalier! Il a été la coqueluche de toutes les maisons où l'on cause, et l'on peut dire qu'on se l'est positivement arraché. Mais ce qui devait arriver est arrivé! D'Annunzio emporte la réputation ... d'un aimable "poseur de lapins" mondain. Dame! sollicité de toutes parts à déjeuner et à dîner, l'enfant de volupté promettait de tous côtés et alors qu'arrivait-il? On réunissait des amis intellectuels, on se promettait un fin régal et, dans le bec haletant de l'assistance, tombait généralement, à défaut du dieu lui-même, une grande enveloppe à belle écriture droite: "Je ne viens pas!" ... Quand d'Annunzio reviendra, il aura bien des petits lapins à se faire pardonner. ... Mais il n'aura qu'à paraître et à sourire, car, je vous le dit en vérité, les femmes sont pour lui.[10]

The complaint most often heard against the poet concerned precisely his failure to honor invitations after accepting them. Many a Parisian gathering, including one at the salon of Princess Mathilde, waited in vain for his appearance. In some cases he even failed to make the proper excuses for breaking his promises. José-Marie de Hérédia, with his three beautiful daughters and future sons-in-law—Henri de Régnier, Pierre Louys, and Maurice Maidron—spent an entire evening futilely awaiting him. The author of *Les Trophées* disappointedly confided to a friend the following day: "Je ne suis pas riche! ... J'avais fait quelques frais. ... Il m'a laissé mon dîner sur l'estomac."[11] D'Annunzio did not even send a word of excuse. It later became known that the poet generally accepted five or six invitations for the same day and that at the last moment, while dressing for the evening, he would decide whom to honor with his presence, neglecting to excuse himself with the others. But "quand on le revoyait ensuite il était si charmant, si empressé, éblouissant et délicieux, qu'on lui pardonnait."[12]

This extraordinary reception was due, of course, to his literary success. D'Annunzio was already, by that time, more than a European celebrity; he was an epidemic. "Les critiques," remarked Luciano Zuccoli in the *Mercure de France,* "voient le jeune maître partout; à travers les pages des autres, surtout; il suffit d'employer un adjectif qui sente l'épidémie pour être classé parmi les suivants de l'auteur de l'*Intrus*."[13] The epidemic affected mostly the women; enchanted by his verbal magic, Francis de Croisset amusingly described a reception taking place immediately after the performance of *La Ville morte,* where D'Annunzio, besieged by fashionable ladies, bestowed his smiles "comme on sème des fleurs." At times silent, said Croisset, "il méditait, et ces dames attendaient, palpitantes. L'éclair aux yeux, il se tournait alors vers une voisine—l'Élue—et lui adressait une phrase ciselée avec un geste d'offrande. Ainsi aux jeunes Bacchantes pâmées, Silène distribuait ses coupes."[14] His personality left a slightly different impression from that imagined by the readers of his novels. Jules Huret, tracing a "portrait physique et moral" of the poet, remarked that his bearing revealed no signs of his exuberant sensuality; his physiognomy was rather aloof and cold. Huret defined D'Annunzio as "un cérébral," master of himself, and more prone to be moved by beautiful verse than by human suffering. Did not the poet write, said Huret: "Complete freedom at all costs, even 'dans l'ivresse' "?[15]

D'Annunzio's literary and political activities were followed in France with much curiosity. In 1900, during a tumultuous session at Montecitorio, the poet made a spectacular political move when suddenly he passed from the right to the extreme left wing with the statement: "As a man of intellect, I go toward life!" While he did not really embrace socialism, he meant nevertheless to show his displeasure with the attitude of the rightists. In the left wing he saw a group of energetic and eloquent men determined to defend their ideas; on the opposite side he saw only moribunds muttering futilely. He chose to abandon the dying and join the living. The left-wingers received him with wild enthusiasm. But the bold stroke did not change the substance of his individualism. When a French journalist from *Le Temps* questioned him on the subject, he answered:

> Do you really believe that I am a socialist? I am what I have always been. Between me and the socialists there is an insurmountable barrier. I am, and I will always be, an extreme individualist—an irreducible one. . . . In Italy socialism is an absurdity. There is in our country only one possible political principle—that of tearing down the present political order. Whatever exists now amounts to nothing; it is only decay—death opposing life. We must destroy. One day you will see me in action in the streets.[16]

In June of that year D'Annunzio ran again for election, this time not in his native Abruzzi, but in the constituency of Florence. He was defeated and this setback ended his political career for the time and brought him back entirely to his writing. The electoral campaign of the new rebel seeking the support of the most aristocratic district in Florence was viewed in the *Mercure de France,* September 3, 1900, as a great absurdity after his move to the extreme left. Furthermore, the ideas and the temperament of the deputy-esthete sharply conflicted with the principles of the social-democratic party. In his works he had always expounded the religion of pleasure and his extreme Nietzscheism, and had always shown supreme scorn for bourgeois morals. His position was therefore illogical whether he was to represent aristocracy or the lower classes, and his rebellion could not dispel the suspicion that his political attitude was bound to shift according to his unpredictable moods.

The year 1900 was not a lucky one for D'Annunzio personally, although his literary production was flourishing. To his political failure was added the campaign against *Il Fuoco* both in Italy and in France. He began to be regarded as a menace to decency. Strict moralists denounced his works and his scandalous life. This, of course, did not stop D'Annunzio from living in his own inimitable way or from displaying in his writings his customary sensuality beyond and above all accepted norms of morality. In 1908 a slanderous pamphlet, circulated and pub-

licized especially in France, warned the public about his works. Against
the would-be champions of decency leading the crusade to discredit the
author of *L'Enfant de volupté* rose Marcel Boulenger who, in an article
in the *Nouvelle Revue française,* defended the poet with noble indignation.

> Les jeunes hommes de notre génération doivent beaucoup à Gabriele
> d'Annunzio. Il me souvient encore du temps où nous lûmes l'*Enfant de
> volupté.* ... Certains de nous étaient au régiment, d'autres en sortaient. Ce
> livre tout imprégné d'art, ce véritable bréviaire du dilettante élégant, ce
> roman dont le héros montait en courses et citait du latin, voire du grec,
> se battait en duel comme un démon, gravait à l'eau-forte, faisait des vers
> exquis, avait tout lu, savait tout, avec cela, s'habillait comme Brummell
> et ne laissait pas de séduire toutes les femmes, et quelles femmes! —Oh!
> comment eussions-nous résisté à ce nouveau Cortigiano? Combien d'entre
> nous, jaloux d'égaler le merveilleux Sperelli, se sont avec fougue remis à
> l'étude et promenés éperdument dans les musées! Gabriele d'Annunzio,
> on ne l'a pas assez dit, apparut avec son *Enfant de volupté* comme un
> incomparable pédagogue. Jamais on ne saura combien de collégiens, entre
> 1894 et 1900, auront mieux soigné leur dissertation ou leur version latine
> après avoir lu d'Annunzio. Et ne fût-ce que pour cette cause touchante et
> toute modeste, je voudrais qu'on le louât publiquement en Sorbonne. ...
> Il faut, dans l'intérêt même des choses belles, qu'il existe de bruyants
> apôtres.[17]

Boulenger's article, as the passage shows, is not only an eloquent defense of D'Annunzio, but a clear indication of the poet's impact on the
young intellectuals of the time and of the positive influence exerted by
the very book labelled as dangerous by the moralists. His stand in support of D'Annunzio was highly commended in the *Mercure de France*
by Charles-Henry Hirsch who, in commenting on the article, hailed
the fact that a French writer countered these calumnies and defamations
by expressing his gratitude "envers l'un des plus justement glorieux
parmi les écrivains de l'Europe actuelle."[18]

19. The French "Exile"

TOWARD the end of March 1910, D'Annunzio arrived in Paris as an
ordinary tourist, accompanied only by his faithful servant Rocco Pesce.
At first he gave the impression of having come to the French capital for

a short stay in order to settle some business with his publishers, and during the first week he refused all social invitations. But circumstances were to keep him there until May 1915. The poet's long sojourn in France was complacently, though improperly, called his "exile"; in reality he had not been banished from his own country; no ostracism had been decreed against him. D'Annunzio left Italy voluntarily, in order to escape his pack of creditors. Generally he seemed little inclined to move from place to place, and did so only when pursued by creditors or women.

Since 1898 he had been living at La Capponcina, in Settignano, near Florence. There he had created an opulent setting, worthy of a great nobleman of the Renaissance, with his fifteenth-century furnishings, rare works of art, oriental rugs, and his library of fourteen thousand richly-bound volumes. He had made of his home a temple of art and refinement.[1] It was at La Capponcina that he wrote his most remarkable works, and it was there also that his transports of passion for Eleonora Duse reached a climax. Surrounded by about fifteen servants, ten horses, forty greyhounds, and two hundred pigeons, D'Annunzio spent so lavishly that his large income was insufficient for his huge and sumptuous household. Gradually his debts increased to fantastic proportions, and when he was no longer able to keep ahead of his creditors, he took refuge in France. A few months later La Capponcina was sold at auction, and day by day he followed in the Parisian press the dispersal of his treasures and the final despoilment of the home which, for over ten years, had been the realization of his dearest youthful dreams.

On his arrival in Paris, D'Annunzio had moved into the Hôtel Meurice (rue de Rivoli)—the address of the foreign celebrities of the time. Donatella, desperately in love, had been awaiting him there. Despite his lack of adequate funds, the poet continued to live magnificently, even "dangerously" (the danger, to be sure, being to the management of the hotel). During the first week he consumed all of the money he had, and he spent the second week trying to find more. Concerned with his financial plight, his friends approached the Société des Auteurs on his behalf and negotiated a loan for him of sixty thousand francs; Gaston Calmann-Lévy provided an additional forty thousand, and this tidy sum seemed to be enough for the moment.[2] He threw himself into the Parisian whirl and once again experienced the inebriation he had known, in his youth, in the elegant salons of Rome. French high society was at first cautious and reserved toward him. His living with Donatella under the same roof (her idea), without saving at least the appearances of social decency, created at first a somewhat embarrassing situation. Under the circumstances, she was not always acceptable where the poet was invited and feted. But she was more interested in parading her liaison and publicly claiming her rights as his mistress than in shining beside him at all social gatherings. On the other hand, D'Annunzio could not accept invitations which did not include Donatella. As a result, in the beginning, she was rather a hindrance to the poet. He later decided to leave her at home occasionally. D'Annunzio soon became the most sought after figure of the season. All doors were wide open to the newcomer. Women pursued him everywhere; he was surrounded especially by actresses, and for about five months his life was filled with parties, balls, dinners, theaters, races, and romantic adventures. He became a Tout-Paris whose presence was deemed essential to the success of any social gathering. In the circles where renown implies social rank, in the world of celebrated cosmopolitan beauties, D'Annunzio was received with the kind of manifestations which are a tribute to greatness. He loved France, particularly Paris; but above all things he loved women and his own glory. In the French capital he seemed to be living only for the gratification of his senses and to add to his reputation as a great lover and a man of the world. He deliberately paraded his relationships and sentimental attachments, and made himself more conspicuous as a social figure than a man of letters. He was seen more frequently at the theater and in the company of women than at meetings of academicians. Fifteen years earlier, Melchior de Vogüé, Gaston Deschamps, Édouard Rod, Henry Bérenger, Philippe Gille, René Doumic had fostered his literary reputation in France; now the official literary arbiters remained rather aloof. They were no longer as favorable toward him as they had been at the time of his brilliant introduction in France, when Brunetière accepted him in the *Revue des Deux Mondes* and Vogüé hailed him as the champion of a new Latin renaissance. However, although the enthusiasm for his novels was almost over and he no longer figured among the avant-garde writers, his personal prestige was considerable. His last great novel, *Forse che sì forse che no,* had just appeared in *La Grande Revue* and, if it failed to arouse the same enthusiasm as the "Novel of the Rose," it did not lack wide success.

The Paris of the time was overflowing with life and pleasure. Refinement, elegance, joie de vivre, insouciance had reached vertiginous heights, and the search for physical enjoyment was seemingly the only aim in life. There was, according to the chronicles of the period, an atmosphere of general debauchery and inebriation; the Golden Age seemed to have returned for the happy inhabitants of the earth, before the horror and the sufferings of the approaching war. The Russians were lavishing the enchantment of their ballet upon an enthusiastic public, theaters were displaying an unusual activity, and all kinds of amusements were within easy reach. In this world of balls and dinners, of horseback riding and elegant gatherings, of intimate meetings and gala parties, D'Annunzio broke his working habits and for five months he never stopped to think or to open a book. His slightest move was commented upon, admired, parodied, criticized. Robert de Montesquiou, his public relations man and companion in dissipation, organized parties in his honor, forced all doors for the entry of the new star on the Parisian scene, and shielded him from the attacks of the envious. Cécile Sorel, an actress of the Comédie-Française, was among the first to open her home to the poet and to have occasionally the honor of sharing his bed, of which she was proud.[3] In the luxurious apartment of Donatella where, in the words of Albert Flament, "tout puait le luxe, la sensualité, le factice, le carnaval, l'imbroglio, la mystification et le suspect," he reigned as a god.[4] Donatella was very much in love with him and she suffered untold jealousy because of his inconstancy. Her rivals soon grew in number, since D'Annunzio was not the man to resist this sort of temptation. As the days went by, her doom became inevitable, despite her desperate efforts to retain the vanishing affection of the poet.

This period of Parisian life, so rich in adventures and physical pleasure, was most varied and kaleidoscopic, most brilliant and exciting, but it was also completely futile, dissipated, and wasteful. D'Annunzio allegedly squandered no less than a hundred thousand francs. Soon, however, the demon of creation recaptured him and aroused in him a yearning for the solitude of the country. Remarkably enough, this would-be man of the world was an exceptionally hard worker and spent most of his life away from cities, almost as a hermit. The atmosphere of the great metropolises was not conducive to the realization of his artistic endeavors and, after a time, always produced in him a deep revulsion, moral lassitude, and regrets. In this particular instance, however, there was an added reason for leaving Paris—Donatella's angry scenes of desperate jealousy, which had become unbearable. D'Annunzio therefore let himself be lured to the peaceful villa Saint-Dominique, in Arcachon (near Bordeaux), by Romaine Brooks, a talented American painter and at the moment Donatella's major rival. There Mrs. Brooks planned to give him refuge and hoped, among other things, to be able to paint his portrait without distractions.

The poet had met her in Florence in 1909, and it is hard to guess the real nature of their relations. According to Guglielmo Gatti, under her inspiration D'Annunzio had conceived a novel, *La Violante dalla bella voce,* which was never written. However, Gatti states, "he included some fifty pages of it in his *Libro segreto* and devoted to her two long *memoranda* published in the *Corriere della sera.*"[5] In his *Libro segreto,* in fact, the author speaks of an unknown "fragment" of his entitled *La Violante dalla bella voce* and narrates a sad story which occupies several pages of the book. "Violante," says D'Annunzio, "was a friend of mine of non-Latin blood, very much loved and desired, whom a tragic event separated from me without love and without death."[6] The setting of the story is the Settignano hill and the account ends with the violent death of his favorite greyhound which, given to the woman as a bond of their mutual devotion, had turned against her and marred her beautiful face. Whether or not the story had been inspired by Romaine Brooks is of relative importance.

Their relations continued in Paris; he confided in her his misfortunes, his sadness, the strain to which he was subjected by his official mistress, and Romaine Brooks sincerely felt that her protective love could somewhat relieve this unhappy genius. Taking advantage of the opportunity offered by her, D'Annunzio decided to depart from Paris in strict secrecy, in order to prevent Donatella from following him to the new destination. When he disclosed his plan to his friend Robert de Montesquiou, the latter was enchanted with the idea, and, as a worthy descendent of D'Artagnan whose friendship for Aramis was similar to his own for D'Annunzio, he gladly organized the flight toward the pineland of Arcachon, where Romaine Brooks was waiting. At midnight D'Annunzio slipped out of the Hôtel Meurice and quietly boarded a train for the South. Robert de Montesquiou and Tom Antongini (the poet's personal secretary) were to look after the transfer of his personal effects and other details. To prevent news of his whereabouts from leaking out, they arranged for any correspondence arriving for him at the Hôtel Meurice to be forwarded in care of

Monsieur Henri (one of the plotters) at Chatou (S.-et-O.) who in
turn would see that it reached Arcachon, where D'Annunzio had
arrived under the assumed name of Guy d'Arbres. In Paris it was
believed for a time that he had withdrawn to Chatou, though, of
course, he was not seen there. To anyone inquiring about him, Robert
de Montesquiou would reply mysteriously: "Ma foi, je n'en sais rien!
Il a disparu ... tout simplement!" Donatella's despair and humiliation
were extreme. She questioned his friends and was given various and
conflicting explanations—all meant to console her. But she could not
resign herself to the situation.

Once away from Paris, D'Annunzio began a new life. A few weeks
after his departure he wrote to Hérelle: "J'étais malade de fatigue, et
j'ai recouvré mes forces en ce marveilleux pays de sables et de pins, de
sel et de résine. Maintenant je suis bien et recommence à travailler."[7]
He established himself at the villa Saint-Dominique as the guest of
Romaine Brooks and seemed finally to be enjoying peace and solitude
between the pine trees and the wide ocean.

Although the companionship of his hostess was very congenial, the
poet did not remain at the villa long, for he could never feel completely
at ease as a house guest. In addition, there had been some unusual
incidents which had created a rather embarrassing situation. One day
a woman, while climbing the high iron gate surrounding the villa with
the obvious intention of reaching D'Annunzio's quarters unseen, was
caught by Mrs. Brooks' chauffeur and gently sent on her way. On
another occasion an actress, Mme Roger, had her hair pulled by the
hostess when found in the poet's rooms at an odd hour. These incidents
hastened D'Annunzio's move to the nearby villa Charitas where he
could be completely free. Meanwhile, following an exchange of conciliatory letters, Donatella had come to take her place again beside the
poet, although she did not officially live under the same roof. Romaine
Brooks packed and returned to Paris, sad and heartsick, realizing the
futility of loving a man no one would be able to possess and who could
not but destroy his victims. Thus, the spell was broken without any
dramatic outcome. Her pride as a talented artist helped her to regain
control of her feelings, and she resumed her normal life devoting herself to her art and refusing to descend to the level of ordinary females
—easy prey of the faithless charmer. D'Annunzio admired her stoic
attitude, the lucid mastery over herself which kept her from yielding
to his seduction. Their relations, instead, developed into an enduring

friendship inspired by a growing esteem and affection maintained on an intellectual rather than sentimental level. In 1913 Romaine Brooks finally painted D'Annunzio's portrait, now in the Musée d'Art Moderne in Paris. The painting, simple and vigorous in its lines, shows D'Annunzio from his knees up, wearing a wind-blown cloak, at the edge of a reef; a cloudy, windy sky and the high, foamy waves of the ocean form the background—a background allusive of a stormy life —against which the poet stands restfully with a rather sad and aloof glance, expressing a feeling of disappointment and emptiness. He dedicated to Romaine Brooks a sonnet in French (1914), inspired by a portrait she painted of herself against a similar, though less stormy, background. The sonnet pays high homage to her strength of character which the poet was unable to break:

> Nul sort ne domptera, ni par fer ni par flamme,
> le secret diamant de ton coeur ingénu.
> Debout entre le ciel morne et le flot chenu,
> tu ne crains pas le choc de la dixième lame.
>
> Voici dans tes grands yeux le feu qui fut l'espoir
> du souverain amour, avant que ton plus noir
> regard mirât l'intacte horreur de la Gorgone.[8]

D'Annunzio posed again for her in December 1915 in Venice, for a portrait in his military uniform, and the sittings are recollected in *Il Notturno* where the name of Cinerina (Romaine Brooks as renamed by the poet) recurs several times: "Cinerina is there, with her strange, inspired expression . . . with her eyes larger than ever and her glance permeated by a mysterious mixture of irony and sadness"; and further: "Cinerina is there, all eyes, all chin, no longer a woman, but a will to create."[9]

With her departure from the villa Saint-Dominique, D'Annunzio was able to move back in as the only tenant. This villa, which he transformed into a new Capponcina, was his favorite abode for the four years of his stay in France. With his usual extravagance he spent over half a million francs in an attempt to create a comfortable place—a place which met the standards of his over-refined taste and satisfied his artistic whim and his illusions of a Renaissance nobleman. He squandered huge sums to improve the premises and no less considerable sums to furnish the house sumptuously. He built a kennel like the one he had at La Capponcina, and in a short time had also collected a library of about five thousand volumes, most of them elegantly bound by Gruel. He called this his "bibliothecula gallica," and he loved to cover the front of its bookshelves with such inscriptions as: "L'ouvrier se cognoist à l'ouvrage," "Laissez-moi penser à mon ayse," "Tais-toy," "Le temps vendra," "Plus hault," "Le temps et moi," "Labora, ora et invenies," and so forth.

At the villa Saint-Dominique he resumed his normal rhythm of life. There he composed *Le Martyre de Saint Sébastien, Le Canzoni della gesta d'Oltremare, La Pisanella, Parisina, La Contemplazione della morte, Le Faville del maglio, Le Chèvrefeuille.* He wrote, he rode, he received distinguished visitors, and began once again to contract debts. He went to Paris occasionally on business, that is, to see publishers and theater directors and to raise money—his constant problem. But his visits to the capital, though frequent, were rather short. If during the first months of his sojourn in Paris he had been the "enfant de volupté" of the fashionable world, he now frequented the literary and artistic circles. He was often seen at the home of Anna de Noailles or at that of Henri de Régnier. He was noticed at dinner with Paul Hervieu, Pierre Loti, Léon Blum, Henri de Régnier, Pierre Louys, Mme Catulle Mendès, Boni de Castellane, Maurice Barrès, Henri Lavedan, and many others. Robert de Montesquiou was always at his side. On his first visits, D'Annunzio stayed at the Hôtel Iéna; but later on, as his stays became more prolonged, especially during the periods of rehearsal and production of his plays, he took furnished apartments. Until August 1914 his life was divided between Arcachon and Paris, although his official residence was the villa Saint-Dominique. The memory of the years spent in Arcachon remained linked in D'Annunzio's mind with his most enjoyable meetings with Henri de Régnier. It was there that he was captivated by the figure of the French poet—so haughty in appearance, yet so gently and warmly human. The moving sonnet which Régnier devoted to the "demeure océanique" of his Italian confrere was cited previously.

D'Annunzio expressed himself in admirable French. He possessed as rich a vocabulary in that language as in his own, and he spoke distinctly, though with a slight lisp similar to that noticed in Cardinal Mazarin by his contemporaries. His personal magnetism stemmed from his brilliant language, always colored by poetic imagery. He was far from a handsome man; pale, bald, and short of stature, he possessed little physical attractiveness. But the beauty of his verbal expression enchanted all women. Isadora Duncan wrote in her memoirs:

> Perhaps one of the most wonderful personalities of our time is Gabriele d'Annunzio, and yet he is small and, except when his face lights up, can hardly be called beautiful. But when he talks to one he loves, he is transformed to the likeness of Phoebus Apollo himself, and he has won the love of some of the greatest and most beautiful women of the day. When d'Annunzio loves a woman, he lifts her spirit from the earth to the divine region where Beatrice moves and shines. In turn he transforms each woman to a part of the divine essence, he carries her aloft until she believes herself with Beatrice. . . . There was an epoch in Paris when the cult of d'Annunzio rose to such a height that he was loved by all the most famous beauties. At that time he flung over each favourite in turn a shining veil. She rose above the heads of ordinary mortals and walked surrounded by strange radiance. But when the caprice of the poet ended, this veil vanished, the radiance was eclipsed, and the woman turned again to common clay. . . . So great a lover was Gabriele d'Annunzio that he could transform the most commonplace mortal to the momentary appearance of a celestial being.[10]

D'Annunzio, of course, did not fail to make advances to the American dancer; but her friendship and admiration for Eleonora Duse and the ingratitude of the poet toward the celebrated actress created in the mind of Isadora a strong feeling against him. She avoided making his personal acquaintance for some time; but one evening D'Annunzio was taken to her home contrary to her wishes, and in the presence of his irresistible personality she was unable to maintain her severity toward him. After this first meeting the poet planned the conquest of the beautiful dancer. He made several attempts, but he was repelled each time. "I thought," she wrote, "I would be the only woman in the world who would resist him. It was a heroic impulse." The figure of Duse rose like a barrier between Isadora and D'Annunzio. "When d'Annunzio wants to make love to a woman," she continued, "every morning he sends a little poem to her with a little flower expressing the poem. Every morning at 8 o'clock I received this little flower, and yet I held to my heroic impulse."[11] She remembers in her memoirs a walk with D'Annunzio in the "Forêt de Marly" at Versailles; they paused a moment in the silence of the woods and the poet began: "Oh, Isadora, it is only possible to be alone with you in Nature. All other women destroy the landscape, you alone become part of it. . . . You are part of the trees, the sky, you are the dominating goddess of Nature."[12] Although she was very receptive to this flattery, she insists that she did not give way. However, the version of the affair given by one of D'Annunzio's biographers implies the contrary.[13] In December 1910 Isadora entertained lavishly at a dinner and reception in honor of D'Annunzio at the Hôtel Biron with full attendance of the elite.[14] This might indicate that her strong feelings against the poet were not completely unshakable.

Elisabeth de Grammont wrote in her *Mémoires:* "Ce génie savait susurrer des paroles sublimes aux oreilles des femmes, mais il changeait souvent, trop souvent d'objet."[15] But despite his inveterate unfaithfulness, women could not resist his seduction: "C'était le temps," continued Grammont, "où elles se l'arrachaient." Men treated him generally with more reserve than sympathy. They were a bit irritated by this foreigner with his ornate speech and elegant dress. Women, on the contrary, were especially attracted to him by the magic uplifting they hoped to receive from his praise. And for this glory many of them "avaient quitté leur honneur comme un manteau léger."[16] Count Boni de Castellane, who in his luxurious apartment always reserved a place of honor for the poet, among such distinguished guests as Edmond Rostand, Henri and Marie de Régnier, Anna de Noailles, and others, said of him: "Sa réputation était celle d'un homme dangereux. ... Peu de femmes résistaient à ce petit homme. Une fois tombées sous sa coupe, il les dominait. Son influence est comme celle des parfums. ... On ne sait si elle vient de la curiosité qu'il suscite ou du magnétisme qu'il dégage."[17] Castellane occasionally found him extremely amusing. One evening he had invited some friends to dinner in order to meet the poet. To everyone's surprise, D'Annunzio arrived a little late wrapped in a black cloak of the kind worn at one time in Venice and his face covered by a black mask as though for a costume ball. The night was cold and he pretended to have dressed so in order to protect himself from the rigors of the winter weather. Before leaving, he again put on the mask with extreme self-assurance and departed in the manner of a Venetian condottiere. "Son appartement," wrote Castellane, "ne ressemblait à aucun autre. Il n'avait jamais d'argent, malgré qu'il touchât pour ses livres des sommes énormes. Il les dépensait sans compter, et c'est un des traits les plus sympathiques de son charactère. Après moi, il est l'homme le plus luxueux et le plus prodigue que j'aie connu."[18]

The adventures of the new Don Juan in the French capital were closely followed by the curious public, and every day "dans ce monde particulier, corrompu, amoral, brillant, intellectuel et 'rosse', quelque histoire nouvelle était colportée soutenue d'une citation piquante de celui qui en était le héros."[19] It was inevitable that his name should appear frequently in the "échos" of the press. His private secretary Tom Antongini related that one day, while in the post office sending some telegrams, he himself was mistaken for the poet by the postal clerk who, encouraged by the friendly smile of the supposed D'Annunzio, said: "Que le monde est méchant, tout de même! Dire qu'on raconte que vous êtes complètement chauve! Vraiment il ne faut jamais croire à ce que l'on dit." Antongini, amused, left without revealing his true identity to her. A few days later the journal *Comoedia* gave the following "écho": "M. d'Annunzio s'éprit, l'hiver dernier, d'une belle actrice romaine: Bianca Liguardi. Celle-ci le repoussa: 'Jamais je ne pourrais aimer un homme chauve!' L'auteur des *Victoires mutilées* souffrit beaucoup de l'échec. Et, aujourd'hui, il a orné son chef d'une perruque ... adéquate."[20] Among the stories circulating about him there were amusing as well as slanderous ones. On leaving a party one evening—it was reported—D'Annunzio accidentally dropped his handkerchief and, when his hostess hurried to pick it up and hold it out to him, he said, with the pride of the superior male: "You may keep it!" The lady turned and threw the handkerchief into the burning fireplace under the indifferent eyes of her distinguished guest. But if his manners and eccentricities were the object of irony, they were as well the object of imitation. There was a time when everyone copied him and "lorsque, dans les rues, on voyait passer un jeune homme ganté de blanc, le buste cambré, la mine impérieuse, portant la moustache fièrement retroussée, on disait: 'C'est un Annunziano.' "[21]

The poet was a bit superstitious and liked occasionally to consult fortunetellers. In France he had the most flattering as well as the most frightening predictions about his future. In the village of Gazinet, about forty miles from Arcachon, was an old sorceress credited with the power of performing miracles. One evening D'Annunzio, out of curiosity and without revealing his identity, visited the woman who, looking at him, said: "Tu seras roi!" When the poet occupied Fiume, everyone recalled the words of the sorceress which came true on September 12, 1920, when, by the creation of the Italian Regency of Carnaro, he became a head of state. But the prediction which deeply troubled his mind was Gabriel Trarieux's in 1912, according to which D'Annunzio would die in 1914. The author stoically awaited the fatal hour to strike,

but it did not. The *Mercure de France*, April 16, 1919, recalling Trarieux's prediction, warmly congratulated the poet, laughing away the
fortuneteller's predictions.

D'Annunzio had a particular fondness for racing dogs, and at the
villa Saint-Dominique he devoted part of his time to the breeding of
greyhounds. He especially liked the borzois (Russian wolfhounds).
Through Donatella he was able to acquire two at first, then to increase
this number to four, then to twelve, and finally to no one knows how
many. He kept them together with his numerous Scottish greyhounds.
His kennel was governed by strict rules, with feeding schedules that
established not only the hour but also the menu written out carefully
in his own hand. The poet spent hours among his dogs—playing with
them, studying their rivalries, stimulating their impulses, and watching
their frolics with childlike enjoyment. Paul Fort, after observing
D'Annunzio amidst his pack, described him in *La Petite Gironde* as a
shepherd followed by his sheep. The number of dogs increased so
rapidly (he had about sixty) that in 1913 the kennel had to be moved
from Saint-Dominique to a farm called Dame-Rose between Saint-
Cloud and Versailles, where the army of hounds could enjoy more
space. Every day it took the meat of an entire horse to feed them adequately. At the beginning of 1914 the sport of dog racing was at its
height, owing to numerous breeders such as Marcel Boulenger, Madame
Lillaz, Madame Hubin, and Donatella herself. It was then that D'Annunzio, with his White Havana, won the Prix de Berri on the Saint-
Cloud racetrack, and thereby aroused the resentment and envy of the
other breeders. He soon became an authoritative member of the Greyhound Club of France and was regarded as an expert on matters of
racing and breeding. He became so enthusiastic about dog racing that
he decided to write a book to be entitled *Vies de chiens illustres* devoted to their admirable deeds. He even hinted that the work was
already in progress and that the manuscript would soon be turned over
to Gaston Calmann-Lévy for immediate publication. The work never
came to light; but since *Le Temps* had announced the author's strange
project, a flood of letters were addressed to the poet from everywhere.
Dog owners hurried to send him long biographies of their own Pou-
pette, Bibì, Azor, Mimì, Ketty, and so on, pointing out with pride the
exceptional qualities, the intelligence, and the devotion of their beloved
pets which they wanted immortalized in this extraordinary book of
canine glories. In order to stem the tide of enthusiasm, D'Annunzio had

to clarify his intention immediately. He dictated a letter and had it sent to the *Gil Blas* with Tom Antongini's signature declaring that *Vies de chiens illustres* was not a collection of pet dog biographies, as was indicated by Georges Docquois in *Le Temps,* but simply the "journal de son chenil." He stated further that what he liked and admired in dogs was not faithfulness and obedience, but gracefulness, strength, and, above all, indomitable courage, and that his book would contain only his personal observations of his own "généreux coursiers."[22] With this declaration he meant to stop the avalanche of sentimental stories coming from the many worshippers of decrepit pets and "bâtards vagabonds."

The letters had the expected result and the project went no further. More than with the life of illustrious dogs, D'Annunzio began now to be concerned with the problem of feeding his racers, for the cost had become exorbitant. It seems that he wrote *Cabiria* for the sole purpose of providing food for these noble animals.[23] D'Annunzio's and Donatella's dogs were soon brought together at the kennel of Dame-Rose in Villacoublay, and during the spring of 1914 they won several prizes. The poet immortalized the names of these braves in the pages of his *Leda senza cigno (Licenza)* just as he had done in *Il Fuoco* with his favorites in the kennel at the Capponcina. But eventually the story of his dogs came to a rather tragic end. The outbreak of the First World War marked the beginning of the end of D'Annunzio's kennel. His noble animals were subjected to the alimentary restrictions imposed by the events, and their life became increasingly precarious. When he left for Italy in May 1915, Donatella, unremittingly in love with the estranged poet, tried desperately to keep his dogs alive. But her means were soon exhausted. The Russian revolution ruined her rich and indulgent husband, and the generous allowance she had been receiving from him was sharply cut. She appealed to the French authorities for help, but they had more important matters to attend to than providing food for the poet's hounds. By the end of the war, D'Annunzio's kennel was finished, and Donatella—herself forsaken, disillusioned, and the victim of her own undying passion for the poet—languished in loneliness, ending her days in the blackest misery (November 1941).[24]

20. The War

AT THE BEGINNING OF 1914, D'Annunzio established himself in Paris, moving from one furnished apartment to another. Although he was still the tenant of the villa Saint-Dominique, which he retained until 1919, he spent only short periods of time there for rest and work, as the capital was conducive to neither. Biographers give conflicting explanations concerning the poet's departure from the solitude of Arcachon where everything had been to his liking. According to Camillo Antona Traversi, French creditors had begun to besiege the poet at the villa and legal action had been taken to sequester his possessions there early in 1914.[1] This, however, was contested by Tom Antongini, at least as far as concerns the dates.[2] While it is true that D'Annunzio's financial affairs were going badly, no confiscation seems to have taken place during the time he was in France. He continued in fact to use Saint-Dominique freely for occasional stays until his departure for Italy.

D'Annunzio spent the first six months of 1914 in a state of uncertainty, almost completely idle, with moments of intense nostalgia for his native land. He even seemed to be contemplating a return to Italy. He observed with distaste the spectacle of Paris so stirred up over the Caillaux Affair,[3] yet so unconcerned with the increasing tension in the international situation. For the first time he began to feel that the Latin race was in a state of decay and that only a war could regenerate it. In a conversation with Maurice Paléologue (June 16, 1914), then French ambassador to Petersburg, D'Annunzio expressed his views in these words:

> La crise que la France vient de traverser m'a secoué dans toutes les fibres de mon patriotisme. Nous vivons à une époque infâme, sous le règne de la multitude et la tyrannie de la plèbe. ... Jamais encore le génie latin n'est tombé si bas; il a totalement perdu le sens des énergies altières et des vertus héroïques; il se traîne dans la fange, il se complaît dans l'humiliation. ... La guerre, une grande guerre nationale, est la dernière chance de salut qui lui reste. C'est par la guerre seulement que les peuples abâtardis s'arrêtent dans leur déclin; car elle leur donne infailliblement ou la gloire ou la mort. ... Si le génie latin n'est plus capable de recouvrer son antique noblesse, eh bien! qu'il meure, qu'il s'ensevelisse dans les

décombres illustres de son passé! ... Donc cette guerre prochaine que vous
semblez craindre, moi, je l'appelle de toutes les forces de mon âme! ...[4]

This declaration clearly defines his position and explains his behavior during the war and the immediate postwar period. D'Annunzio's
philosophy of regeneration through bloodshed—which echoed that of
the Nietzschean superman—took the form of extreme nationalism.
The poet was obsessed by the great shadows of the past, by their
grandiose deeds and misdeeds, by their spirit of domination; he wished
to recreate a heroic race, thus reviving the glories of past ages. It never
came to his mind that perhaps there was a better religion to live by—
that of human brotherhood and social progress which eventually might
regenerate mankind without violence and bloodshed. But the age was
too intoxicated with nationalism to see the absurdity of a bloody conflict, and the few voices raised against this heroic ideal were submerged
by the wave of blind patriotism for which humanity had to pay with
immense destruction.

D'Annunzio's attitude in the face of the approaching war was the
inevitable outcome of his philosophy of life. The Sarajevo incident on
June 28, 1914, was in a way what he had wished for. It was soon to
pull him out of his relative idleness and to throw him into the whirl of
political events. The outbreak of the war filled him with excitement and
awakened in him a combative spirit and patriotic exaltation. The main
concern which had occupied his mind in the wake of the rising international tension had been the uncertain political situation in Italy.
Should she be drawn into the conflict on the side of Austria, what should
he, what could he, do? But Italy's immediate declaration of neutrality
relieved his mind for the moment.[5] While hopefully waiting for the
supreme decision of his country, he made the French cause his own.
Instead of leaving Paris menaced by the invader and returning to
Arcachon away from danger, he chose to remain in the capital and face
the enemy. And amidst the general despair, he composed his *Ode pour
la résurrection latine,* dedicated to "la victoire certaine" at a moment
when every hope seemed to be lost. The poem, published in *Le Figaro,*
August 13, 1914,[6] is a war cry addressed to hesitant Italy in the name
of Latin brotherhood:

> Voici ton jour, voici ton heure,
> Italie; et, pour cette heure,

des années merveilleuses,
la plénitude de tes allégresses! ...

Malheur à toi si tu doutes,
malheur à toi si tu hésites,
malheur à toi si tu n'oses jeter le dé.

D'Annunzio's ode (eleven stanzas of twenty lines each, in blank verse) is not among his best patriotic poems. The French fails to communicate the brilliance and suggestive power of his high-flown imagery. One feels a strain and a certain lack of musicality. The poet's talent was deeply rooted in the Italian language; his poetic images were perfectly molded to the Italian form. The attempt to clothe them in a rather artificial French expression leads to their deformation. Furthermore, historical references and cumbersome parallels often overburden the natural flow of lyrical expression, and the poem falls into lifeless erudition and sheer rhetoric. Yet the ode has some suggestive passages, especially when the poet's emotion becomes more direct and spontaneous, and the closeness to Italian permits sucessful transposition:

Je crie et j'invoque: "O Italie! O France!"
Et j'entends, par-dessus les sépulcres fendus
et par-dessus tes lauriers hérissés,
Victoire, le tonnerre des aigles
qui se précipitent vers l'Est
et de toutes leurs serres déchirent la nuit.
Le jour est proche! Voici le jour! ...

Ta soeur se tient debout dans le soleil.
Elle a vêtu sa robe guerrière de pourpre.
Elle a mis de doubles ailes à ses pieds nus. ...
Elle est prête à chanter, comme l'alouette,
sur tous les sommets de la mort.
Rassise, de ses mains infatigables,
elle tissera la toile du monde nouveau.
Qui est contre elle, sinon le barbare?
Et qui sera près d'elle, sinon toi?

The poet sent the manuscript of his *Ode* to Marie de Régnier with these words: "Chère Suora Notte, ... Daignez accepter, en témoignage de mon amitié reconnaissante, le manuscrit de l'ode *Pour la résurrection latine*. Le jour de la victoire, vous le brûlerez 'sacri thuris honores' à notre dieu."[7] But Mme de Régnier did not burn the manuscript, which she considered precious: "Relisez, cette ode, qui d'un mouvement de victoire, porte en son essor ce cri de héros et de poète, ce cri d'amour pour la France, enfin unie à la patrie qui est la sienne."[8]

In his *Envoi à la France* (*Licenza,* in *La Leda senza cigno*), D'Annunzio in 1916 evoked in moving pages those unforgettable days of heroic struggle. Confined to complete darkness and immobility by an eye wound suffered in the war, he relives the tragic hours of the invasion of France during the first weeks of the conflict—hours of trepidation, despair, hope, and, finally, the "French miracle." The battered cathedrals, the bell-towers falling in flames, the royal forest of Compiègne half destroyed, the villages sacked, the towns ravaged, and the gloomy aspect of Paris under a dark sky—of the Paris which seemed to be in its last hour—and the image of France, insufficiently armed but undaunted, unfold before the bandaged eyes of the poet in this book of memories and devotion. He finds himself with Marcel Boulenger at the family table one evening in August 1914:

> Heures inoubliables d'amitié, de résolution, d'espérance. Nous étions assis autour de la table familiale. Les lampes n'avaient pas été allumées. Une à une, les choses étaient abandonnées par la lumière du jour qui s'en retournait vers l'Occident. ... Nous parlions à demi-voix comme si l'ombre de cette soirée eût été d'une grandeur inaccoutumée. Nous laissions l'argutie se refroidir dans notre bouche et le thé dans nos tasses. L'ennemi n'était pas seulement à la frontière, mais sur notre seuil. Le seuil de la maison et la frontière de la patrie étaient une seule et même sainteté qui pouvait être profanée. Il fallait se dresser et combattre. Alors Marcel vint en souriant, avec son visage pâle et affilé comme une épée nue qui repose sur une dalle de carrare. Il vint et apporta sa tunique bleue, son képi de fantassin, tirés du fond d'une armoire. ... Nous n'aurions pas été plus émus si nous avions été effleurés par les plis du drapeau flottant. Chacun de nous palpa la rude étoffe. Quelqu'un, peut-être, la vit tachée de sang. ... A partir de ce soir-là, nos deux patries n'en furent qu'une seule pour nous.[9]

Despite the gravity of the situation in Paris and the entreaties to the poet to leave the capital, which was being evacuated by the civilians, he did not want to move. He secretly bought a military overcoat and prepared to fight from the window if Von Klück's troops entered the city. Under the date of August 30 he wrote in his *Envoi:* "Aujourd'hui, l'envahisseur est à La Fère. Ses chevaux descendent sur Paris par la vallée de l'Oise; ils piétinent déjà le vrai coeur de la France; ils foulent la plus sensible partie de la terre affligée; à chaque pas, ils profanent un souvenir, offensent une beauté, renouvellent une douleur."[10] The wounded arrive in Paris, "chair sanglante entassée dans les camions; mais on ... n'entendait pas une plainte, pas une imprécation. Tous ces hommes me paraissaient beaux. Le visage de la France était sur chacun de ces visages. Là, en des reliefs d'os et de muscles était sculpté le destin le plus mâle."[11] It was during these days that he read on the afflicted face of Maurice Barrès the suffering and hope which were to bring the two men closer than any meeting in literary or social circles had done. D'Annunzio recalled with Henry Bordeaux this fraternal friendship with an accent of deep emotion in 1929: "J'ai lu sur le visage crispé de Barrès toute l'angoisse de la patrie. Cette expression qui dépassait infiniment tout souci personnel, où l'homme tout entier se perdait, se mêlait au sort du pays, est demeuré dans mes yeux, inoubliable."[12]

Two days before the glorious battle of the Marne, General Gallieni, the military governor of Paris, who was prepared to defend the city or die on the spot, seems to have received Tom Antongini with a message from the poet expressing his firm desire to remain in Paris and share her fate. Gallieni's answer, as reported by Antongini, was highly appreciative of the strong feeling of solidarity shown by the poet: "... Je suis très heureux que votre grand poète me propose courageusement de partager notre sort. ... Dites-lui qu'à partir d'aujourd'hui je le considère comme un soldat français. ... Je vous ferai donner deux uniformes, si c'est nécessaire."[13] But, after these dark days, the Marne miracle was accomplished. The prayer, wrote D'Annunzio, "fut exaucée du plus profond de la terre au plus profond du ciel! ... Qui dira la beauté de la nuit où tourna le sort, où se dessina le prodige?"[14]

Filled with enthusiasm and more than ever eager to visit the front lines, D'Annunzio addressed a letter to his friend Captain Gheusi,[15] General Gallieni's aide-de-camp, on September 12:

> ... Je vous envoie aujourd'hui un messager sûr, M. Antongini, pour vous demander un sauf-conduit qui me permette de sortir du camp retranché de Paris, en automobile. J'en userai avec discrétion; et je m'engage à n'écrire, sur ce que je pourrai voir, que des impressions de poète, et d'un poète qui a fait de la France sa seconde patrie bien-aimée.[16]

On September 16, D'Annunzio was received by General Gallieni,[17] and was granted the required pass to visit the front. The next day, and again on the 19th and the 20th, he was able to get a close-range glimpse of the war in which he was soon to take an astonishingly heroic part.

The Marne victory averted danger for the moment, and the poet adapted himself to the new situation. He took a great interest in the founding of an Italian military hospital in Paris, which had been planned by Duchess Camastra at the beginning of the conflict. He wrote an appeal to the Italians for their support:

> Tous les peuples libres et dignes de grandir sont témoins que le sang de la France ne fut jamais si précieux. Il sert aujourd'hui à sauver la plus belle espérance de notre race et à honorer la plus haute pensée de la vie. Il servira demain à écrire les tables nouvelles pour la génération prochaine. ... Tout hôpital de guerre est ici un lieu mystique pour une apparition glorieuse. Toute offrande est un acte de fidélité à la cause noble.[18]

Until the spring of 1915 D'Annunzio lived through hours of hope and disappointment. Firmly convinced that Italy should and would enter the war on the side of France, he was impatient to hail the moment. Things were moving too slowly and every attempt to rouse the Italians to action seemed to be hindered by numberless obstacles and to be doomed to failure. During these long months of waiting, D'Annunzio was not inactive. He spoke, he wrote, he sent messages to awaken his countrymen and incite them to take up arms beside their French brothers. He worked with passion to bring about the Italian intervention. In his view, the cause of France was the cause of the Latin race. "La France et l'Italie formeront un bloc indestructible: elles soulèveront le monde; elles y seront les gardiennes de l'idéal et de l'ordre, de la bonne grâce et de l'harmonieuse beauté."[19] During the most somber days he showed unshakable faith in the final victory. In February 1915 at a "Banquet de l'Union latine," he delivered an inflamed speech forecasting Italy's entry into the war:

> Si les pressentiments du poète sont plus profonds que la cécité du politicien, si la vertu du sang est plus forte que les ferments de la corruption, si la voie romaine est toujours la plus droite et si le ciment romain est toujours le plus efficace pour lier les pierres de toute grandeur civile, aujourd'hui je vous annonce la certitude qui est pour moi fatale comme l'éclosion du printemps, comme l'entrée du soleil dans le signe du Bélier, la certitude de notre guerre, de celle que je prêche depuis vingt ans.[20]

At the ceremony Mlle Madeleine Roch, of the Comédie-Française, declaimed his *Ode pour la résurrection latine,* and the press commented enthusiastically on the poet's speech, hailing him as the prophet and the staunchest advocate of Italian intervention. Maurice Barrès reprinted in his *Cahiers* the last lines of the allocution:

> La France aujourd'hui n'est seulement le champion de la liberté latine. Elle est, et il faut le proclamer très haut, et il faut le répéter sans cesse— elle est le champion de toute la liberté du monde. Qui donc sera près d'elle, sinon sa soeur en armes, debout? ... Elle y sera demain, je vous le dis. J'en ai enfin dans mon âme la certitude enivrante. Et vraiment, mes frères, les aurores les plus belles ne sont pas encore nées.[21]

In the course of the winter of 1915, the leaders of the Garibaldini movement in France,[22] impatient over Italy's hesitancy and fearing an eventual victory of the "neutralists," were planning, with the consent of the French government, a landing of Garibaldini in Liguria in the spring, in order to press the awaited Italian decision. A landing of 2,000 red shirts would have been a psychological shock leading to the rally of the entire country.[23] D'Annunzio was in close contact with Peppino Garibaldi, the commander of the Garibaldini regiment, which had already distinguished itself for bravery on the Argonne front, and worked with him on the plan. He was also in correspondence with Ettore Cozzani, a young interventionist writer from La Spezia, who was preparing the ground for the triumphal return of the poet to Italy. On March 16, in the company of Ugo Ojetti and Joseph Reinach, D'Annunzio visited Reims, whose famous cathedral had been almost completely destroyed by bombing and fire. He was cordially welcomed by the mayor of the stricken city. He called on Cardinal Luçon, and the sorrow and respect he expressed for the destroyed cathedral led the Cardinal to suspect that the author was far from being the impious pagan he was thought to be. In his *Envoi à la France,* the poet evoked in brilliant pages the beauty of the cathedral ending in flames.

But his great hour was drawing near. Upon returning from "his pilgrimage" to Reims, D'Annunzio received the long-awaited invitation from the mayor of Genoa to deliver the official address for the inauguration of the monument to Garibaldi at Quarto on May 5. The patriotic significance of the celebration was the sign of a new political orientation in the direction wished by the poet. D'Annunzio now envisioned the landing of the Garibaldini and his dedicatory speech at Quarto as a combined action which, in his view, would result in a stirring patriotic manifestation; he dreamed for a moment of arriving in Genoa by sea at the head of two thousand red shirts.

The days which followed were full of activity and preparations for the great event. On April 5, D'Annunzio left Paris for Arcachon and there spent the whole month composing his fiery address. At the end of the month he returned to Paris to prepare for departure; meanwhile plans had been changed in part; no landing with two thousand Garibaldini, but a peaceful arrival in Genoa by train. The presence of red shirts would be limited and symbolic, since the turn of events had made the landing unnecessary. Intervention now seemed inevitable. Toward the end of April, Italy committed herself secretly to enter the war on the side of the Allies, and it was necessary now to prepare public opinion and to overcome the resistance in the Parliament.

D'Annunzio wanted to take leave of his "seconda patria" with a poetical farewell—four "sonnets d'amour" entitled *Sur une image de la France croisée peinte par Romaine Brooks*. He sent the four poems to Alfred Capus, the editor of *Le Figaro*, with these words: "Je pars pour Gêne, on va jeter le dé! Ce qui n'est pas arrivé sous le 'Signe du Bélier' va arriver sous le signe du Taureau. ... De Gêne vous recevrez de grandes nouvelles. J'ai composé quatre sonnets d'amour pour la France et je les publie au profit de la Croix-Rouge de France, du Vestiaire des Blessés et de l'Hôpital auxiliaire du Val-de-Grâce n° II (Institution italienne). Ils sont inédits. J'aimerais les donner au public français en guise d'adieu. Voulez-vous les publier dans le *Figaro* le matin du 5 mai? A la même heure nous serons des alliés."[24] Romaine Brooks' painting, portraying a Red Cross nurse standing against the background of a burning plain, symbolized "la France croisée" in the poet's imagination. And the first sonnet in fact is the evocation of this image of the nurse:

> Ont-ils haussé l'éponge âcre au fer de la lance
> contre sa belle bouche ivre du Corps Très-Saint?
> La Croix sans Christ, qui souffre au-dessus de son sein,
> n'est que la double entaille acceptée en silence.
>
> Mais son oeil est plus clair que la claire Provence,
> mais son coeur est plus doux que le printemps messin.
> Elle oint de sa douleur la force qui la ceint,
> elle noue à ses pieds percés la Patience.

. . . .

The second and third sonnets exalt the heroism of France:

> O face de l'ardeur, ô pitié sans sommeil,
> courage qui jamais n'écarte le calice,

force qui fais avec tes chairs ton sacrifice
et ta libation avec ton sang vermeil!

Sur quel bûcher, sous quel signe, pour quel réveil,
à quel Avent ta foi chantait dans le supplice?
Plus haut que l'alouette à l'aube du solstice,
on vit soudain ton coeur bondir vers le soleil.   (II)

. . . .

(The third was highly praised by critics and is the best known):

France, France, la douce entre les héroïnes,
bénie, amour du monde, ardente sous la croix,
comme aux murs d'Antioche, alors que Godefroi
sentait sous son camail la couronne d'épines,

debout avec ton Dieu comme au pont de Bouvines,
dans ta gloire à genoux comme au champ de Rocroi,
neuve immortalement comme l'herbe qui croît
aux bords de tes tombeaux, aux creux de tes ruines,

fraîche comme le jet de ton blanc peuplier
que demain tu sauras en guirlandes plier
pour les chants non chantés de ta jeune pléiade[25]

ressuscitée en Christ qui fait de ton linceul
confalon de lumière et cotte de croisade,
"France, France, sans toi le monde serait seul."[26]

The fourth poem is an incitement to fight, and most of it is adapted
from lines of the *Chanson de Roland:*

Et voici le printemps de notre amour. Exulte
dans ton sang et jubile au bout de ta doubleur,
quand même tu n'aurais à cueillir d'autre fleur
que le héros jailli de la racine occulte.

"Sonnerai l'olifant," dit l'Ancêtre. O tumulte
de tes chênes! O vent de l'immense clameur!
Hauts sont tes puys, tes vaux profonds. On meurt, on meurt,
et chacun de tes morts dans ta beauté se sculpte.

Entendez le signal, combattants, combattants,
âmes prises aux corps comme aux ceps le printemps,
comme aux poignets les fers, les bannières aux hampes.

Roland le comte sonne; et tout en est fumant,
et en saigne sa bouche, en éclatent ses tempes.
"Frappez, Francais, frappez! C'est mon commandement!"

With this exhortation the poet took leave of "la douce France" on May 3, accompanied by Peppino and Ricciotti Garibaldi, Jr., Tom Antongini, and others. It is difficult to state whether he was really certain of the success of his mission. From the various declarations he made before his departure he seemed firmly convinced that his speech in Quarto on May 5 would have a decisive effect. "A la même heure nous serons des Alliés," he said in his letter to Capus. However, according to Antongini, D'Annunzio did not believe that Italy was as yet morally prepared for war, and he had serious doubts concerning the outcome of his inflammatory address. The poet seemed to be envisaging a return to France after the ceremony, there to await the decrees of Fate. But the enthusiastic reception on his way from Modane to Genoa must have revealed to him that the Italian people had already passed the period of indecision. The resistance from the "pacifists" was nonetheless still strong, and it had to be overcome. On May 5, from the foot of the monument to the "Thousand," D'Annunzio delivered his historical address, and his words aroused a great patriotic fervor which soon turned into a veritable battle cry from one end of the peninsula to the other. He had now the clear sensation that the cause for intervention was almost won. Italy's entrance in the war would soon be a reality. The nation was in favor of it. The moment had come to discredit the opponents in Parliament. From Genoa D'Annunzio moved to Rome; at the station he was awaited by a cheering crowd of eight thousand and when, a few moments later, he appeared at the balcony of the Hotel Regina to say that Italy was neither a hotel nor a museum nor a garden for honeymooners, but a living nation, there was a storm of wild applause. When he added: "There is the smell of treason around us, and this treason is perpetrated in Rome; we are about to be sold like cowardly sheep," the crowd roared: "Death to the traitors!"

With his speeches at the Campidoglio and the Teatro Costanzi he continued to stir up feelings and beat down the last resistance. Now the word "intervention" was the most reasonable, logical, and irresistible. In a meeting with Minister Salandra, D'Annunzio extolled the heroism of the French army, giving an account of his visit to the front lines.

The French followed the poet in his triumphal march culminating in the alliance and the brotherhood-in-arms of the two nations. Jean Carrère, who witnessed D'Annunzio's crusade for war, wrote that he had never seen an orator like him, facing with blazing eyes and the

assurance of a dominator the excited multitude.[27] Camille Mallarmé
reported from Italy during these feverish days of May 1915:

> ... D'Annunzio dirige le formidable orchestre d'un geste précis, sans
> crainte, sans recul, avec sa parole incisive, impitoyable et tranchante
> comme une épée. ... Il est plus roi que le roi en Italie, en ce moment. Et si
> l'Angleterre et la France voient cette nouvelle alliée à leurs côtés pendant
> la guerre, elles la doivent à Sonnino d'abord, à d'Annunzio ensuite.[28]

On May 21, Maurice Barrès sent the poet a long and enthusiastic letter:

> Depuis que vous nous avez quittés, vous êtes plus près que jamais de nos
> coeurs. Par delà l'horizon, notre regard vous accompagne, ô triomphateur,
> dans les cortèges que vous menez au milieu des acclamations des deux
> rives d'Italie. ... Réussissez, Annunzio, faites-nous voir, comme vous
> l'annoncez, "apprès le miracle francais, le miracle Italien," et nous
> inscrirons sur un cippe, dans les bois d'Arcachon, la date et la louange des
> revêries solitaires que vous y poursuiviez en méditant les hautes destins de
> votre patrie. ... Je joins ma voix à celle de vos auditoires frémissants pour
> acclamer l'Italie.[29]

On the evening of May 23, D'Annunzio answered Barrès with this
moving telegram:

> Je lis vos grandes paroles à l'heure même où la déclaration de guerre
> éclate dans la ville enfiévrée. On chante la Marseillaise autour de la
> colonne Trajane. Le vert et le bleu de nos drapeaux font une seule couleur
> dans le soir qui tombe. Je sais que le même souffle passe sous nos arcs de
> triomphe et sous le vôtre. Nous avions deux patries, et, ce soir, nous en
> avons une seule, qui va de la Flandre française à la mer de Sicile. C'est la
> poésie qui fait ce don réel et merveilleux à notre amitié militante. Fidem
> signemus sanguine.[30]

In his *Chronique de la Grande Guerre,* Barrès devoted three pages of
meditations to D'Annunzio's words. "De telles images," he wrote, "qui
font à cette minute le tour de France, resteront dans l'histoire pour
rendre sensible cette amitié latine à qui nous ferons produire une mission illimitée."[31] The *Annales politiques et littéraires,* May 30, 1915,
exalted the figure of the poet: "D'un grand coup d'aile, il vient d'entrer
dans la gloire. ... Étrange et magnifique figure, que celle de Gabriele
d'Annunzio! Être exceptionnel, marqué du sceau du génie! ... En lui
s'incarne l'âme italienne."[32]

The war made of the "enfant de volupté" a man of action and a leader. He had spent the last months in Paris in an apartment where the atmosphere was that of an alcove impregnated with the scent of perfume and decorated with sumptuous colors. This man, who seemed enervated and doomed to slow consumption, was soon to display so much energy and courage as to astonish both friends and enemies. The war revealed in him the toughness of a condottiere. A few days after the Italian intervention he joined the combat troops. This action was highly praised in the French press; the poet appeared now under an unsuspected light—that of the soldier ready to pay in person for the war he preached. "Dès maintenant," wrote André Lichtenberger, "quelle que soit sa vie, quelle que soit sa mort, il demeurera, au siècle des siècles, un sujet d'envie et de pieuse exaltation pour les écrivains. ... Gabriele d'Annunzio a réalisé le grand miracle dont le voeu nous hante tous: celui de se projeter au delà de la médiocre destinée individuelle qui nous enserre."[33] Gabriel Maugain singled him out as one of the most fervent friends of France—a long-standing one as proved by the touching lines of the "Chanson à Hélène de France," written in 1911 (*Laudi*, IV): "O douce France, ô soeur unique ... ."[34] In an article entitled "La leçon de Gabriele d'Annunzio" (*Le Temps*, October 28, 1915) Paul Souday described the poet, often accused of weakness and debauchery, as a man of great courage and high principles.

During the war D'Annunzio served in the army, the navy, and the air force, volunteering for all sorts of perilous missions; he was present wherever the risk to himself was greatest; he sought the thrills of danger. This refined egotist transformed himself into an example of devotion and physical and moral courage. If up to that time he had lived solely for the flesh, he now scorned it completely; his conduct in war astonished those who knew only the D'Annunzio of the social and literary salons. During these years of bloody struggle the superman in him appeared in a new light. To elevate himself above the common mortal was for D'Annunzio no longer merely a literary attitude or a poet's dream. His ideal of the superman could no longer be lived intellectually; it had to be realized in heroic deeds. The war years were his most active ones. He wrote and delivered speeches to the soldiers; he frequently visited the front lines, bringing his enthusiasm to the fighting men; but, above all, he fought with a supreme disregard for danger. "I have a horror of the immobile work with pen, ink, and paper—things which have now become futile. Danger is the only shining god to whom I wish to devote my unexpressed poetry."[35] He said to Maurice Barrès in 1916: "Que sont ... ces rêves de domination et d'autres rêves encore? Je ne désire plus que de retrouver ces minutes où le moindre homme devient quelqu'un qu'il n'avait jamais soupçonné."[36]

His numerous war actions on land, in the air, on the sea; his air raids on Trieste, Pola, Cattaro; his torpedo-boat raid in the Bay of Buccari, his presence in all sectors of the front; finally his spectacular flight over Vienna—all were superb examples of his abnegation and patriotism, showing complete dedication to the cause he advocated. Although his age (he was in his fifties) could have spared him from the dangers of the war, he did not want to remain safely in the rear as did many propagandists of the conflict. In an airplane landing in February 1916, he lost his right eye. But he never complained of the injury. Maurice Barrès sent the wounded poet this telegram:

> Vos amis francais s'inquiètent. Dites-nous que vos yeux, au service de votre génie, continueront de puiser des images dans la beauté du monde. La barbarie serait trop heureuse de détruire un regard faiseur de chefs-d'oeuvre. Je vous embrasse, mon cher et glorieux ami, soldat de Cadorna. Nous vivons dans l'angoisse de la bataille de Verdun; mais la ruée allemande ne parviendra pas à rompre nos magnifiques soldats, et plus que jamais nous avons la certitude du complet triomphe de la civilisation. Vive l'Italie! Fraternellement vôtre.[37]

D'Annunzio replied with the following message:

> Que la lumière s'affaiblisse ou s'éteigne dans mes yeux, peu importe aujourd'hui! Un combattant en vaut un autre, et je serai bien remplacé. J'ai pu m'incliner sur la figure sainte du héros de Laibach quelques heures avant d'entrer dans la nuit. Mais il faut que la lumière ne s'éteigne, ni ne s'affaiblisse dans le monde menacé de la plus vile obscurité par ces barbares qui, déjà trop de fois, ont tenté d'interrompre ou fausser l'harmonie des esprits et des formes inventées par notre race créatrice. Le sang français n'est aujourd'hui que de la lumière jaillissante, et le ciment informe de Douaumont est plein de vie idéale, comme les blocs du plus beau marbre d'où sortent les statues. De ma douloureuse immobilité toute mon âme se tend vers la bataille sublime. Nous voudrions tous combattre à vos côtés en cette heure de danger et de gloire suprême. Ne vous inquiétez pas de mes yeux, mon frère, mais sauvez la beauté du monde pour les yeux nouveaux. Vive la France![38]

In May 1916 Barrès visited the convalescent poet in Venice, and he gave a moving account of this visit in the *Annales politiques et littér-aires* for October 5 of that year. He left interesting pages of his conversation with D'Annunzio in his *Chronique de la Grande Guerre,* in which he exalts the soldier-poet and his role in the war:

> Aux jours les plus tragiques, il a précipité le destin, tout en maintenant l'accord du roi et du peuple, et de Gênes à Rome, à grands coups de discours pareils à des odes, il a poursuivi, écrasé le parti de l'étranger. L'histoire dira qu'il répandit une brûlante beauté sur les calculs qu'il fallait bien que l'on fît, mais qui risquaient d'amener un refroidissement de l'âme populaire.[39]

After his recovery D'Annunzio resumed his Icarian flights over the battlefields, despite the orders of his physicians, who feared serious consequences to the other eye. He reserved for himself the most dangerous missions, challenging death fearlessly. In January 1917 Captain Gabriele D'Annunzio received his first French Croix de Guerre for bravery; the decoration was accompanied by a letter from the Minister of War, General Lyautey, to whom the poet replied that he was extremely proud to receive the decoration worn by the brave of the Marne and Verdun who saved the world. In August of that year D'Annunzio was wounded on his right wrist during an air raid at low altitude while returning from his mission with his aircraft riddled by bullets. A second Croix de Guerre was conferred upon him in September 1918 by General Pétain. Poincaré made a trip to Italy for the purpose of decorating this glorious ally.

In his *Vita segreta di d'Annunzio,* Tom Antongini reports that he never saw the poet so anxious and disturbed (except for the disaster of Caporetto) as he was during the German offensive in the spring of 1918. After the battle of Chemin des Dames (June 1918) the batteries of General Ludendorff thundered close to Paris; the French capital was being threatened for the second time. "I cannot tell you," D'Annunzio wrote to Antongini, "my emotion and admiration for the heroism which desperate France is showing. I have not been able to sleep for the past two nights. Neither yesterday nor today was I able to eat. I feel my breath choked off by distress. . . . I am so anxious to come to France at the head of my planes. Who knows?"[40] On September 26, 1918, he flew over the French lines at the Aisne and dropped a message over the sector held by the Italian Army Corps under the command of General Albricci. He remained at the French front for a week; he visited the Italian troops, and he was received everywhere with enthusiasm. General Berthelot invited him, the "Animator," to a camp luncheon at Ay. And on this occasion D'Annunzio made a brief address as a salute to the French Army:

> Je vous apporte, mon général, la reconnaissance de tous les Italiens pour le sévère amour que vous avez témoigné à nos soldats, à notre sang fraternel, aux bienheureux qui sont morts sur votre sol en signant—selon le mode mystique—cette fraternité vermeille et en confirmant la promesse en notre avenir. J'ai été autrefois l'hôte dévoué de la France douloureuse; je suis aujourd'hui l'hôte ébloui de la France victorieuse. Le sang de la nation libre n'eut jamais tant d'éclat. Il est comme la splendeur présente de la foi que nous confessons. Debout les morts! On a jeté ce cri, chez vous, quelque part, dans la nuit. Mais les morts n'étaient pas à terre. Ils restaient debout, tous: crucifiés sans sépulcre. Pour avoir accompli chaque jour humblement un acte de fidélité à sa cause noble, je suis peut-être digne, mon général, de saluer en vous l'Armée francaise—cette immense vague de gloire qui soulève tous les sacrifices et domine tous les horizons.[41]

On October 4 he left for the Italian front where a few days later he participated in the battle at Vittorio Veneto, which ended with the surrender of Austria on November 4. On the 11th of that month, the day of the final victory on the French front, the poet sent the following telegram to his friend Boulenger: "Toute parole est vaine. J'embrasse en vous mes chers frères de France!"[42] A few days later Boulenger visited him in Venice, and this was a happy occasion for them to evoke the epic struggle against the common enemy and the sacrifice and heroism of the two nations.[43]

By the end of the war, D'Annunzio had received five silver medals, one gold medal, three Croix de Guerre, the Légion d'honneur, the Cross of the Order of Savoy, three promotions for military merit, and several wounds on the battlefield. Among foreign decorations, besides the French, were the Military Cross conferred upon him by King George of England, the Silver Medal given him by the king of Montenegro, and the Croix de Guerre bestowed by King Albert of Belgium.

21. After the Victory

AFTER the final victory, D'Annunzio's relations with France regrettably underwent a period of misunderstandings. The Versailles Peace Conference left the Italian people disappointed and humiliated in their national aspirations. Political and economic interests united England, France, and America against Italy's territorial claims, in complete disregard of her contribution to the common cause—the destruction of her national resources, over seven hundred thousand dead, one and a half million wounded and disabled, and the brilliant victory at Vittorio Veneto which brought about the surrender of Austria. The port city of Fiume (populated almost completely by Italians), despite its expressed will to be united to Italy, was destined for the Croats by the negotiators of the Peace Treaty. Jealous of political competition in the new settlement of Europe, France and England saw with distaste the emergence of Italy as a European power; they therefore treated their former ally with no sympathy. The opposition to Italy's annexation of Fiume had evident political overtones. The British expected to set up a base in the city and there establish a shipping company, thus having free access to the Balkans. Taking advantage of the economic difficulties in the newly created state of Yugoslavia, English high finance was planning large capital investments in industrial enterprises there, which would have served economic as well as political purposes. In view of this, British diplomacy had engineered, with the support of the French and American delegates at the Peace Conference, the concession of Fiume to the former enemy and paid little heed to the strong Italian protests. To Italy's demands, the cold answer was that no stipulation concerning Fiume had been made in the London Treaty by which Italy entered the war on the side of the Allies. This was unfortunately true, but it was equally true that the sacrifice and effort demanded from Italy in the course of the war far exceeded those contemplated in the London Treaty.

In the controversy engaged in at the Peace Conference by the Rome delegates and the other allies, the Italians expected to find the French on their side. But Clemenceau showed himself to be, instead, firmly opposed to Italy's claims. His attitude was sharply stigmatized even by the French press. M. Mirtil, in an article in the *Mercure de France*, entitled "La grande désillusion de l'Italie," wrote:

Quant à l'ensemble du peuple francais ... qu'il n'oublie jamais qu'en 1915, alors que les Russes reculaient en Galicie, nos voisins n'ont pas hésité à jeter noblement leur épée dans la balance. L'Italie a dédaigné les avantages honteux de la neutralité. Elle a obéi à la voix du sang et son sang a coulé. Grâce à elle plus d'un million d'Austro-Hongrois n'ont point tenu les tranchées en Lorraine ou en Champagne. Cette circonstance seule doit être la cause de notre éternelle reconnaissance envers les soldats du Carso.[1]

But Clemenceau's views were quite different, and to Emmanuele Orlando's request for the annexation of Fiume to Italy he flatly answered with the unfortunate phrase "Fiume c'est la lune!" D'Annunzio could never forgive the French statesman for these words which hurt and outraged the Italian people. The reaction of the press in Italy was violent, not only against Clemenceau, but also against Wilson who supported the English haggling. The American President was covered with the most derogatory epithets and presented to the Italian public as the false prophet of the time.

At the end of the war Fiume had been occupied immediately by contingents of allied troops. The French and the English sided with the Croats against the Italians, thus creating a tense situation with frequent clashes between Italian soldiers and civilians on the one side and French, English, and Croats on the other. Cabaret brawls, disputes between garrisons, and other misunderstandings convinced the Italians that France was helping to set up another Austria where Italy had overturned it, and that French soldiers were in Fiume to give Italy's enemies a strong hand in order to harass the Italian population in the occupied city. In June 1919 French soldiers were reported to have snatched from Italian girls the tricolored cockades that they wore. The incident resulted in serious disorders which prompted the Nitti government to withdraw the Italian contingent in order to avoid further clashes.

D'Annunzio followed with increasing distress all of the diplomatic maneuvers, the declarations, and the propaganda preceding the opening of the Peace Conference in January 1919. The ingratitude shown by the other allies toward Italy from the very beginning of the negotiations at Versailles disappointed and embittered him more and more. The "engineers" of the peace—Clemenceau, Lloyd George, and Wilson —deliberately minimized the Italian victory at Vittorio Veneto,[2] and this unfortunate and unjust course of events aroused D'Annunzio to action. His speeches and writings, collected in *Sudore di sangue* (January–September 1919), clearly express his resentment for the "mutilated peace" imposed upon Italy by her three strong partners dominating the peace table. In his first cry of indignation—*Lettera ai Dalmati* (January 1919)—he emphatically denounced the other allies' maneuvers against Italy's territorial claims on the Dalmation coast. In this cutting message full or irony and anger, he imprudently used words recalling the "Pasque veronesi" (a massacre of French soldiers in Verona on the day after Easter in 1797):

> So great is the weight of the Italians' suffering that it suffocates even anger. And may this suffering also be blessed. The other day, turning to the façade of St. Mark's Basilica to seek the absent horses, they did not want to remember who took them away one hundred and twenty years ago. Nor, when from overseas blows the customary insolence, do they want to think that in the Lions of your maritime doors could dwell the demon of the Veronese Easter. Let us exorcise, let us avert a brotherly tragedy.[3]

The allusion, distorted and misconstrued by the official press in France, grieved his numerous friends across the Alps. The Paris newspaper *Le Matin* (January 27, 1919), in an article entitled "Les poètes parfois oublient," expressed deep regret over D'Annunzio's attacks against France. Marcel Boulenger, the poet's closest friend, sent him a long letter discussing the misunderstanding and lamenting his impatience in judging the French attitude in the dispute over Fiume.[4] In *L'Action française* Jacques Bainville deplored D'Annunzio's bitter words against France, emphasizing that his country was more interested in the Rhine than in the Adriatic and that "elle sait très peu, très mal qu'il existe des Yougoslaves et elle ne sait pas où."[5]

The *Lettera ai Dalmati* was followed about a month later by *Aveux de l'ingrat* (February 1919), a long message, partly lyrical and partly polemical, in which he appeals to the French public, carefully spelling out Italy's sacrifice and defending her demands. The work is divided into four parts—"Toujours et quand même," "La mesure unique," "La tragédie des méprises," "La lettre aux Dalmates." Like a deceived lover, D'Annunzio reaffirms in the first part his unchanging affection for France, reminding the forgetful of what he had done in May 1915 when "Je partais tout seul de Paris menacé, vers l'Italie tombée aux mains des trafiqueurs et des traîtres, tout seul avec ma foi, pour jeter le grand appel."[6] He evokes again the first months of war on French soil, the Marne victory, his hours of anxiety and exaltation. "Ce mot 'le miracle francais', adopté par l'admiration du monde entier et par votre orgueil victorieux, je veux enfin le revendiquer. Je l'ai écrit le premier, en Septembre 1914, revenant des lignes de bataille ... : 'Tel est aujourd'hui *le miracle francais*. En chacun de vos soldats toute la France s'exprime avec tous ses héros vigilants. ...' Si les paroles de ma ferveur on les oublie déja, qu'importe? J'en dirai d'autres, plus belles."[7]

But if on the one hand he explains the misunderstanding apologetically, on the other he does not hesitate to polemicize on the faults of the "Latin sister" and to inveigh in an inflamed philippic against the denigrators of the Italian contribution to the common victory. To those reproaching Italy for Caporetto,[8] he replies that while it is true that the Italian lines had been broken there (had not the same thing happened to the French in 1914 and in 1918?) it is equally true that a few days later the enemy was stopped on the Piave by the Italians alone and destroyed there the following year by the Italian troops. Once more he deplores the political intrigue designed to favor Italy's enemies and the lack of "mesure unique" in assessing the sacrifice of each winning country. He finally laments the attitude of the French soldiers in the disputed Fiume and presents the true context of his misconstrued *Lettera ai Dalmati,* explaining his reasons for writing it.

D'Annunzio intended to publish the manuscript in one of the widely circulated journals, possibly *Le Figaro.* But, despite the efforts made by his friends, especially Marcel Boulenger and Achille Richard, no editor dared to take a stand for Italy's claims against "Tiger" Clemenceau. Only the publisher Bernard Grasset made the courageous gesture of printing the work in book form in March 1919. Clemenceau did not oppose the circulation of the volume. He was well aware that a book, read by a limited number of people, could not have the same influence on public opinion as an article being read by thousands simultaneously. The press, however, failed to give any publicity to D'Annunzio's plea and consequently the voice of the poet never reached the tribunal of public opinion.

If *Aveux de l'ingrāt* is an expression of grievances and a cry of protest, it is no less a message of undying love and an act of faith to the fraternal pact "signé avec le seing rouge, qu'on ne doit plus rompre, qu'on ne peut pas violer."[9] D'Annunzio's indignation was directed against the Quai d'Orsay and in particular against Clemenceau, the

"Docteur ès étoiles." "In the decrepit Celtic Tiger," he wrote later, "there is not the whole of France, not certainly the young and eternal France—the one we love, the one by which we wish to be loved."[10] The poet's affection for France remained untouched: "Si vous avez oublié mon amour d'hier, que m'importe? Je saurai bien me faire aimer davantage, demain. Il faut que chacun tue son amour pour qu'il revive sept fois plus ardent."[11] His many friends fully understood his feelings and his duty to defend his own country, victorious in war and humiliated at the peace table; they held no ill will against him. On July 14, 1919, the poet dispatched a pilot to bring the following message to the French people:

> A la France éternelle, qui célèbre aujourd'hui sa fête héroïque pour les vivants et pour les morts, l'Italie victorieuse et déçue envoie la parole de son sacrifice et de son espoir, par la plus rapide et la plus forte de ses ailes. Que les combattants italiens de l'Ardre et de l'Aisne la recueillent pour la crier sous l'Arc de Triomphe.[12]

After the signing of the Versailles Peace Treaty (June 28, 1919) D'Annunzio, completely embittered and disheartened, withdrew into silence and for a time there were rumors that he was preparing a spectacular flight from Rome to Tokyo. But before long events brought him back to the political scene. On September 12, 1919, challenging the Versailles Peace Treaty and the Italian government which had signed it, D'Annunzio at the head of a group of war veterans occupied Fiume without firing a shot. The Allies' contingent withdrew from the city and the poet became the master of the situation amidst the ovation of soldiers and civilians alike. Confronted with the embarrassing and difficult situation, the Italian government repeatedly ordered him to leave Fiume. But, strongly supported by the Italian public, he ignored the orders.

On September 22, 1919, he appealed to the French people: "Frères de France, vous savez ce que nous avons fait, sous l'inspiration et la protection de notre Dieu!" He explained the reasons which drove him to occupy the martyred city, stressing the determination to defend it, even at the cost of his life. He was certain that the French, who for long sad years had suffered for their own enslaved cities, would not condemn him. "Le combattant," he said, "qui se dévoua ardemment à votre cause en août 1914; le même qui ne s'éloigna de l'Ile de France que pour aller prêcher la guerre en mai 1915; le même qui survola le front de l'Aisne en septembre 1918; celui-là même vous salue sans espoir ni crainte du haut de la ville assiégée."[13]

The Fiume episode (September 12, 1919 to January 18, 1921) aroused divergent reactions in France. The poet's numerous friends rejoiced at the heroic deed of the Animator; official circles on the other hand sharply stigmatized the ruthless act which they considered worthy only of an adventurer. Many articles—some of them condoning D'Annunzio, others condemning him—appeared in the French press. Gonzague Truc wrote a most unsympathetic piece, "D'Annunzio ou les dangers des poètes," for *La Grand Revue*, October 19. Paul Rival, in the *Revue hebdomadaire* of September 11, 1920, ridiculed the dictator of Fiume with biting irony, giving a satirical picture of the poet in the occupied city, analyzing his lyrical speeches, and presenting him as a man possessed. A complacent commentary of Rival's article, written by Charles Henry Hirsch for the *Mercure de France,* November 1 of that year, pokes fun at the lyrical dictator, who is described as governing the city by the power and the splendor of his images. But a completely different picture of D'Annunzio was subsequently given by Marcel Boulenger, who visited him in Fiume with Achille Richard. "Il est difficile à l'auteur de ses lignes," wrote Boulenger, "de parler de Gabriele d'Annunzio sans une émotion profonde. Animateur sans égal, ce chef, ce puissant maître des âmes demeure le plus extraordinaire créateur d'énergie et de beauté que notre age ait connu."[14] In expressing his admiration and enthusiasm for "ce magicien, conducteur de foules," he voiced his support of the cause of Fiume, clearly pointing out that the city had been destined for the Yugoslavs with the obvious aim of serving the interests of English financiers. This, in his opinion, was the main reason for the labyrinth of complications at the Peace Conference where facts had been so distorted as to present Italian national aspirations as imperialistic dreams. Furthermore, Boulenger stressed that Italy's effort in the war had been a considerable one, and that if the Italians claimed Fiume they were entitled to it for ethnographical reasons and because it was the expressed desire of the people of Fiume to be united with Italy.

In the *Journal des débats,* December 28, 1920, Auguste Gauvain sharply attacked the poet shortly before the end of his reign over Fiume. Gauvain had already made known his animosity against D'Annunzio in a previous article for the same periodical (August 29, 1919) a few days before the occupation of Fiume, when the name of the poet appeared on all the walls of the awaiting city. But Gauvain now went so far as to make the ridiculous accusation that the poet changed his name from Gaetano Rapagnetta to Gabriele D'Annunzio (Gabriel Nuntius)[15]—a more fitting one for his messianic ambitions. Furthermore, Gauvain emphasized that D'Annunzio's life had been but a series of scandals and that immorality was abundantly displayed in his works. This, however, could have been overlooked, in the critic's mind, if D'Annunzio had remained in the literary world. But, since he had chosen to become a political figure as well, he must be nothing but a madman. In Gauvain's opinion D'Annunzio had now obliterated whatever good he may previously have done the Allied cause. With this the critic could cancel out the debt of gratitude that France owed the poet.

Fortunately, except for a few like Paul Rival who renewed his attacks against D'Annunzio in the *Mercure de France* a few days after the epilogue of the Fiume episode, the French did not share Gauvain's views. Rival's second article, entitled "Un acteur tragique," presents the poet as a showman living in a make-believe world. The Fiume adventure was the result of his egotistical aspiration as a superman. His obsession for power, in Rival's views, and his scorn for common law led him to the foolish conquest of Fiume. Thus, Paul Rival intended to explain the Fiume affair—a national problem—by unsympathetically analyzing the nature and character of the superman D'Annunzio for whom, according to Rival, Fiume was not an end but a means for the realization of his egotistical dream of "dépassement." The heroic life of the soldier, altruistically devoted to his country, failed to carry any sort of message to Paul Rival, and he took pleasure in presenting the wounded war hero as a despicable figure and vulgar comic. "L'impulsion du corps, la ferveur du sang, l'élan du coeur provoqué par le vent du matin, la chaleur du soleil ou la proie sexuelle qui fuit, l'instinct physique préféré à la pensée, voilà D'Annunzio."[16] Rival added that D'Annunzio had fought for no one but himself; he commented that the war, which was sacrifice, idealism, devotion to a noble cause, was for D'Annunzio (who had offered his life many times!) nothing but "réveil de la force animale, de l'instinct de puissance, du désir de tuer."[17]

Rival's article aroused immediate reaction. Letters of protest were sent to the *Mercure de France,* among them one by Marcel Boulenger expressing shock at such a vicious attack against Lieutenant Colonel D'Annunzio, "mutilé de guerre, décoré de toutes les croix militaires italiennes et françaises, croix gagnées au feu." He pointed out that the brilliant role played by D'Annunzio in May 1915 and during the war commanded respect and that the public might be astonished to see Rival's slander published in France. "Cette lettre," concluded Boulenger, "ne vous porte que l'expression de mon affectueux chagrin, auquel se joint celui de très nombreux amis du poète—ou plutôt, non, laissons le poète: du soldat ... de l'homme qui, à cinquante ans passés (on l'oublie vraiment trop), prodigua son énergie, son talent, sa santé, son sang, pour la cause commune et contre l'ennemi commun, pendant toute la guerre."[18]

But the Fiume episode, the polemics, the harsh words, and the incitement to hate were soon to fall into oblivion on both sides. After Fiume it was rumored in the French press that D'Annunzio would retire to France and devote himself to the theater. Ida Rubinstein awaited him there in order to stage his *Martyre de Saint Sébastien* once again. But D'Annunzio did not move from Italy. In the fall of 1921 when his *Envoi à la France,* translated by Andre Doderet, was published by the *Revue hebdomadaire* even his worst slanderers could not help but recognize his deep and sincere affection for France, which clearly emerged from the pages of his work. In 1922 Paul Hazard visited him in the small town on Lake Garda which was soon to become Il Vittoriale and devoted a touching article to the visit:

> Je n'oublierai jamais, pour mon compte, qu'il nous a donné un peu de son coeur; et je me rappellerai toujours qu'il fut avec nous à l'heure suprême. C'est le danger de la France qui l'a transformé, dilettante et sceptique qu'il était, en croyant, en soldat, en chef, c'est le danger de la France qui a fait surgir de cet incomparable artiste un homme d'action. Sans lui, sans la puissance de son verbe, sans l'effort de sa volonté, la grande flamme qui illumine la conscience italienne aurait malaisément jailli. Il ne fut pas de ces ingrats qui, aimant les plaisirs, que leur offrait la France, n'aimaient pas son âme et l'ont trahie: il a compté, au contraire, parmi ceux qui ont voulu lui rendre en sacrifices ses dons des jours heureux.[19]

In June 1923 the French press enthusiastically announced that D'Annunzio was expected in Paris for the performance of his *Phèdre* at the Opéra. His return to the French capital was to symbolize the happy ending of the political drama and the official reconciliation of the poet with his "seconda patria." He was due to arrive in Paris by plane on June 3, and on the following day he was to deliver a speech at the Trocadéro where an immense crowd was awaiting the opportunity of acclaiming him. The *Annales politiques et littéraires* for June 3 carried the following announcement:

> A l'heure où paraîtront ces lignes, Gabriele d'Annunzio nous arrivera par les chemins du ciel. Et demain, dimanche, la foule pressée dans la salle du Trocadéro l'acclamera. ... Il revient à Paris auréolé de gloire. Le soleil luit de nouveau, après d'épais nuages, et plus ardent que jamais. ... Les Parisiens accueilleront chaleureusement l'illustre poète, qui a su chanter avec lyrisme, avec amour, le beau pays de France.[20]

For the occasion the editor of the journal had asked Louis Barthou of the French Academy for an article of "souvenirs inédits" which appeared in the issue of June 10 with this introductory note:

> Le retour de Gabriele d'Annunzio à Paris dénoue heureusement une situation un peu tendue. L'auteur du *Feu* considérait ... la France comme sa seconde mère. Il lui prouva son dévouement en stimulant l'ardeur patriotique de l'Italie, en l'entraînant vers nous, en se battant lui-même héroïquement pour la cause commune. Plus tard, des paroles injustes lui échappèrent. Nous en fûmes émus et attristés. Nous attribuâmes cet emportement à l'excès d'une passion généreuse. Le fond de nos sentiments réciproques n'en fut atteint. Aujourd'hui, ces ombres sont dissipées et le soleil brille sans nuages.[21]

Barthou's pages evoke a dinner in June 1910 at which the academician and statesman had as guests D'Annunzio, Pierre Loti, Edmond Rostand, and Adrien Hébrard. He speaks movingly of the part D'Annunzio took in the war on behalf of France, of the Fiume expedition, and of the appeal made by the poet to the French people in September 1919:

> Il n'y a de vrai grand homme qui ne renferme en lui plusieurs hommes, mais peu furent aussi riches de dons variés que Gabriele d'Annunzio. Poète, il a fait vibrer toutes les cordes d'une lyre qui n'a rien eu à s'ajouter pour être complète. Romancier, il a exprimé la vie ... dans des oeuvres dont aucune ne ressemble à l'autre que par l'unité de la beauté et par l'éclat rayonnant du génie. ... Homme de lettres, il a voulu être et il a été un homme d'action. ... Quand la paix trompa son espoir, il fit l'expédition de Fiume: il y a des heures où il faut vaincre l'hésitation des hommes et violer le destin. ... Je salue dans Gabriele d'Annunzio le génie, vivant et puissant, de la Resurrection Latine.[22]

Printed beside Barthou's article was a column of brief judgments on D'Annunzio by eminent French writers of the time. The first was by Maurice Barrès: "Les amis de d'Annunzio peuvent montrer de lui, en l'honneur de la France, mieux encore que ses innombrables écrits: des actes. Quel homme de bonne foi ... pourra nier que cet Italien ne soit en même temps un grand et utile Français?" Georges de Porto-Riche wrote: "Maintenant que Tolstoï n'est plus là, Anatole France, d'Annunzio et Thomas Hardy sont, d'après moi, les cerveaux les plus puissants du monde." Robert de Flers pointed out that if in the *Lettre aux Dalmates* the poet struck at France on political grounds, "il n'en demeure pas moins que si nous voulions réunir en une anthologie les pages les plus belles et les plus tendres dédiées à la France, plusieurs d'entre elles porteraient cette signature: Gabriele d'Annunzio." And finally J. H. Rosny, after mentioning that the men of letters unjustly mocked "l'aventure de Fiume" and the poet who lived as a great man of the Renaissance, said: "Je me borne à envier et à admirer ce poète qui, pendant une année entière, a imposé son vouloir aux hommes d'État d'Europe et d'Amérique."[23]

But to the disappointment of the public and his personal friends D'Annunzio did not go to Paris. The *Annales politiques et littéraires* in a note entitled "Il n'est pas venu," expressed deep regret for his failure to visit the French capital. His arrival by plane had been announced in detail: "trente aéros italiens l'escortaient; vingt-quatre appareils français se disposaient à voler à sa rencontre. Ce devait être une apothéose. ... Nous l'attendions. ... Nous avons été deçus. Gabriele d'Annunzio ... n'a pas voulu venir chercher ici les lauriers et les roses qu'on se préparait à lui offrir."[24]

In the hermitage of Il Vittoriale he quietly spent the twilight of his life, haunted by the memories of his brilliant past. His French friends often sent messages or paid him visits, and French writers crossing into Italy were unfailingly attracted to Il Vittoriale for a meeting not with "l'enfant de volupté" but with the war hero and ardent friend of their country. He received French visitors with great joy and never allowed them to leave Il Vittoriale without a souvenir. To honor them and their country he often ordered the cannons to be fired as many times as the solemnity required. The presence of Frenchmen reopened for him the book of his memories, and he relived in his mind the glorious years of his sojourn in France and the tragic but no less glorious hours of the war, thus reviving the brotherhood-in-arms of the two

Latin nations. Many of his visitors devoted articles to Il Vittoriale which sheltered and shaded the soldier-poet in his declining years. There was so much curiosity about him that Paul Guiton in an article in the *Mercure de France* (March 1, 1924) tried to establish the reasons for the poet's complete baldness in order to satisfy those who wondered at his loss of hair so early in his life. Even those who did not particularly care for him could not resist the temptation of visiting him in his retreat whenever they happened to be in Italy. The actress Georgette Leblanc was one of these. Although she admired his works, she had no liking for D'Annunzio as a man. "Il m'irritait," she wrote, "à cause de ses airs vainqueurs devant les femmes. Son assurance, son italianisme, son romantisme exaspéré me gênaient. Je l'avais recontré plusieurs fois à Paris et je ne parvenais pas à reconcilier l'homme et l'oeuvre."[25] Nevertheless, she wrote him from Milan to inform him of her presence there and while waiting for a reply she read *Il Notturno* for the first time. In the simplicity and conciseness of the book she could detect but little of the hand that had written *Il Fuoco*. Upon receiving her note, D'Annunzio sent her many flowers and gifts with a letter evoking the friendship he felt for her—"une amitié sagace et fuyante, qui noua nos mains une seule fois"—in the Paris days when he hid his heroic predestination beneath a life of pleasures: "En ce Vittoriale, glorieuse prison et voluptueux ermitage," he said, "je ne veux voir personne ... nessuno; mais dans le sens homérique d'Ulysse. Je ne veux voir que des esprits décharnés et des chairs lumineuses. En mon souvenir, chère Armide, vous étiez tour à tour l'une et l'autre."[26] Two days later Georgette Leblanc arrived at Il Vittoriale. D'Annunzio hurried toward her and kissed her hand. At the sight of her he suddenly found again the youth and vigor of the past. "Je ne savais pas," she said, "que nous étions si amis." To which he replied: "Certes, vous étiez si peu gentille avec moi." "Mais vous n'êtes plus le même," she said. This man, whom Georgette Leblanc had known at the time of his Parisian conquests, now appeared to her in a completely different light. He was no longer the "child of pleasure"; he was the poet, the soldier, the war hero, and the master of Fiume.

In 1927, when relations between Italy and France were very tense, there were rumors that D'Annunzio would be sent to Paris to smooth them. The French minister Briand had extended to D'Annunzio an invitation to this effect. The poet wrote quickly to his French friends to inform them that he would be arriving by plane accompanied by the brilliant aviator Francesco de Pinedo. The poet's visit was to coincide with the performance of his *La Torche sous le boisseau* at the Comédie-Française. But once again Paris waited in vain. D'Annunzio sent Prime Minister Poincaré the following message on the occasion:

> Puisque la Comédie-Française me fait le grand et insolite honneur de m'accuellir, je peux me croire à nouveau reconnu par ma seconde patrie. Et cette générosité rappelle en ma mémoire notre recontre de guerre au front italien et la croix d'honneur par moi reçue de vos mains sur le champ de bataille. Aujourd'hui, mon sévère et loyal ami, je vous renouvelle ma reconnaissance et mon dévouement.[27]

And Poincaré replied:

> Très touché de votre aimable télégramme et profondément sensible à l'inaltérable souvenir que vous évoquez, je me réjouis que la représentation d'un de vos chefs-d'oeuvre sur la scène du Théâtre-Français fournisse aux Parisiens l'occasion d'acclamer votre nom. Je vous prie de recevoir, avec mes chaleureuses félicitations, la nouvelle assurance de mon admirative amitié.[28]

Despite his absence, however, the theatrical event (December 7, 9, 11) was a semiofficial manifestation of Franco-Italian friendship. The president of the Republic, the prime minister, and the minister of education shared a box with the Italian ambassador in what seemed to be a warm expression of unity between France and Italy. The name of the poet linked them in a spirit of Latin brotherhood.

Early in the spring of 1929 Henry Bordeaux, on tour through "la claire Italie," stopped at Il Vittoriale for a visit. D'Annunzio had met Bordeaux for the first time in 1910 at Notre-Dame in Paris. Later an incident in the literary world brought the two writers together. The incident occurred when Robert de Montesquiou published a book entitled *La Petite Mademoiselle,* being unaware that such a title had already been used by Bordeaux. In writing his excuses to Bordeaux for the error, Montesquiou enclosed a note from D'Annunzio who apologized for his friend. The occurrence soon brought about a close and lasting friendship between Bordeaux and D'Annunzio. Bordeaux's visit at Il Vittoriale was undoubtedly a happy occasion. The two friends evoked the past together—the glorious days in Paris, the sad days of war, the luminous days of victory. Many names of friends were recalled in their conversation, especially that of Maurice Barrès, the unforgettable Barrès who was always present in the heart of the poet. At the start of the visit, D'Annunzio handed his friend two copies of *La Contemplazione della morte*—one meant for Paul Bourget "qui vit dans les profondeurs," and the other for Philippe Barrès, the son of "mon grand Maurice bien-aimé" and "jeune frère d'armes." He gave a copy of *Le Faville del maglio* to Bordeaux himself—"émule en travail acharné."[29] In the long article the French writer devoted to this visit he said: "L'auteur des *Laudi* et du *Nocturne* est un des plus grands poètes de tous les temps."[30]

In May of 1929 Constantin Photiadès brought to the solitary of Il Vittoriale two letters from France—one by Marie de Régnier, the other by Anna de Noailles. "Anna de Noailles et Marie de Régnier," D'Annunzio said to the new visitor, "seraient émues, sans doute, si elles pouvaient deviner le battement de mon jeune coeur à la lecture de leurs lettres inattendues. Il y a des souvenirs qui tourbillonnent, autour d'un poète memoriosus, comme les feuilles de la Sybille."[31] To celebrate the happy occasion the Comandante gave orders to fire a six-gun salute— one for France, one for Italy, one for the two poetesses who sent him a "souffle de la *France dulce*," one for all his French friends, and one for the visitor.

He spoke to Photiadès of his friendship with Claude Debussy— "Claude de France"—a friendship strengthened by their common passion for music and a marked affinity which D'Annunzio felt in their respective artistic tastes. When in 1918 he received the news of Debussy's death, he told Photiadès, he was grieved as never before. He read the telegram a moment before taking off for an air raid over Pola. He left for the mission and descended to an altitude of only twelve hundred feet over the city amidst the inferno of the antiaircraft batteries, as though life no longer mattered to him. He recalled his walks with Anatole France, his attachment to Barrès (this was an unavoidable theme), the visits of Marie and Henri de Régnier at Arcachon. "Elle m'avait prié d'écrire des vies de saintes pour une collection déterminée. Apprenez-lui," said the poet, "que j'ai esquissé, à son intention, en français, trois vies de saintes imaginaires, avec des noms choisis."[32] He had in fact planned to write in French the lives of three imaginary saints and to dedicate the work to Marie de Régnier—*Les Trois Riantes Martyres sans liens excluses de la Légende d'or: Sainte Erbeline de Ruissel; Sainte Salmendre d'Ardour; Sainte Guittette de Roussée.* This fanciful book was never written, but its title is included in the national edition of D'Annunzio's works with the notes prepared for its composition.

Touched by the misfortunes and infirmity of Anna de Noailles, D'Annunzio expressed his desire to have her at Il Vittoriale for a period of rest: "... Tout le monde serait ici à ses pieds." D'Annunzio asked about life in Paris with great nostalgia. According to reports, he said, the Parisian women seem to be more elegant than ever—their "toilettes" more refined and more luxurious. "Est-ce vrai?"

It was the 23rd of May, the eve of Italy's declaration of war on Austria fourteen years earlier. "Ce soir, il y a quatorze ans, Maurice Barrès entendait de loin mon cri et la cloche du Capitole, qui rapprochait la France sanglante à l'Italie réveillée." Telegrams and letters of congratulations arrived at Il Vittoriale by the hundreds from France and Italy. "Journée trois fois glorieuse!" said the poet to his guest. "Pour l'amour de la France, j'ai fait sonner ... à toute volée la grande cloche du Capitole."[33] The following day, May 24, the guns began to fire their salute in the mountains around Lake Garda in observance of the anniversary of Italy's entry into the war. "Mon ami," said D'Annunzio, "qu'il vous souvienne que c'est le matin de la journée victorieuse (24 mai 1915)! Le vert du drapeau italien 'bleuit' par amour du bleu de France, comme alors!"[34]

The flight of Professor Piccard to the stratosphere in 1932 gave D'Annunzio the opportunity to break his long silence. He wrote the hero of the air two sensational letters (*Mercure de France*) exalting his audacity. The flight of the new Icarus rekindled in the poet his dream of heroism, his desire for action. After his landing (near Lake Garda) Piccard visited D'Annunzio and received a gift as a token of his admiration. "Veuillez m'empêcher," the poet wrote to Piccard, "de mourir entre deux draps honteux dans le miasme qui sert d'esprit et dans le méphite qui sert d'âme à tous les bipèdes humains."[35]

At Il Vittoriale D'Annunzio once more turned his attention to "la langue d'oïl," constantly striving to prove his unfaltering love for France. In 1930 he finished *Le Dit du sourd et muet,* the first and only volume of a trilogy which he intended to write under the general title *Li Trois Livres Oscurs dou Trésor de Brunet Latin.* The second and third volumes, entitled *Le Lai des Plaisirs Parlants, de la Salmendre Lubrique et du Canardeau d'Abailard Chastré à matines* and *Le Jeu de la Rose et de la Mort,* remained only in the mind of the poet, now in its twilight. The first volume was published in Rome in 1936, with the bizarre title *De Gabriele D'Annunzio qu'on nommait Guerri de Danpnes: Le Dit du sourd et muet qui fut miraculé en l'an de grace 1226.* This book, which he defines as a sort of "fableau tour à tour choral dialogué dansable," is dedicated "Aux bons chevaliers latins de France et d'Italie ... pour opposer hardiment un lumineux témoignage d'amour à des ombres importunes." D'Annunzio narrates, in an archaic prose crammed with confused historical reminiscences, a miracle performed by Saint Louis in the Sainte-Chapelle. Although the subject matter of the tale is religious, the voluptuous note is still present in D'Annunzio's pages; panting bodies of women, virgins filled with desire still disturb the crepuscular dreams of the poet.

In 1935 when the Italo-Abyssinian conflict was brought before the League of Nations, D'Annunzio wrote a long message addressed again "Aux bons chevaliers de France et d'Italie, pour lealté maintenir." The message, consisting of about fifty pages of desultory fancies, is a pathetic document of a declining intelligence. D'Annunzio's mind seems to have been invaded by all kinds of phantoms. He now addresses himself to France as an "écrivain combattant français," calling her to the side of Italy in the name of Latin brotherhood. He patches together passages from *Le Dit du sourd et muet* and the *Aveux de l'ingrat,* quotes repeatedly the *Ode pour la résurrection latine,* and lapses constantly into the *déjà dit.*

This was his last tribute to the French language. His use of French was prompted by his constant desire to prove his unfaltering love for France. His effort to gain mastery of her language and to assimilate her vast culture was, indeed, admirable. But his artistic talent was too strongly established in his native tongue to be susceptible of radical metamorphoses, under whatever influence. His linguistic and cultural acquisitions remained, artistically, a foreign world superposed on his native world. His endeavors as a French writer lack artistic spontaneity and, as a result, fall short of his expectations. His literary French is an amalgamation of disparate linguistic elements derived from different texts. It is fragmentary and never felt as an organic expressive system, a psychological experience. Archaic forms are often mingled with modern, noble terms with popular, which results in incoherent and anachronistic combinations that represent not one language but the confusion of juxtaposition of many. The only criterion for D'Annunzio's choice of words and phrases is their rarity. His French is similar to that of the "rhétoriqueurs." The artistic use of a language requires the assimilation of its historical traditions, so that it may be felt as an expressive experience. D'Annunzio assumes the new medium in its abstract form, as a mere system of signs and sound for the eyes and for the ears. This passage, taken from *Le Dit du sourd et muet*, offers an interesting example:

> Mestre gindre, voici que vous avez multuplié vos pains. Jusqu'à l'aube la pâte va surabonder. Ayez d'autres coffres auges huches. Mestre, je vien d'escole; mais je ne veuil d'aumone. Je vous achète, en nom Dieu, un petit pain à chanter, avec ces cinq livres parisis que je vous donne en sus pour que vos hommes boivent à sainte Abondance et au bon escolier errant. Taverne ai moult amée et li bon morsel m'ont la borse voidée. ...[36]

Furthermore, in his choice of words, as well as in the construction of his phrases, D'Annunzio always followed his personal instinct and his artistic taste, without perceptible concern for ordinary usage of the language. He often boasted to his French translator Georges Hérelle that he never conformed to the common usage of the Italian language. This was true of his French as well. D'Annunzio is adamant in his determination to convey his favorite images through his new expressive medium. Whether the syntax is forced, whether the common usage is violated, whether the words are old or new are for him questions of secondary importance.

22. French Friendships

D'ANNUNZIO's sojourn in France extended the circle of his social and literary friends considerably, and it would be a difficult task to trace the relations he had with all of them. Anatole France, Pierre Loti, Maurice Barrès, Marcel Prévost, Edmond Rostand, Louis Barthou, Henri Bataille, Paul Hervieu, Henri Lavedan, Georges de Porto-Riche, Anna de Noailles, the brothers Margueritte, Henri and Marie de Régnier, Henry Bordeaux, Marcel Boulenger, Pierre Louys, Léon Blum, André Gide, Robert de Montesquiou, André Suarès, Paul Adam, Romain Rolland, and many others in the social, theatrical, artistic, and literary worlds were among those with whom, at one time or another, he formed varying degrees of friendship. He met Pierre Loti and Anatole France at the home of Gaston Calmann-Lévy. He admired both of them greatly—one, for his exquisite poetic sensibility, the other, for his extraordinary erudition, the purity of his style, his caustic spirit, his broad philosophical knowledge, and his stimulating conversation. In 1896, when the poet was accused of plagiarism in Italy, Charles Maurras in defending him in the *Revue encyclopédique* (February 8) expressed his regret that D'Annunzio, instead of drawing from Maupassant, Péladan, and Flaubert, had not sought inspiration in Anatole France. The reason was obvious. Despite his admiration, D'Annunzio was never really attracted to the works of this cold Voltairean—all intelligence and irony. His own artistic nature and extreme sensuality were leading him in a completely different direction. He could not stand irony. After meeting D'Annunzio in Florence at the end of 1895, André Gide made this pertinent remark: "Talking of irony, he says that he cannot endure it, that in using irony you oppose yourself to things whereas it is only through love that you penetrate them, and that that is the important."[1] Nevertheless, the personal relations between D'Annunzio and Anatole France were extremely pleasant and inspired by cordial friendship. André Doderet wrote, in his *Vingt ans d'amitié avec d'Annunzio* (p. 83), that whenever he returned from a visit to D'Annunzio in Italy he invariably was invited to lunch with Calmann-Lévy and Anatole France who was always particularly eager to have "des nouvelles de Gabriele" and to hear some spicy stories about him. For, said Doderet, if men such as Barrès and Suarès always asked about new literary works by the poet, the elderly Anatole France "s'intéressait surtout aux maîtresses."

André Gide was among D'Annunzio's first French acquaintances. Relations between them had, however, a rather odd destiny. They began with warm esteem in the 1890's, but by the time of the founding of the *Nouvelle Revue française* (1908) the idyll was over. Gide's literary interests were so far from D'Annunzio's esthetics that the French writer took a sharp critical stand against the poet. The first expression of his admiration for D'Annunzio is found in a letter to Valéry in March 1895: "Je lis l'*Intrus* et j'admire."[2] It is certain that Gide was familiar with D'Annunzio's novels which around that time were appearing in French translation. In December of 1895 the two writers met in Florence and the entries in Gide's *Journal* relative to their first personal contacts attest to mutual sympathetic feelings.[3] Gide found D'Annunzio charming, a man of a delicate sensibility, a perfect literary artist. Their conversations during Gide's short stay in Florence indicate a definite understanding between them. This was the time when Gide, striving toward liberation from his puritanism, was evolving in the direction of the exasperated hedonism of his *Nourritures terrestres*. Both writers underwent the influence of Nietzsche at about the same time, and the philosophy of the superman, the theme of "dépassement," sensuality, and egotism might have given Gide the impression of a certain kinship with D'Annunzio. The publication *Nourritures terrestres* in 1897 brought this remark by Paul Valéry: "Ce qui fait l'amusement de ton petit Baedeker, c'est qu'il y a un peu de tout. Il y a un peu de d'Annunzio, des Soukhns, des Donatelli, et des fruits qui sont à la mode."[4] The cynical hedonist Ménalque of the *Nourritures* and the cruel superman Michel of *L'Immoraliste* were very close to D'Annunzio's literary world.

But Gide's intellectual growth, his evolution from estheticism to a more serious concern with the problems of life explain his departure from his early admiration for D'Annunzio. The founding of the *Nouvelle Revue française* brought about a complete break. The first issue of the new review (November 15, 1908), which carried an enthusiastic eulogy for Gabriele D'Annunzio by Marcel Boulenger, irritated Gide.[5] The article, entitled "En regardant chevaucher Gabriele d'Annunzio," in which the Italian writer was called the "Jules Verne de l'humanisme," the "maître des images inoubliables," the "prodige superbe, l'artiste incomparable," the man devoted exclusively to Beauty, seemed to be in sharp disagreement with the stern moral attitude of the *Nouvelle Revue française*, whose founders were Calvinists. D'Annunzio was considered to be the representative of literary snobbery. Gide detested his ostentatious stylistic display, his pompous linguistic artifice which, while not a sign of creative poverty, conflicted with his own sobriety and sincerity of form. This attitude, mainly inspired by Gide, clearly explains the criticism constantly levelled at D'Annunzio by the writers of the *Nouvelle Revue française*—especially Henri Ghéon and Jean Schlumberger. For them artistic beauty springs from the discovery of the relations between thought and form. If this rapport is suppressed, the beauty vanishes even if the work is made of rare gems. Real beauty is central, not peripheral; it is not the pompous and resplendent embellishment of external dress with disregard for the body wearing it. In the light of the classical principles they practiced, D'Annunzio seemed to them to be a decadent whose esthetics led not to beauty but away from it. This evident preoccupation with moral content—as opposed to sheer formal beauty—turned Gide against D'Annunzio by 1908. Gide's religious nature, his inner conflict, his keen concern with ethical and social problems revealed him as a moral philosopher struggling with fundamental human issues, although it would be hard to define his credo. He could not remain faithful to the doctrine of pure art, for he had something to say which was more important than the manner of saying it. He strove for sincerity and simplicity of expression, devoid of affectation and decoration. The austerity of his style, so bare, so rapid and spontaneous was in complete contrast to D'Annunzio's flamboyant expression in which the man is completely obliterated by the artist.

In 1910 Gide wrote in his *Journal:* "Yesterday, lunch at Rouché's with Gabriele d'Annunzio. I had originally refused, caring very little about seeing him again; and I replied to Rouché that I had too good a memory of my meeting with d'Annunzio fifteen years ago to risk spoiling it by seeing again a writer for whose talent I no longer had much esteem."[6] Although he always considered him a charming person, Gide no longer thought of D'Annunzio as a great artist. He was in fact outraged when, in 1938, André Suarès wrote in the *Nouvelle Revue française*[7] that D'Annunzio was the greatest writer of Italy in the last three centuries: "And what of Leopardi?" Gide questioned.[8]

D'Annunzio's relations with Romain Rolland ran more or less a similar course. They began in 1897, grew into a close but short friendship, gradually deteriorated into indifference, and finally ended almost in bitterness in 1914. The war irremediably brought the men into sharp ideological conflict; but the break never obliterated the memory of their early personal friendship. In 1940, in fact, Rolland devoted a long and touching article to his relations with D'Annunzio,[9] which is a serene and sympathetic judgment of the man. The sincerity with which D'Annunzio devoted himself to the cause of the war, the courage he displayed during the four years of hardships, the personal price he paid in the loss of one eye always commanded, if not the approval, the respect of Rolland.

The beginning of their relations was due to no affinity of character or literary taste but to pure chance. In 1897 Rolland, who was then on the threshold of his literary career, had submitted his first book, *Saint-Louis*, to the *Revue de Paris*. Although the work was a serious one, its author was still completely unknown, and the editor of the review,

Louis Ganderax, in order to counterbalance the effect of Rolland's book, wished to print concurrently a work different in nature. Strangely enough, he was considering for the purpose D'Annunzio's *Le Feu*. But since D'Annunzio had postponed the publication of his novel, Rolland's *Saint-Louis* was coupled with a humorous work. A few months after this attempt to bring the names of the two writers together in the *Revue de Paris*, Rolland was introduced to D'Annunzio in Rome, at the home of Countess Ersilia Locatelli. "Dans ce beau cercle de railleurs courtois à l'affût," wrote Rolland, "d'Annunzio boudait sur un canapé: Je fus bien supris de le trouver d'apparence et de manières si peu italiennes. Un fashionable de Paris, un démodé: ... rien d'un poète, rien d'un artiste. On eût dit un attaché d'ambassade très snob."[10]

During the two weeks that Rolland stayed in Rome, he saw D'Annunzio almost every day, and the two quickly became friends. Although they were far removed from each other by ideology and by moral and artistic temperament, they seemed at the beginning to find a basis for their friendship in their love for music. Music was in fact the ground on which they were able to associate and communicate intellectually. Another link between them was Eleonora Duse, greatly admired by Rolland. The two writers met again in Paris, in January 1898, during the production of *La Ville morte*, and in Zurich, in September 1899, when D'Annunzio accompanied Eleonora Duse there for a series of performances. At this time Rolland drew very close to both of them, attempting to smooth their relations now being strained by misunderstandings, passion, and jealousy. Duse had learned, through the indiscretion of friends, that *Il Fuoco*, which was soon to appear, contained uncomplimentary details about her relationship with the author. She became extremely bitter against "l'enfant de volupté" who had described in his novel all the secrets of their intimate life for public display. D'Annunzio, although determined to preserve the integrity of his work, tried to appease her in some way and to bring about a reconciliation. Romain Rolland became their confidant and made all possible efforts to end the stormy crisis. Duse, in a state of moral depression, was unapproachable; D'Annunzio, furious at her hostility, threatened suicide. Rolland soothed their torment with his music and, during their stay in Zurich, he was a sympathetic mediator between them. At the moment of their departure, said Rolland, D'Annunzio "m'embrassa, en m'appelant son cher Romain." The publication of *Il Fuoco* seemed to bring about the end of relations between the two lovers; but D'Annunzio soon won over his mistress again, and despite the deep hurt, she resumed her life with him at the Capponcina. Rolland's reaction to *Il Fuoco* and his correspondence with D'Annunzio in this connection were mentioned earlier. However, in 1902, while in Rome, Rolland received a telegram from D'Annunzio summoning him to Milan. He spent a few days there with the poet, and some time later was a guest at the Capponcina for a week. Duse had herself been drawn into friendship with the French writer, and at the Capponcina she revealed to him all her suffering, her bitterness, and her passion. She was to leave for America in a few weeks, perhaps in order to save D'Annunzio from financial disaster, and she well knew that she would soon be replaced by another woman in the mobile heart of her lover. In his article, Rolland recalls this sadly and is still unable to condone or justify D'Annunzio's detestable behavior toward such a sensitive and delicate woman as Eleonora Duse. When he left the Capponcina, D'Annunzio invited him to return soon: "Votre présence musicale," he said, "remplit ma solitude." Rolland went back a few months later. Eleonora had left for America and he sensed that someone else had already taken her place; although he preferred to pass over this in silence, he tacitly condemned D'Annunzio's amoral attitude.

Rolland disliked in D'Annunzio "l'homme public," his "prodigieux dandysme," his "scandales amoureux," his "exploitation de la beauté appariée à la volupté," and "toute cette odeur d'Adonis de mauvais lieu."[11] But he soon realized that under this flamboyant mask was a different and truer D'Annunzio—a serious and weary man, tired of his prostituted glory and of his official role which he judged with bitterness. Despite his many faults, he had some high virtues—among them his sincerity and loyalty to his friends. However, Rolland considered him to be "le plus tranquillement meurtrier des génies." In his cruel selfishness, D'Annunzio showed no concern for the moral anguish of his mistress, who sailed for America fearful of dying there, alone and abandoned. "La seule chance de salut," wrote Rolland, "c'était que d'Annunzio crût littérairement (et il le croyait peut-être) que la voie royale du génie mène de l'égoïsme à l'altruisme, de la volupté d'amour à l'amour charité."[12] But D'Annunzio was "un monstre de génie" like his Renaissance masters, and although Rolland admired heroic ideals, he had no sympathy for the condottiere types.

During the following years a high wall gradually rose between the author of *Jean-Christophe* and the author of *L'Enfant de volupté*. The antinationalism of Rolland and the extreme nationalism of D'Annunzio were to jeopardize their friendship irremediably. The marriage of the German genius to the Latin genius, so dear to Rolland, was soon to run against the "haine des barbares" aroused in the Latin nations by such men as Barrès and D'Annunzio. However, their personal relations still remained rather cordial. In 1903 there was an exchange of books. D'Annunzio sent *Laus Vitae;* Rolland reciprocated with *Beethoven,* inscribed: "To the only Poet of our times, with all my heart." In one of two letters to the poet in 1904, Rolland hints at the possibiliy of his giving a course on D'Annunzio's theater at the École des Hautes Études Sociales. In 1906 there was one more letter from Rolland; in the meantime two plans for meeting—one in 1904 and the other in 1906—failed to materialize.[13] Rolland's warm interest in the writers of *La Voce* (founded in 1908), whose program was a reaction to the ethical and esthetic principles D'Annunzio stood for, began to create the final intellectual break between them—a break which was inevitable in any event. "J'étais pris par le grand flot de mon *Jean-Christophe,*" wrote Rolland, "qui m'éloignait décidément de lui. Et ce Christophe menait son Olivier français tambour battant; il ne lui passait pas ses indulgences et ses faiblesses pour un monde qu'il condamnait; peut-être était-il jaloux de l'affection cachée qu'Olivier gardait pour Gabriele."[14]

Despite the growing intellectual differences separating them, the poet's deep affection for Rolland remained untouched. In 1910, when the French writer was struck by a car and badly hurt, D'Annunzio immediately wrote him from Arcachon:

> Nous sommes séparés par la distance, par le silence, et par d'autres choses encore; mais je vous aime beaucoup, puisque la nouvelle de votre infortune m'a agité et affligé si vivement. ... Accueillez mes voeux fraternels. J'espère que vous ne souffrez pas trop et que vous serez guéri en quelques jours. Je n'ai pas oublié nos belles heures d'amitié et de musique. Je vous ai suivi dans vos oeuvres toujours plus hautes.[15]

Rolland confessed that he was not sure whether he ever answered this letter and he expressed regret for failing to take the hand stretched out in a reaffirmation of generous friendship. Actually he did answer:

> ... Votre lettre m'a profondément touché. Moi aussi, je pense à vous avec affection. Quoi que la vie et l'art puissent faire pour nous éloigner l'un de l'autre, je suis peut-être plus près de vous que ceux qui vous font la

cour. En tout cas, je sais combien vous êtes supérieur aux hommes de lettres parisiens; mon principal regret, justement, est que vous restiez dans ce milieu délétère. Certes, il ne manque pas à Paris, de grands esprits et de grands coeurs; mais ils vivent à l'écart. Je vous souhaite de vaincre, à Paris, mais de n'y pas rester.[16]

The publication of the *Canzoni della gesta d'Oltremare* (1912) must have widened their differences, although there was no reaction from Rolland to these patriotic poems. Just before the outbreak of the war the two writers happened to be at a "gala" at the Opéra. The poet, sitting beside his St. Sebastian—Ida Rubinstein—a few rows ahead of Rolland, was whistling "avec fureur" a ballet by Richard Strauss. "Je ne fis rien pour l'aborder," said Rolland.[17] He felt that it was futile to begin again, to renew ties that were destined to be broken, and he kept away from him.

Strongly opposed to the men who propagandized the war as a holy crusade against barbarity, Rolland followed with distaste D'Annunzio's wartime activity, and, while he had words of high praise for his heroism, he bitterly attacked his propaganda. Commenting on the *Ode pour la résurrection latine*, Rolland wrote in the *Journal de Genève*: "Kipling et d'Annunzio chantent des hymnes de guerre, Barrès et Maeterlinck entonnent des péans de haine."[18] In his *Journal des années de guerre* there are several references to D'Annunzio. On the speech at Quarto he made these bitter remarks: "Cet homme, qui est le mensonge littéraire incarné, ose se poser en Jésus! Il *joue* Jésus, et refait le Sermon sur la Montagne, pour exciter l'Italie à violer ses traités et à faire la guerre à ses alliés d'hier. ... Cette infâme comédie soulève naturellement l'enthousiasme des deux tiers de l'Europe. Les hommes ne savent même pas ce qu'est la vérité. ... Quant à d'Annunzio, sa personnalité n'existe pas. Il est un conglomérat de pastiches. Il refait l'Evangile, comme un discours latin."[19] D'Annunzio's speech at the Capitole was commented upon with the same bitterness: "Gabriele d'Annunzio, au Capitole, (17 mai) se fait instantanément l'âme de Marat, le pourvoyeur de la guillotine. En ce jour où il lance l'Italie dans la guerre, non satisfait encore, il l'excite à la haine civique. Il déchaîne la fureur de la populace contre le seul homme qui tente de s'opposer au délire public: Giolitti."[20]

His hostility to D'Annunzio did not prevent him from asking the poet in the fall of 1914 for his signature on a pamphlet protesting "la destruction barbare de Reims et le Louvain."[21] He soon had to recognize that D'Annunzio was quite different from many other war propagandists who preached bloodshed while never exposing themselves to danger. The announcement that D'Annunzio had joined the fighting troops in June 1915 brought this remark from Rolland: "En ceci du moins, il se montre supérieur aux Barrès, Daudet et autres héros du patriotisme, qui se contentent de faire se battre les autres."[22] And later Rolland expressed regret for his attacks against D'Annunzio the soldier who affirmed on the battlefield his principles, however evil: "J'aime ceux qui, comme Jean Richard Bloch et comme d'Annunzio mettent leur vie pour enjeu de la patrie."[23] In 1919, referring to his own remarks on D'Annunzio's speech at Quarto four years earlier, Rolland wrote: "Je regrette la violence de ces lignes contre d'Annunzio. Mais je ne puis pas m'abstenir de les écrire et de les récrire."[24] Although his pacifism and his distaste for the false rhetoric of the war advocates had not changed, he did justice to D'Annunzio the writer and the hero:

> J'admire le génie verbal de d'Annunzio et sa force vitale. Je l'ai même connu assez intimement pour apprécier le meilleur de sa nature, —qu'il semble cacher jalousement au monde, pour n'étaler que le pire; —j'aime ce qui subsiste, au fond de ce terrible rhéteur, de naïf, de jeune, d'ardent, de jaillissant, surtout son sentiment très haut de l'amitié. Et depuis, il a donné la preuve au monde (pour moi, je n'en doutais pas), de son héroïsme. Seul des rhéteurs de la guerre, il a payé de sa personne, il a signé sa rhétorique de son sang.[25]

The immediate postwar period left Rolland no less disappointed than D'Annunzio. The French writer saw the political meddling, the upsurge of appetites, pride, and hate as the premises for new catastrophes. He did not approve the Fiume episode, yet he did not condone the attitude of the Allies in this respect, and he applauded D'Annunzio's denunciation of Wilson. Despite the events and the conflict of ideas, their friendship was not completely extinguished. In 1922, when D'Annunzio fell from a window and fractured his skull, Rolland broke a long silence with a message of good wishes: "J'apprends avec peine que vous êtes, une fois de plus, blessé gravement; je fais des voeux pour votre prompte guérison. Voici bien des années que nous sommes profondément séparés par les destins qui commandent à nos vies et à nos pensées. Mais je n'ai jamais oublié les belles journées de Settignano et notre intimité fraternelle."[26] Two years later their signatures appeared together in a formal protest made by several writers against the exile of

Miguel de Unamuno. The death of Eleonora Duse in the United States
in 1924 prompted one more and perhaps the last letter from Rolland
to D'Annunzio. Instead of sending condolences to the official representative of the Italian government, as the occasion would have required, Rolland addressed them to D'Annunzio, as the person closest
to the heart of the actress: "... C'est à vous, cher Gabriele, que j'adresse
la fleur de mon souvenir triste et tendre, cueillie dans mon coeur. ...
Vous êtes, en ma mémoire, l'un à l'autre immortellement liés. Et
j'évoque, à cette heure, avec mélancolie, les jours passés ensemble à
Settignano et à Marina di Pisa."[27]

In his pages of memoirs in 1940, his sympathetic judgment on the
man "qui avait fait un pacte avec la victoire ou la mort," is the best
eulogy to D'Annunzio, the more so since it came from one who did
not share the poet's views:

> ... Je n'oublie pas ses vols d'Icare héroïque et les blessures, dont le grand
> rhéteur a scellé ses harangues de combat. Il n'était pas comme la plupart
> des gens d'écritoire, un combattant de l'arrière. Quoi qu'il ait écrit son
> sang le loue. ... Homme, il fut loyal envers les hommes; et il fut brave.
> Sa vie fut un hautain défi à une époque lâche et fourbe, qui l'admirait en
> le dénigrant, en le guettant, prête à le mordre, qui l'eût dévoré s'il ne
> l'eût domptée.[28]

To Rolland D'Annunzio was a true and authentic artist, but a man
living on erratic principles: "his philosophy is false but his art is
true."[29] He was a vital if not a moral force, capable of heroism in a
world of apathy and mediocrity and, as such, he deserved respect if
not approbation. On the other hand, D'Annunzio admired Rolland not
so much for his art as for the moral greatness of his works.

Robert de Montesquiou was the first prominent figure in the social
world to approach D'Annunzio upon the latter's arrival in Paris in
1910. Their friendship was both social and literary. Montesquiou had
met the Italian writer in 1898 when *La Ville morte* was presented in
the French capital at the Théâtre de la Renaissance. They were introduced by Sarah Bernhardt, who was playing the leading role in the
tragedy. A typical dandy, a decadent poet of a refined and morbid
sensibility, Montesquiou was, like D'Annunzio, a "dilettante of sensations" with a taste for baroque erudition and for the rare and the
strange in both language and images. Therefore he felt a certain affinity
with the Italian poet. Montesquiou lacked depth of inspiration and,

despite the publication of his many collections of poems, he had little reputation as a poet. But he was quite a figure in the social circles of the time. His aristocratic insolence and sharp tongue made him fearsome. It is well known that he served as a model for Huysmans' Jean des Esseintes (*A rebours*) and later for Proust's Baron de Charlus (*A la recherche du temps perdu*).

When D'Annunzio arrived in Paris, Montesquiou appointed himself his mentor. He made of D'Annunzio his idol. "Nous devîmes," he wrote, "comme on dit, les meilleurs amis du monde, et je goûtais l'enivrement capiteux de me croire tendrement aimé par un homme de génie."[30] He made it a point to impose his new god upon the social and literary circles, to force open all doors to him. The first day that the poet visited him at his Palais Rose (accompanied, of course, by some women), Montesquiou recited the following poem he had composed to express his esthetic pleasure and tenderness:

> Seul, le silence pourra dire
> Ce que la parole tairait;
> Ce n'est pas assez qu'on admire,
> Un culte doit être secret.
>
> Le mystère, seul, est suprême;
> L'ineffable est-il proféré?
> Ce n'est pas assez que l'on aime,
> L'office doit être sacré.
>
> Ce qu'au fond de son coeur, on crie,
> Au dehors n'apparaît que peu;
> Ce n'est pas assez que l'on prie,
> L'inconnu monte seul à Dieu.[31]

Montesquiou was outraged at the fact that D'Annunzio had not immediately received official recognition in the high literary circles, except for individual expressions of esteem. "Tous nos bonnets de lettres faisaient les sourds, les aveugles et les morts, pour ne pas voir ce qui leur crevait les yeux, la possibilité d'honorer un maître des maîtres."[32] This led Montesquiou to prepare the ground for D'Annunzio's entrance into the high world with the honors he deserved. He removed all obstacles so that D'Annunzio would be accepted and feted. He accompanied the poet everywhere and organized parties in his honor; he brought D'Annunzio together with Barrès; he introduced him to Ida Rubinstein, and was thus instrumental in the creation of the *Martyre de Saint Sébastien* of which he took the grave responsibility of correcting the manuscript. But this enthusiasm was not to last long; it seems to have occupied "l'espace d'un matin." The "engagement sentimental et presque religieux" taken by Montesquiou was only for one year, during which he did all in his power to conquer the heart of his guest. D'Annunzio wrote the preface to Montesquiou's *La Divine Comtesse. Études d'après Mme Castiglione* (1913), and it seems that their friendship died there. Some critics have insinuated that once Montesquiou had received what he wanted from D'Annunzio (the preface) his courtship ended. But his version is quite different. D'Annunzio was not an easy man to deal with. He would not give in to all the manifestations of friendship on the part of Montesquiou. He showed himself extremely kind with the obvious intention to please; "quoique je pense," remarked Montesquiou, "plutôt pour le plaisir qu'il ressentait à exceller dans ce genre, comme il faisait dans son art, mais sans que l'émotion vînt communiquer à sa grâce le frisson qui la divinise."[33] Friendship played an important role in D'Annunzio's novel *Forse che sì forse che no;* he knew all the nuances of the sentimental manifestations of it, but this did not mean, in the opinion of Montesquiou, that D'Annunzio felt it. "Il y avait, entre nous," said Montesquiou, "un obstacle plus insurmontable, un propos plus divergent, une affinité plus divellente: 'L'amitié, disait-il, est le terrain de la liberté'; je répondais, moi: 'C'est le seul terrain de l'enchaînement.' Et ces paroles restèrent entre nous, comme une menace qui s'est réalisée."[34]

By his "terrain de la liberté" D'Annunzio meant to avoid the threat of a yoke and completely preserve his freedom. As a result their relations thereafter became somewhat cooler, with occasional exchanges of books and notes evoking their earlier friendship.

Undoubtedly D'Annunzio's most prominent friend in France was Maurice Barrès. Their friendship was motivated by both artistic and patriotic reasons. They shared the same nationalistic feelings, the same hate for the Germans; and they fought together for the same cause—the defense of the Latin world against the German menace. Their intellectual evolutions present some striking affinities. Both gradually progressed from extreme individualism, completely detached from political and social concern, to extreme nationalism; from the individual ego to the national ego; from pure estheticism to the position of national leaders; from dilettantism to political action. Despite certain differences in their temperaments, Barrès' cycle of the "Culte du moi"

corresponds to D'Annunzio's "Romanzi della rosa." Barrès is endowed with a keen spirit of analysis lacking in his Italian confrere;
he is more cerebral, D'Annunzio more sensual. Their passage from the
first to the second phase of their intellectual attitude followed different
routes. From *Il Piacere* (1889) with the well-known reference by
Andrea Sperelli (the protagonist of the novel) to the soldiers who died
at Dogali as "four hundred brutes who died brutally" to the *Canzoni
della gesta d'Oltremare* (1912) exalting Italian colonialism and the
valor of the conquerors of Libya, D'Annunzio does not seem to have
undergone a real inner evolution; the change in his attitude is somewhat external; the passage is motivated by the desire to expand the
ego, and the nation is an instrument for this expansion. There is, therefore, no real inner renovation.[35] Barrès, who had a deeper moral con-
sciousness, passed from the "culte du moi" to the "Roman de l'énergie
nationale" through his effort to overcome egoism. The "culte du moi"
cannot achieve well-being through the breaking of imposed laws or
through the imposition of its own law. It can be achieved through love.
This led him to the cult of country, to nationalism, in which love and
piety can be promoted. In Barrès egotism tends to transcend itself in
love of country and is presented as a crisis leading to such a logical
development; in D'Annunzio egotism seems to remain static in its
primitive form, with no perceptible evolution. His nationalism thus
appears as an instrument for bolstering his ego, which becomes more
and more exacting, seeking higher and higher experiences in an effort
to reach the Olympic altitude of a god. The love of country does not
dissolve the individual ego into the nation; it does not effect any expansion of the individuality toward others.

But whatever the differences between the two men may have been,
they were bound, perhaps by the course of events, to a lasting friendship and a sincere reciprocal admiration which never lessened. They
met for the first time in the summer of 1910 in Paris. In his *Les Pas
effacés*, Robert de Montesquiou, who arranged the meeting, described
the event in great detail. In order to bring the two writers together,
he organized a dinner in honor of D'Annunzio. However, according to
Montesquiou, Barrès at first showed a strong reluctance to accept the
invitation. He said to Montesquiou: "De prime abord, je n'aime pas
cet Italien."[36] D'Annunzio's reputation as a Don Juan and the sensuality of his works had produced an aversion in Barrès for Montesquiou's

idol. But Barrès was in the end persuaded to attend. The dinner took place on June 30 at the fashionable Pré-Catelan (Bois de Boulogne). The event was magnificently elaborated and the guests carefully selected—Barrès, Edmond Rostand, some celebrities of the theatrical world (Cécile Sorel, Berthe Bady, Marie Leconte, and Julia Bartet who acted as hostess). The pomegranate—D'Annunzio's emblem and the symbol of intellectual pleasure—adorned the cover of an album entitled *Dîner de Grenade* which each guest found in his plate. To solemnize this event Robert de Montesquiou, always ready to pour out his money, his perfumes, and even his perfidies, rose at the end of the dinner to recite oratorically the following poem which he had composed for the occasion:

> La Grenade, ce fruit que vous avez fait vôtre
> Et qui loge des grains de rubis dans son coeur,
> Mais d'un rubis vivant, plus suave que l'autre,
> Un rubis que l'on mange, ayant un goût de fleur ...
>
> La Grenade, ce fruit qui porte une couronne,
> A qui donc serait-il, si ce n'est à des dieux?
> Toute la Poésie, en vos livres se donne,
> Et ces rubis vivants sont notre amour pour eux.
>
> Faites-en le collier qu'à cet arbre notoire,
> Votre noble héroïne attache dans la nuit.
> Les grains de ce bijou disent votre victoire
> Et, pour vous entourer de tendresse et de gloire,
> Nos coeurs se sont réglés sur les grains de ce fruit.[37]

Afterward Mme Bartet declaimed the passage at the beginning of *Il Fuoco* where Stelio Effrena, the hero of the novel, tells Foscarina why he made the pomegranate his own emblem.

Barrès seemed to be quite charmed by D'Annunzio,[38] yet he maintained a cautious attitude: "On peut causer avec lui parce qu'il a un terrain, un bon sens."[39] But as he had a chance to know D'Annunzio better, Barrès developed an increasing admiration for his artistic talent. The image of D'Annunzio as a Don Juan of the social salons of the French capital was gradually obliterated by the image of the accomplished artist, the writer of genius. The dedication of the *Martyre de Saint Sébastien* to Barrès, although at first seeming to disturb him because of the condemnation of the work by the Church,[40] strengthened their relations, at least on the literary level. Barrès was aware of the pagan inspiration in the work, but he did not hesitate to admit its artistic qualities. He could not overlook the fact that in the *Martyre* high homage was being paid to France and her culture by a foreigner who was eager to express his love for whatever was French. After the play, the *Canzoni della gesta d'Oltremare* and the invectives against the Hapsburgs ("Canzone dei Dardanelli"), the exaltation of the brotherhood between the two Latin countries ("Canzone d'Elena di Francia") constituted an additional tie between the two writers whose political views brought them closer and closer. On the other hand, D'Annunzio could not be indifferent toward this Latin brother who had extolled the beauty of Italy, who had found the most moving inspiration in Pisa, in Siena, in Parma, at the tombstone of Dante in Ravenna, in the gardens of Lombardy.[41] Their exchange of messages indicates a growing understanding between them.[42] A strong advocate of the Latin union, firmly opposed to the Triple Alliance, D'Annunzio was bound to be Barrès' friend. Their relations, however, developed into a feeling of brotherhood only with the outbreak of the war. They were now bound unalterably together: their countries become as one to face the enemy of the Latin race. D'Annunzio's action for the common cause, his heroic life drew constant admiration from Barrès. Messages, dedications of books, and the beautiful pages Barrès devoted to D'Annunzio in his *Chronique de la Grande Guerre, Mes Cahiers, Dix Journées en Italie,* clearly express the feelings and ideas which bound them together. In evoking with Henry Bordeaux his friendship for Barrès, D'Annunzio said: "Je suis ... le seul, ou l'un des seuls à avoir connu la douceur barrésienne. Chez ceux de ma race, comme de la sienne, la douceur n'existe guère. Elle n'en a que plus de prix. Il est beau d'avoir vu dans la guerre et dans la vie deux hommes taillés pour être des rivaux se comprendre ainsi et s'aimer."[43]

The misunderstanding arising at the end of the war and D'Annunzio's occupation of Fiume did not affect their friendship. Barrès, while always speaking of D'Annunzio with admiration, did not completely approve of the Fiume episode. He felt in all fairness that D'Annunzio's action did not solve the Fiume problem, but aggravated it.[44] He maintained that the possession of Fiume would add nothing to the power of Italy once she had Trieste and Vallona. He expressed the view that the Slavs also had a right to the Adriatic Sea and that a policy of compromise and friendship should be adopted between Italy and Yugoslavia. Barrès was unquestionably well balanced and more reflective. Although at times he felt somewhat shocked by D'Annunzio's exuberance, he remained in a way close to his Italian confrere. In Tome XIII of *Mes Cahiers* (published in 1950) he gives this judgment: "Annunzio —poésie d'opéra, peinture de décor, de la virtuosité, de l'éclat. Ni sévérité, ni excellence de goût. Mais, il y a, par dessous, de la virilité."[45] But these reservations concerning the artist change to unconditional praise for the man and the ally when Barrès evokes the dark days of 1914:

> Annunzio—Il était à Paris (en 1914) quand une partie de Paris se déversait vers le Midi. Je me rappelle l'avoir rencontré place Vendôme, dans un de ces jours où la grande ville, solitaire et pleine d'espérance, se raffermissait pour supporter bientôt (sans défaillir de joie) la nouvelle fameuse: "La bataille s'achève en une victoire incontestable." Il ne nous quitta que pour soulever sa patrie. Il écouta la mélodie de ces grands jours et donna l'essor à son chant intérieur. Chacun a loué sa pompe. J'aime sa solidité.[46]

Barrès never visited D'Annunzio at Il Vittoriale, but his affection remained unaltered. In 1923, when Montesquiou's *Les Pas effacés* were published (posthumously), some remarks in the book disturbed Barrès. Montesquiou related a conversation he had had with him concerning the *Martyre de Saint Sébastien* and indicated that Barrès had been distressed at the dedication of the play to him. This unpleasant revelation prompted a letter by Barrès assuring D'Annunzio of the appreciation he had for and the pride he took in the dedication of the work: "Une chose est certaine, le profond plaisir que j'ai éprouvé et que je continue de ressentir pour cette dédicace où vous m'avez fait l'honneur d'inscrire mon nom. Un tel témoignage c'est un plaisir pour toute ma vie, et sur ma mémoire un honneur immortel."[47]

It is to be noted, however, that this friendship lacked close familiarity. It was patriotic and literary. Both D'Annunzio and Barrès are pagan; their cult of the land is pagan. The God of the Christians is absent in D'Annunzio's works, and whenever Christian religion appears in them, it is mixed with sensuality. He worships antiquity and his only god is Beauty. Barrès, although essentially pagan, professes the desire for perfection and the Divine. Catholicism is for him a form of violence which he accepts as a restrictive discipline. However, their attitudes were in sharp contrast with their time. The positivistic ideas stemming from Auguste Comte drew attention to science and society. Barrès and D'Annunzio scorned both as an expression of academicism. They are romantic, lyrical; they identify with their characters: Barrès is Philippe of *Le Culte du moi;* D'Annunzio is Andrea Sperelli of *Il Piacere.* Both are enemies of the commonplace, the bourgeois; both love rare sensations, voluptuousness, blood, death—elements which form a rare mixture in their works. In temperament, however, they were completely different. Barrès was rather aristocratic and distant; D'Annunzio was friendly and warm, and he felt a spontaneous affection for Barrès. But both were "animators," and contributed greatly in bringing France and Italy together in a time of danger.

One of the most faithful and sincere friends of the poet was Marcel Boulenger. His admiration for D'Annunzio is eloquently expressed in the first issue of the *Nouvelle Revue française* (November 15, 1908), in which he exalts in the Italian writer "le Jules Verne de l'humanisme, de la haute culture et du raffinement intellectuel," recalling the enthusiasm with which the young men of his generation had read *L'Enfant de volupté* fourteen years earlier. In the *Licenza* of his *Leda senza cigno* D'Annunzio devoted touching pages to Marcel Boulenger, evoking their camaraderie and reciprocal affection. Boulenger's works comprise several novels and various volumes of "chroniques." He was highly appreciated as a polemist and a publicist. A sportsman, he shared with D'Annunzio a passion for racing dogs, and also a taste for high life and culture. Their friendship was both patriotic and literary, and they worked together at the beginning of the war for the "rapprochement franco-italien." In 1916 D'Annunzio, half blind, telegraphed him: "J'espère guérir pour revoir les allées de Chantilly et le verger de l'amitié."[48] It was at Chantilly, where Boulenger had a beautiful mansion, that the two men had spent together many hours in friendly conversation. Boulenger visited D'Annunzio in Fiume in 1920 and ardently defended him against the attacks levelled at the poet in France on the occasion of the occupation of Fiume. In 1922 he devoted a book to his friend—*Chez Gabriele d'Annunzio*—that is moving in its simplicity and sincerity.

D'Annunzio and Anna de Noailles met for the first time in May 1910. It is hard to say whether the French poetess had at that time any knowledge of D'Annunzio's poetic works, of which little had yet appeared in French translation. No one knows, either, whether she had enough familiarity with the Italian language to be able to read his verses in the original. She was undoubtedly well acquainted with D'Annunzio's novels and dramatic works available in French translation. In her *La Domination* (1905) there are evident echoes of *Il Trionfo della morte*, and her admiration for D'Annunzio clearly emerges from a copy of her book, sent to him with the dedication: "En hommage d'extrême admiration."[49] The Italian writer seems to have had a high opinion of her works. Their first meeting made a strange impression on her. What struck her most strongly in D'Annunzio was his pride: "Comme il paraît sûr de lui, comme il a l'air de porter ses destinées entre ses mains! Sait-il, ce Don Juan, ce que c'est que l'amour? L'orgueil seul fait trembler son coeur."[50] But whatever this first impression might have been, they met again and again in the various literary circles; he accompanied her to the cinema and to the Bois de Boulogne. He particularly loved her conversation, in which he found an extraordinary charm. One day, while they were on their way to the Bois de Boulogne, D'Annunzio asked her jestingly if she was satisfied with him as a companion: "Contente, cher ami? Non, mais vraiment heureuse, comme on peut l'être en compagnie d'un égal." The poet confessed many years later. "Je me le tins pour dit. Après quoi, je n'essayai plus de lutter avec cette Muse."[51]

Their relations became more and more cordial as they came to know each other better and to appreciate each other's works. Her initial impression was obliterated before long and she began to discover in D'Annunzio a noble and gentle heart far different from the proud and vain Don Juan of their first meeting. Invitations and notes from Countess de Noailles attest to her desire to see D'Annunzio and to converse with him. In August 1913 she made a sort of Nietzschean pilgrimage to Weimar and, knowing that the poet had devoted a poem to the German philosopher ("Per la morte di un di struttore," *Laudi*, II), she wrote D'Annunzio: "La cité fameuse est toute emplie de votre gloire. Hier, dans la maison de Nietzsche, nous avons lu avec vénération votre poème aux ailes géantes; ce chant d'un aigle à un autre aigle montant si haut!"[52] The same year she published her *Les Vivants et les morts* of which she sent a copy to the poet with this dedication: "A G. d'A., au génie éclatant et total, —à la bonté duquel je crois—et à qui je voudrais adresser les louanges que lui-même donne à la Terre, au Feu, à l'Eau, à l'Air."[53]

The war interrupted their exchange of notes and messages. No trace of further correspondence seems to exist until 1923, when the French poetess extended an invitation to him to join the committee in charge of the celebration of Ronsard's 400th birthday: "Le plus grand poète du monde, que vous êtes, ne peut pas refuser à Ronsard cette fraternité à travers les siècles."[54] There was on this occasion an exchange of telegrams and letters; then followed a silence of six years. The visit of Constantin Photiadès at Il Vittoriale in May 1929 and the letter he brought to the poet from Anna de Noailles renewed the exchange of messages and rekindled the old affection. "Il n'est aucun être," Anna de Noailles' letter said, "pour qui votre oeuvre immense écrite ou dessinée sur le monde ne soit une surhumaine image qui suscite l'adoration, —le seul sentiment qui console"; it brought back to the mind of the poet the memory of Maurice Barrès who had died in 1923: "Votre gloire le comblait d'enthousiasme et de cette satisfaction sublime que la perfection cause aux êtres de génie."[55] There followed a letter by D'Annunzio from his "ermitage païen," evoking the "lumineuses heures latines" and the image of the unforgettable Barrès: "Je vous écris à l'aube du 24 mai: 1915–1929, Maurice Barrès est là, debout. Avec sa noble nonchalance qui cache son ardeur tyrannique, il s'appuie à la vaste hélice d'avion habitée toujours par un esprit du ciel hostile."[56]

Another letter from Anna de Noailles brings their correspondence to a close: "Je sais du fond de ma tristesse et du milieu du désert d'où rien de suffisant ne monte vers mon triste rocher, abrupt, aigu, quel secours c'est de vous lire, de songer à vous puissamment, de se réfugier sous l'auguste aile fraternelle." The letter ends on a loving thought for France: "... cette France que vous aimez ... qui vous attend, qui serait éblouie de votre présence!"[57] She died in 1933, and at her burial there was a wreath from D'Annunzio.

Paul Valéry was one of D'Annunzio's last great friends in France. Their personal relations in fact began after the First World War, when the figure of the Italian poet was fading from the political and literary scene. Although there was little or no affinity between them (except their cult for Leonardo), they soon developed a cordial and fervent friendship. From the few references in the correspondence between Gide and Valéry, it is clear that the latter was familiar with D'Annunzio's works during the 1890's when the Italian writer enjoyed great popularity in France. But Valéry's real interest was far removed from D'Annunzio's despite their contemporary devotion to Leonardo (Le

Vergini delle rocce, and the *Introduction à la méthode de Léonard* were both published in 1895). Much later Valéry admitted borrowing in *La Jeune Parque* (1917) an image from D'Annunzio's *La Pisanelle,*[58] and this was all. On the other hand, D'Annunzio did not seem to be acquainted with Valéry's works before the war. It was during his occupation of Fiume that, most probably through André Doderet, he became interested in the French poet. He read *Le Cimetière marin* with great enchantment, impressed especially by the solid architecture and the musical qualities of Valéry's poetry. He often told Doderet that in the tumult of Fiume "il s'était isolé dans la poésie et le silence du *Cimetière marin* que Valéry venait de lui envoyer."[59] Immediately after the Fiume interlude Doderet brought the two poets together.

Early in 1921 there began an exchange of books with enthusiastic dedications between D'Annunzio and Valéry. The Italian poet sent from Il Vittoriale a copy of the *Ritratto di Luisa Bàccara:* "A Paul Valéry, pour son admirable *Cimetière marin* qui, dans le tumulte de Fiume en armes, me fut une 'pause musicale' comme celle-ci, que je lui offre."[60] In the fall of the same year D'Annunzio sent Valéry a second gift—a copy of *Il Notturno,* just published: "Au pur poète Paul Valéry, ce thème sans lyre est offert."[61] In June 1922 Valéry reciprocated with *Charmes:* "A Gabriele d'Annunzio colle mie scuse di non poterle mandare un esemplare più degno di Lei. Omaggio d'Ammirazione e profonda simpatia" (Italian incorrect).[62]

At this point direct contact was established between them. On August 13, 1922, D'Annunzio mysteriously fell from a window and injured himself; Valéry a few days later sent him a short message of good wishes for his recovery. The name of D'Annunzio is always present in his exchange of notes with Doderet. Valéry constantly asks to be remembered to the Italian poet. In June 1923 the author of *La Jeune Parque* was in the front row with Doderet and Marcel Boulenger at the presentation of D'Annunzio's *Phèdre* at L'Opéra. In the spring of the following year, during a lecture tour in Italy, Valéry finally made the personal acquaintance of D'Annunzio at Il Vittoriale. Ugo Ojetti in his *Cose viste* (Vol. III) briefly described this first meeting as related to him by Valéry himself. In Ojetti's account, when the French poet reached Desenzano, a diabolical motor-launch dispatched by D'Annunzio took him at high speed to Gardone "amidst clouds of water and bursts of wind that threatened to strip him of hair, clothes and skin." When he entered D'Annunzio's home, says Ojetti, Valéry saw the poet come toward him, "all shaven—beard, moustache, eyebrows: 'Me voilà'—so that he seemed to have shaved for him. And they embraced." This was for Valéry "l'accolade d'un roi."[63]

It is not possible to determine the length of the visit, but it was extremely cordial. They seem to have talked mainly of their favorite subject—Leonardo. D'Annunzio might have also entertained Valéry on a subject which had been occupying his mind—the "terzo luogo," a psychic state which he never clearly defined and which he seems to place at times beyond, at times between, life and death. Valéry left Il Vittoriale amused and enchanted. He offered D'Annunzio the *Introduction à la méthode de Léonard* accompanied by a series of "quatrains" in French and Italian. D'Annunzio heaped upon his guest books and photos with the most extravagant dedications: "Au grand poète hermétique Paul Valéry, cette image mystique de son frère"; "A Paul Valéry, le flibustier de Fiume"; "A Paul Valéry, le Borgne Coclès"; "A Paul Valéry, le pirate de Buccari," and so on.[64]

The French poet kept a lasting remembrance of D'Annunzio's lyric hospitality. In the correspondence which followed this first and only meeting they immediately passed from the polite to the familiar form of address: "Mio carissimo Paolo," "Caro Gabriele." Some of Valéry's notes and messages are in bookish and flowery Italian. When in 1925 Valéry was elected to the French Academy, D'Annunzio conspicuously contributed to the purchase of the sword for the new academician. On New Year's Eve of 1926 a group of friends gathered at Countess Béhague's in Paris, and on this occasion they sent D'Annunzio a message in which each one of them wrote a few words. Marie de Régnier wrote: "Cher Foco! Je voudrais tant vous revoir! Suora Notte"; Henri de Régnier: "Revenez-nous!; Paul Valéry: "... Nous crions à la nouvelle année: D'Annunzio! D'Annunzio!"[65]

The dialogue between D'Annunzio and Valéry continued until 1933, always cordial, and seemingly inspired by a deep reciprocal admiration. The last note in their correspondence was one by Valéry, reminiscing on his visit at Il Vittoriale nine years earlier, on the warm welcome received, and the sensation he had and still retained "d'avoir connu la personnalité absolue du Poète—l'Être qui est contre le temps." "Tu es le dernier ..." says Valéry, "et ton nom marquera un âge révolu de l'histoire profonde de la terre."[66] Was Valéry's admiration for D'Annunzio completely sincere? Henry de Montherlant recently reported, in a sympathetic article on the Italian poet,[67] that Valéry always spoke of D'Annunzio with irony rather than respect. But in the light of their correspondence it is hard to believe Valéry capable of such hypocrisy.

23. The Last Years

THE LAST YEARS of D'Annunzio's life were accompanied by a concert of praise for the writer and the war hero living in the quiet shade of his laurels. In his *Histoire générale du théâtre* (1932), Lucien Dubech refers to D'Annunzio as "l'homme qui domine cette époque, aussi bien dans l'art dramatique que dans les autres ordres de l'art d'écrire," pointing out "le rôle qu'il a joué dans le monde au titre d'homme d'action" and the homage he paid to the French language in choosing it to write among other things "les octosyllabes souples et ornés du *Martyre de Saint Sébastien*."[1] In an introductory note to a biographical article by Robert de Beauplan commemorating D'Annunzio's seventieth birthday, the editor of *L'Illustration* speaks of him as the "grand poète qui a aussi enrichi, par plusieurs de ses ouvrages écrits en langue française, notre patrimoine littéraire et pour qui la France, où il vécut aux heures tristes de sa destinée, fut toujours une seconde patrie."[2] Albert Flament wrote in a long article of reminiscences: "Souvent notre pensée le visite, cherche à percer le mystère et lui envoie, en échange de ses feuilles de laurier, quelques pétales de nos roses de Paris, qu'il a tant aimées et meurtries."[3]

In September 1936 the Société des Gens de Lettres and the Association des Écrivains Combattants sent a committee to Italy to participate in a ceremony at Dante's tomb in Ravenna. It was inevitable that the committee on this occasion should visit the great "écrivain combattant" at Il Vittoriale. D'Annunzio received his French confreres with immense cordiality and took this opportunity to send through them a "message d'amour" to his "frères les écrivains combattants français." The message, written in a visionary style, emphasizes the sentence pronounced by an Italian ascetic of the fourteenth century: "L'Amore non è amato" (Love is not loved). Since D'Annunzio's previous message, a year earlier, had remained unanswered, his allusion to "l'Amore non è amato" sounds like a lover's reproach. "J'offre à nouveau ce message d'amour," he said, "écrit dans le langage qui m'a fait l'émule de Brunet Latin"; and he handed it to José Germain, head of the committee, together with a copy of *Le Dit du Sourd et muet,* luxuriously bound:

> Cher José Germain, chers frères écrivains de France, cet impérial manuscrit lié dans le tissu où le coq de Charlemagne semble entravé, je ne vous le donne point sur le lac de Garde que Sirmio enchante, par les mains de Catulle, en guise de suplex libellus, mais par les doigts décharnés de ce très vieil ascète qui sur la première et dernière page a récrit la sentence désespérante: "L'Amore non è amato" (l'Amour n'est pas aimée).[4]

D'Annunzio's death on March 1, 1938, aroused in France expressions of sincere and deep sympathy. With his passing France lost the most ardent of her Italian friends—the one who had constantly asserted Latin brotherhood and had shown in deeds his devotion to this cause. The many necrological articles appearing in the French press unanimously and movingly eulogized the "French writer," the war hero, and the unfaltering friend. Gérard Baüer wrote in the *Annales politiques et littéraires* "Il ne sut pas séparer dans son coeur, pas plus que dans son esprit, les deux langues où il s'était exprimé, et il les maria dans la défense d'une civilisation. Il n'eut de cesse qu'il n'eût placé sur les champs de bataille sa patrie à côté de la nôtre."[5] In the *Revue des Deux Mondes,* Marie de Régnier acknowledged the loss with a delicate touch of personal admiration and friendship:

> La France perd son ami, son allié, son fervent, le poète qui, étant déjà le plus grand poète de son temps et de sa patrie, voulut ajouter à son laurier natal celui-là qu'on cueille chez nous. ... D'un grand amour, ce Latin magnifique aima la France et il le lui prouva. ... La France doit à Gabriele d'Annunzio une immense gratitude. Il faut qu'elle porte son deuil et célèbre sa mémoire. ... Je regarde sa photographie de guerrier, son profil de condottiere, audacieux et joyeux d'avoir eu sa victoire, et je veux croire que le coeur de la France bat encore avec reconnaissance, avec amour, pour son ami, le glorieux poète d'Italie et son héros latin.[6]

François Porché wrote of him in the *Revue de Paris:*

> ... C'est toute une conception du monde qui s'efface avec cette figure éclatante. ... Les lettres françaises garderont une reconnaissance particulière à ce grand poète italien, ce merveilleux génie bilingue, qui sut couler ses

sentiments, ses rêves légendaires, la vibration de sa lyre épique et sacrée dans notre "doux parler." ... Vint la guerre. On sait ce que la France doit à Gabriele d'Annunzio. ...[7]

The *Illustration* published abundant photographic documentation on the poet and the soldier together with articles and brief expressions of sympathy:

> ... Nous pleurons un grand mort. D'Annunzio fut pendant des années notre hôte, notre ami, notre frère. ... Un instant sur notre sol, il se plut à donner l'expression française à son génie latin. ... Quand vint la guerre, il rassembla, dans la force de l'unité, les âmes de même race. Il fut l'aède exaltant les énergies latines contre la ruée germaine. Plus encore, il fondait sur l'épreuve commune de sang et de gloire la naissance d'un monde nouveau.[8]

Eulogistic articles appeared also in the *Nouvelle Revue française* (March), in the *Mercure de France* (April 1), in the *Revue bleue* (April), and even in *Études* (May 5) despite the strong Catholic reservations concerning the man and the writer.

Marcel Boulenger, who had already passed on, had written in his book *Chez Gabriele d'Annunzio* (1922) that the life of the poet would be later "mise en images d'Épinal." Anatole de Monzie, a former member of the Cabinet, said at the death of D'Annunzio: "Quand nous nous serons reconnus et rapprochés, Italiens et Français, il faudra élever un monument de grâce et de gratitude à Gabriele d'Annunzio, face à l'Océan sur quelque avancée audacieuse de la côte française."[9] In October 1958 a bust of D'Annunzio was erected in the town of Arcachon with the inscription: "La France à Gabriele d'Annunzio"—an expression of admiration and love for a great and sincere friend, the most eloquent advocate of Latin brotherhood.

In France, D'Annunzio the man was no less great than the novelist, the dramatist, the poet. If as a writer he sometimes met with reservations on the part of critics, as a soldier and a friend he won general acclaim. "Ses amis survivants," wrote Marie de Régnier, "ressentiront jusqu'à leur mort l'honneur et le bonheur de l'avoir quelquefois approché, entendu, de s'être illuminés à la lumière de flamme de leur Frate Foco."[10] And Gérard Bauër said: "Gabriele d'Annunzio sut devenir ce qu'il était: plusieurs hommes à la fois. La gloire peut choisir entre eux, car tous furent grands."[11]

Notes

Introduction

1. "Gabriele d'Annunzio et son théâtre," *La Quinzaine*, Sept. 16, 1902, p. 142.

2. See now Thovez's *L'Arco d'Ulisse* (Naples: Ricciardi, 1921). A summary of Thovez's accusations is found in *La Revue des revues*, Feb. 1, 1896, pp. 283–286.

3. For earlier mentions of D'Annunzio's indebtedness to French writers see: *La Liberté*, July 12, 1893 (borrowing from Maupassant), and *La Vie contemporaine*, June 15, 1895 (influence of Bourget). For the debate on D'Annunzio's plagiarisms see André Hallays, *Journal des débats*, Feb. 2, 1896; anon., *La Revue des revues*, Feb. 1, 1896; G. Izambard, *Revue bleue*, Feb. 15, 1896; Gaston Deschamps, *Le Temps*, Feb. 2 and 26, 1896; Charles Maurras, *Revue encyclopédique*, Feb. 8, 1896. For other references to D'Annunzio's sources see Pierre Mille, *La Dépêche*, Dec. 2, 1911; Ernest Bovet, *Lyrisme, épopée, drame* (Paris: Colin, 1911); Jean Cazes, *Mercure de France*, June 15, 1920; Eugène Rouvellon, *Nouveau Mercure Français*, Jan. 1924.

4. Borrowings from Maupassant are rather extensive (see Édouard Maynial, *Mercure de France*, Nov. 1904, pp. 289–315; Lucien Duplessy, *Mercure de France*, Dec. 1, 1927, pp. 345–376, and Nov. 15, 1934, pp. 50–76). D'Annunzio borrowed not only from Maupassant's prose works but from the latter's less known work, *Des Vers* (1880).

5. D'Annunzio's main source was *La Tentation de Saint Antoine*.

6. *La Letteratura della Nuova Italia* (Bari: Laterza, 1922), Vol. IV.

7. *Revue encyclopédique*, Feb. 8, 1896. The article was reprinted in *Barbarie et Poésie* (Paris: Champion, 1925).

8. *Lyrisme, épopée, drame* (Paris: Colin, 1911).

9. In addition to the references given in the above notes, the following are to be added: Giuseppe Marra, "Sulla *Fedra* del Racine e del d'Annunzio," *Rassegna di studi francesi*, Jan.–Feb., Mar.–Apr., May–June 1925; Guy Tosi, "Gabriele d'Annunzio lecteur de Malraux," *Comparative Literature*, No. 2, 1950; J. Bonavita, *Gabriele d'Annunzio et ses emprunts à la littérature européenne dans l'Isottèo, la Chimera* (Rome: Bardi, 1950); Tom Antongini, "D'Annunzio e Baudelaire," *Letterature moderne*, No. 4, 1953, and "D'Annunzio e Balzac," *ibid.*, No. 1, 1953; Jeanne-Frédérique Renauld, "Gabriele d'Annunzio tributaire de Fromentin," *Revue de littérature comparée*, No. 2, 1953; Lucia Culcasi, "Les Rapports de d'Annunzio et de Barrès," *Letterature moderne*, No. 4, 1953; Susanna Gugenheim, "D'Annunzio e Chateaubriand," *Letterature moderne*, No. 1, 1954; Antoine Fongaro, "D'Annunzio et Huysmans," in *Studi sulla letteratura dell'Ottocento in onore di P. P. Trompeo* (Naples: Edizioni scientifiche, 1959); Luigi Salvatorelli, "D'Annunzio e Barrès," *ibid.*; Sergio Cigada, "Flaubert, Verlaine e la formazione poetica di d'Annunzio," *Rivista di letterature moderne e comparate*, No. 1, 1959.

10. Some of his works to which this writer is particularly indebted are: *D'Annunzio à Georges Hérelle; correspondance inédite* (Paris: Denoël, 1946); *Claude Debussy et Gabriele d'Annunzio; correspondance inédite* (Paris: Denoël, 1948); *D'Annunzio en France au début de la Grande Guerre* (Florence: Sansoni, 1961), unpublished notebooks.

1. The Enthusiastic Reception

1. Third book of poems, published in 1883.

2. Book of poems, published in 1886.

3. The title was arbitrarily chosen by the editor of *Le Temps*. To justify the choice it was explained that another novel entitled *L'Innocent* had already been published a year earlier in France (probably by Émile Pouvillon).

213

4. The publication of *Il Piacere* (Milan: Treves, 1889) had already aroused a strong reaction against D'Annunzio's moral indifference. His books displeased especially Giuseppe Chiarini and other eminent critics who had earlier encouraged the debut of the young poet.

5. Georges Hérelle was born in Pougy-sur-Aube in 1848. Among his classmates at the Lycée were Ferdinand Brunetière and Paul Bourget. He formed with the latter a close and lasting friendship. When he became D'Annunzio's translator he was professor of philosophy at the Lycée of Cherbourg. He died in 1935.

6. D'Annunzio, *Correspondance à Hérelle*, trad. et introd. de Guy Tosi (Paris: Denoël, 1946), p. 170. The original letters (in Italian) are still unpublished. They are preserved in the Bibliothèque de Troyes.

7. Only a part of this correspondence, namely, a selection of letters from D'Annunzio to Hérelle, was translated into French by Guy Tosi. The letters from Hérelle to D'Annunzio are still to be brought to light from the archives of Il Vittoriale.

8. *Petits mémoires littéraires*. Work still unpublished and preserved in the Bibliothèque de Troyes. Quoted from Tosi, "Introduction" to *Correspondance à Hérelle*, p. 22.

9. *Correspondance à Hérelle*, p. 111.

10. *Ibid.*, p. 112.

11. *Ibid.*, p. 114: "Il faut rendre plus musicales certaines cadences, certaines chutes de phrases comme dirait votre divin Flaubert. Vous vous êtes aperçu que dans mon roman reviennent souvent comme des thèmes dominants certains groupes de mots, quelque chose de comparable au leit-motiv wagnérien."

12. *Ibid.*, pp. 115–116.

13. *Ibid.*, p. 167.

14. *Ibid.*, pp. 282–283.

15. *Ibid.*, p. 121.

16. Letter of Oct. 29, 1892. See *Correspondance à Hérelle*, pp. 143–144.

17. *Correspondance à Hérelle*, pp. 143–144. *L'Intrus* was published in book form by Calmann-Lévy in 1893.

18. Poet, novelist, and critic, he belonged to the group of the *Revue Wagnérienne*.

19. *Correspondance à Hérelle*, p. 124.

20. *Ibid.*, p. 125.

21. Novelist of the verist school. He had written in *Libri e teatro* concerning D'Annunzio's novel: "In this new volume the prose-writer is completely overshadowed by the poet; the observer is taken away by the colorist and stylist; the bare and sincere vision of reality is covered by an importune cloud of lyricism which irritates and tires." (See *Mercure de France*, Apr. 1, 1893, p. 374, this writer's translation).

22. *Mercure de France*, Apr. 1, 1893, p. 374.

23. "Gabriele d'Annunzio, poète et romancier italien," *Revue hebdomadaire*, June 24, 1893, p. 599.

24. *Ibid.*, p. 602.

25. See *Correspondance à Hérelle*, p. 148.

26. See *ibid.*, p. 159.

27. See *ibid.*, pp. 150–151.

28. *Ibid.*, p. 146.

29. *Ibid.*, p. 154.

2. The D'Annunzian Vogue

1. *Correspondance à Hérelle*, p. 158.

2. See Edouard Maynial, "Guy de Maupassant et Gabriele d'Annunzio. De la Normandie

aux Abruzzes," *Mercure de France,* Nov. 4, 1904, pp. 289–315; and Lucien Duplessy, "Maupassant, source de Gabriele d'Annunzio," *Mercure de France,* Dec. 15, 1927, pp. 345–376.

3. The stories are the following: "Les Cloches" ("Campane") from *Terra vergine;* "La Belle-soeur" ("Nell'Assenza di Lanciotto") from *Il Libro delle vergini;* and "La Sieste" ("La Siesta"), "La Huche" ("La Madia"), "Les Sequins" ("I Marenghi"), "Le Martyr" ("Il Martirio di Gialluca"), "Saint Pantaléon" ("San Pantaleone"), "Le Héros" ("L'Eroe"), "Annales d'Anne" ("Annali d'Anna") all from *San Pantaleone.* "Le Martyr," "Saint Pantaléon," "Les Sequins," "Annales d'Anne" appeared in the *Revue hebdomadaire,* respectively, Sept. 1, 1893; Sept. 2 and June 4, 1894; Jan. 3, 1895. "La Sieste" was published by the *Revue de Paris,* June 15, 1894; "Le Héros," and "Les Cloches" by *Le Gaulois,* Mar. 31, 1894, and a subsequent issue, the date of which is missing. Indications about "La Huche" and "La Belle-soeur" are lacking.

4. See *Correspondance à Hérelle,* p. 176.

5. See *ibid.,* p. 166. Letter of Brunetière to Hérelle, Jan. 16, 1894.

6. *Ibid.,* p. 166.

7. The engraving is now preserved in the museum of Bayonne.

8. *Correspondance à Hérelle,* p. 211.

9. See *ibid.,* p. 241: "Ne craignez pas que les critiques me chagrinent! ... J'ai la peau dure. Et vous ne pouvez imaginer mon impassibilité sur ce point."

10. *Ibid.,* p. 167: "Il est unanimement reconnu, ici en Italie, que la moindre de mes phrases se distingue par une empreinte vigoureuse de personnalité. ... Or, souvent dans votre traduction j'apparais comme un écrivain ordinaire, un peu timide, assez ami des *phrases toutes faites.* Vous vous ingéniez souvent avec beaucoup de peine à effacer de ma prose tout relief."

11. *Ibid.,* p. 178.

12. *Ibid.,* p. 189.

13. See *ibid.,* pp. 189–190: "Je vous répète que lorsque vous suivez de près le texte vous êtes admirable, et votre prose acquiert une saveur plus forte et je ne sais quelle agréable nouveauté."

14. See *ibid.,* p. 219.

15. See *ibid.,* p. 222.

16. *Revue des Deux Mondes,* Jan. 1, 1895, p. 192.

17. *Ibid.,* p. 206.

18. *Correspondance à Hérelle,* p. 228.

19. *Ibid.,* p. 228.

20. *Ibid.,* p. 228.

21. Rome: Sommaruga, 1884.

22. *Correspondance à Hérelle,* p. 117.

23. *Ibid.,* p. 140.

24. Diego Angeli, "Chez d'Annunzio," *Journal,* May 11, 1895.

25. *Correspondance à Hérelle,* p. 172.

26. "Gabriele d'Annunzio et son théâtre," p. 147.

27. *Ibid.,* p. 147.

28. *Correspondance à Hérelle,* p. 177n.

29. *Ibid.,* p. 247.

30. *Op. cit.,* p. 205.

31. "Gabriele d'Annunzio," *Les Jeunes* (Paris: Perrin, 1896), p. 259.

32. Mar. 1, 1896, p. 135.

33. *Op. cit.,* p. 263.

34. "M. Maeterlinck et M. d'Annunzio," *Annales politiques et littéraires,* June 6, 1897, p. 364.

3. D'Annunzio and the "Latin Renaissance"

1. "Gabriele d'Annunzio; poèmes et romans," *Revue des Deux Mondes,* Jan. 1, 1895, p. 191.
2. "D'Annunzio et la Duse," *Oeuvres libres* (Paris: Fayard, 1947), No. 246, p. 4.
3. E. Dupuy, *Les Grands maîtres de la littérature russe au XIXe siècle,* 1885; E.-M. Vogüé, *Le Roman russe,* 1886.
4. See Ugo Ojetti, *Alla scoperta dei letterati* (Milan: Dumolard, 1895).
5. "Gabriele d'Annunzio," *Les Jeunes* (Paris: Perrin, 1896), p. 263.
6. *Op. cit.,* p. 190.
7. "Enquête littéraire italienne," p. 451.
8. *Ibid.,* p. 452.
9. "Gabriele d'Annunzio," *Le Correspondant,* Jan. 25, 1898, p. 272.
10. *Ibid.,* p. 257.
11. Issue of Apr. 1, p. 176.
12. "Lettre à Gabriele d'Annunzio," *Mercure de France,* Mar. 1, 1896, p. 412.
13. "Une Conversation avec M. Gabriele d'Annunzio," *Revue bleue,* May 16, 1896, p. 611.

4. The Novels for the Elite

1. *Correspondance à Hérelle,* p. 253.
2. *Ibid.,* p. 265.
3. *Ibid.,* p. 274.
4. *Ibid.,* p. 275.
5. *Ibid.,* p. 291.
6. *Ibid.,* p. 288.
7. *Ibid.,* p. 288.
8. *Ibid.,* p. 286.
9. *Ibid.,* p. 290.
10. "Gabriele d'Annunzio," *Le Correspondant,* Jan. 25, 1898, p. 266.
11. "Opinions et souvenirs sur Gabriele d'Annunzio," *Dante,* May–June 1938, p. 183.
12. "M. d'Annunzio et M. Maeterlinck," *Annales politiques et littéraires,* June 6, 1897, p. 364.
13. *Op. cit.,* p. 262.
14. See *Correspondance à Hérelle,* p. 251.
15. *Journal,* Jan. 27, 1899.
16. *Correspondance à Hérelle,* p. 288.
17. See *ibid.,* p. 336.
18. *Ibid.,* p. 344.
19. *Ibid.,* p. 354.
20. *Ibid.,* p. 358.
21. *Ibid.,* p. 360.
22. *Ibid.,* p. 355.
23. See Rolland, "D'Annunzio et la Duse," *Oeuvres libres* (1947), No. 246, p. 26.
24. "Revue des livres," *Annales politiques et littéraires,* Jan. 27, 1901, p. 60.
25. *Ibid.,* p. 60.
26. Rachilde, "Gabriele d'Annunzio, le *Feu,*" p. 185.

5. The Last Novel

1. "Revue des livres," *Annales politiques et littéraires*, Nov. 7, 1909, p. 430.
2. *Ibid.*, p. 430.
3. *Correspondance à Hérelle*, p. 292.
4. *Ibid.*, p. 393.
5. *Le Livre secret de Gabriele d'Annunzio et de Donatella Cross* (Padova: Edizioni letterarie "Il Pellicano," 1947), p. 130.
6. "Gabriele d'Annunzio et la vie moderne," July 10, 1910, p. 56.
7. *Ibid.*, p. 58.
8. "La Vigile du poète," Aug. 15, 1916, p. 877.
9. See Tom Antongini, *Vita segreta di Gabriele d'Annunzio* (Milan: Mondadori, 1938), p. 139.
10. *Correspondance à Hérelle*, p. 394.
11. *Ibid.*, p. 321n.
12. "Georges Hérelle traducteur," *Le Temps*, Jan. 7, 1906.
13. See L. Morel-Payen, *Georges Hérelle, traducteur de Gabriele d'Annunzio* (Troyes, 1929), p. 16.
14. *Les Jeunes*, p. 244.
15. "D'Annunzio et la France," *Notre prestige*, Mar. 15, 1938, p. 14.
16. *Le Temps*, Feb. 24, 1912.
17. *Le Temps*, Aug. 23, 1928.
18. "Notes sur la littérature italienne," *Revue bleue*, Jan. 22, 1898, p. 122.
19. *Correspondance à Hérelle*, p. 124.

6. Other Prose Works

1. *Vingt ans d'amitié avec Gabriele d'Annunzio* (Paris: Éditions du Cerf-Volant, 1956), p. 17.
2. *Ibid.*, p. 17.
3. "D'Annunzio devant la mort," *Nouvelles littéraires*, June 9, 1923.
4. Apr. 16, 1917, p. 161.
5. "Impression de guerre de Gabriele d'Annunzio," p. 459.
6. See Doderet, *Vingt ans d'amitié avec Gabriele d'Annunzio*, p. 80.
7. *Essai sur d'Annunzio* (Paris: Perrin, 1925), p. 201.
8. Doderet, *Vingt ans d'amitié avec Gabriele d'Annunzio*, p. 32.
9. *Ibid.*, p. 86.
10. "Gabriele d'Annunzio: *Notturno*," Feb. 1, 1922, p. 818.
11. "Le *Notturno*," *Nouvelle Revue française*, Oct. 19, 1922, p. 495.
12. "D'Annunzio devant la mort," *Nouvelles littéraires*, June 9, 1923.
13. "Physio-pathologie du *Nocturne* de Gabriele d'Annunzio," *Nouvelles littéraires*, June 23, 1923.
14. "*Notturno* de Gabriele d'Annunzio," *Annales politiques et littéraires*, July 27, 1923, p. 161.
15. "La *Contemplation de la mort*," Sept. 1, 1912, p. 196.
16. *Ibid.*, p. 197.
17. "La Contemplation de la mort," *Nouvelles littéraires*, Aug. 18, 1928.
18. "Angelo Cocles: *Cento e cento pagine del libro segreto*," Oct. 1, 1935, p. 193.
19. "Le livre secret de Gabriele d'Annunzio," *Nouvelles littéraires*, Aug. 24, 1935.
20. "Littérature étrangère," *Annales politiques et littéraires*, Nov. 7, 1909, p. 430.

21. *Ibid.*, p. 431.

22. *Episcopo et Cie* was reprinted in 1913; *L'Enfant de volupté*, in 1921; *L'Intrus*, in 1922 (all by Calmann-Lévy); *Le Feu*, in 1919 (by Crès); *Le Triomphe de la mort*, in 1923 (by Mornay, Paris).

23. See Tosi, "Introduction," *Correspondance à Hérelle*, p. 44.

24. *Correspondance à Hérelle*, p. 292. Vera Charnasse in a short novel entitled *Le Charme* (Les *Oeuvres libres*, Apr. 1935, Vol. 166) copied entire passages from *L'Enfant de volupté*. (See Georgetti Béatrix, *Mercure de France*, Sept. 15, 1935.)

25. Paris: Mercure de France, 1896, I, 184.

26. Sergines, "D'Annunzio jugé par les esprits," *Annales politiques et littéraires*, May 12, 1907, p. 205.

27. "Opinions et souvenirs sur Gabriele d'Annunzio," *Dante* (Paris), May–June 1938, p. 180.

28. "Gabriele d'Annunzio," *Revue de Paris*, Mar. 15, 1938, p. 458.

29. Guy Tosi, *op. cit.*, p. 52.

30. "Un prince de la terre," *Nouvelles littéraires*, June 20, 1963.

7. D'Annunzio's Debut as a Dramatist

1. "Le Théâtre de Gabriele d'Annunzio," *Revue des Deux Mondes*, Feb. 1, 1904, p. 655.

2. Sarah Bernhardt, who was at that time director of the Théâtre de la Renaissance.

3. G. Primoli, "La Duse," p. 529.

4. *Correspondance à Hérelle*, p. 319.

5. See *ibid.*, p. 320.

6. Jean Dornis, *op. cit.*, p. 663.

7. *Ibid.*, p. 664.

8. Jan. 25, 1898, p. 276.

9. "D'Annunzio dramaturge," *Revue des cours et conférences*, Jan. 15, 1940, p. 182.

10. *Correspondance à Hérelle*, p. 320.

11. See *ibid.*, p. 322.

12. *Ibid.*, p. 255.

13. *Ibid.*, p. 296.

14. See *ibid.*, pp. 296–297.

15. See *ibid.*, p. 316.

16. See letter to Sarah Bernhardt in *Dante* (Paris), May–June 1938, p. 143.

17. *Ibid.*, p. 144.

18. Paris: Ollendorff, 1906, I, 168.

19. *Théâtre italien* (Paris: Michaud, 1910), p. 200; *Ariel Armato* (Milan: Mondadori, 1931), p. 289.

20. Guy Tosi, "Introduction," *Correspondance à Hérelle*, p. 42.

21. See *ibid.*, p. 42.

22. See Edmond Stoullig et Edouard Noël, *Annales du théâtre et de la musique, 1898* (Paris: Charpentier, 1899), pp. 172–173.

23. *Correspondance à Hérelle*, p. 302.

24. Paul Flat, *Théâtre contemporain* (Paris: Sansot, 1912), p. 40. The chapter on D'Annunzio had appeared in the *Revue bleue* (Oct. 3, 1903) under the title "Théâtre idéaliste. I. Gabriele d'Annunzio." See also Dorothy Knowles, *Réaction idéaliste au théâtre* (Paris: Droz, 1934), p. 220.

25. *Journal des débats*, Jan. 24, 1898.

26. François Carry, "Gabriele d'Annunzio," *Le Correspondant*, Jan. 25, 1898, p. 269.

27. *Illustration,* Jan. 29, 1898, p. 112.
28. *Revue des Deux Mondes,* Feb. 1, 1898, pp. 705–706.
29. *Ibid.,* p. 706.
30. E. A., Jan. 30, 1898, p. 73.
31. *Op. cit.,* p. 668.
32. *Op. cit.,* p. 188.
33. "Gabriele d'Annunzio et son théâtre," *Quinzaine,* Sept. 16, 1902, p. 156.
34. *Op. cit.,* p. 256.
35. *Op. cit.,* p. 706.
36. Sept. 16, 1902, p. 162.
37. Stoullig et Noël, *op. cit.,* p. 173.
38. "Zacconi dans la *Ville morte,*" *Nouvelles littéraires,* Feb. 25, 1933.

8. *La Gloria, La Gioconda*

1. "Le Renouveau musical en Italie," May 16, 1919, p. 220.
2. D'Annunzio changed here the name of Blanche-Marie to that of Hébé. He felt that the former was too ordinary.
3. "Représentations des tragédies modernes de Gabriele d'Annunzio," p. 844.
4. See *ibid.,* pp. 844–845.
5. See *Correspondance à Hérelle,* p. 330.
6. Armand Caraccio, "D'Annunzio dramaturge," *Revue des cours et conférences,* Apr. 15, 1940, p. 135.
7. Jean Dornis, *op. cit.,* p. 660.
8. Léon Blum, *op. cit.,* p. 190.
9. See *Correspondance à Hérelle,* p. 330.
10. *Essai sur d'Annunzio,* p. 141.
11. Paris: Ollendorff, 1900, p. 262.
12. *Op. cit.,* pp. 204–205.
13. Feb. 15, 1905, p. 623.
14. Jan. 29, 1905, p. 74.
15. Nov. 10, 1906, p. 640.
16. *Op. cit.,* p. 215.
17. See *Mercure de France,* February 1, 1905, p. 488.
18. "... le succès littéraire remporté par la *Gioconda* au Gymnase, avec l'ardente Suzanne Desprès, succès littéraire que consacra, dans un de ses plus beaux essais, M. Léon Blum."
19. See Dorothy Knowles, *op. cit.,* p. 471.
20. See *ibid.,* p. 471.
21. *Op. cit.,* p. 59.
22. *Ibid.,* p. 53.

9. A Theatrical Success

1. *Correspondance à Hérelle,* p. 371. "Il convient d'adopter la méthode de la traduction littérale et linéaire en cherchant à conserver à la langue une partie au moins de sa fraîcheur populaire."
2. *Ibid.,* p. 373.
3. *Ibid.,* p. 375. In the *Correspondance* are found some lyrical passages of the play in the form given by D'Annunzio, with a note by Hérelle pointing out the poet's misconception concerning translation "lorsqu'il croyait transporter en français le rythme italien par ses phrases trop souvent maladroites et gauches."

4. *Ibid.*, p. 384.

5. *Ibid.*, p. 383.

6. "Le Mouvement dramatique," *La Revue*, Feb. 5, 1905, p. 531.

7. July 1, 1904, p. 273.

8. See Dornis, *Essai sur d'Annunzio*, p. 180.

9. "La *Fille de Iorio*," *Mercure de France*, Mar. 1, 1905, pp. 132–133.

10. "La Tragédie catholique de Gabriele d'Annunzio," *Mercure de France*, Feb. 25, 1905, p. 505.

11. *Op. cit.*, p. 180.

12. *Op. cit.*, pp. 211–212.

13. "La *Figlia di Iorio*, tragédie pastorale," *Revue des Deux Mondes*, July 15, 1904, p. 466.

14. "L'Année littéraire en Italie," *Nouvelle Revue française*, Oct. 1922, p. 495.

10. Plays Never Presented in France

1. Robert de Beauplan reported in *La Petite Illustration* of Dec. 31, 1927, p. 32, that André Doderet was preparing for "une de nos grandes scènes une traduction de la *Nef.*" Doderet in his *Vingt ans d'amitié avec G. d'A.* (p. 137) mentions casually his translation of the play; but to this writer's knowledge it never appeared.

2. *Op. cit.*, p. 470.

3. Ricciotto Canudo, "La Dernière pièce de Gabriele d'Annunzio," *Mercure de France*, Dec. 15, 1906, p. 633.

4. *"Più che l'amore,"* *Mercure de France*, Apr. 1, 1907, p. 543.

5. Dec. 16, 1907.

6. Jan. 1, 1908.

7. "La Nouvelle tragédie de M. d'Annunzio," *Revue des Deux Mondes*, Feb. 15, 1908, p. 941.

8. *Lyrisme, épopée, drame* (Paris: Colin, 1911), p. 279.

9. *Essai sur d'Annunzio*, p. 185.

10. "La Nouvelle tragédie de Gabriele d'Annunzio," *Mercure de France*, Dec. 16, 1907, p. 146.

11. P. 487.

12. After its publication in the *Revue de Paris*, *Francesca da Rimini* appeared in book form at Calmann-Lévy's in 1913.

13. Feb. 1, 1902, p. 544.

14. *Correspondance à Hérelle*, p. 367.

15. *Ibid.*, p. 367.

16. *Ibid.*, p. 396.

17. *Ibid.*, p. 397.

18. *Ibid.*, p. 398.

19. *Ibid.*, p. 67.

20. *Revue des Deux Mondes*, Apr. 15, 1902.

21. Maurice Muret compared the two plays in *La Revue* of July 15, 1906.

22. "D'Annunzio dramaturge," *Revue des cours et conférences*, May 15, 1940, p. 220.

23. The plot of *La Parisina* revolves around a pilgrimage to Loreto. Parisina dei Malatesti, married to Nicolò D'Este, hated her stepson in the beginning of her marriage, but later fell in love with him. She is escorted by the young man on a pilgrimage to Loreto and when the Saracens attacked the sanctuary he defends it gallantly. Wounded, he is

nursed by his stepmother, and their love is consummated. But they are betrayed to Nicolò and executed at his order. The execution, followed by Nicolò's remorse, is the climax of the play.

24. See Vernon Jarrat, *The Italian Cinema* (New York: Macmillan, 1951), p. 18: "Even nowadays *Cabiria* is still the symbol throughout the world of the cinema for outstanding achievement of the early days."

25. The name meant "born from fire."

26. See Tom Antongini, *Vita segreta di Gabriele d'Annunzio*, p. 241.

27. Paris: Éditions de France, 1932, II, 141.

28. Stoullig et Noël, *op. cit.*, p. 203.

29. See Antongini, *op. cit.*, p. 179.

11. The French Plays

1. Louis Handler, "Avant le *Martyre de Saint Sébastien*," *Comoedia*, May 14, 1911.

2. See É. Stoullig and É. Noël, *op. cit.*, 1911, p. 387; L. Schneider, "Comment d'Annunzio eut l'idée d'écrire le *Martyre de Saint Sébastien*," *Théâtre*, June 1, 1911, pp. 20–24.

3. Stoullig and Noël, *op. cit.*, 1911, p. 387.

4. See Gustave Cohen, "Gabriele d'Annunzio et le *Martyre de Saint Sébastien*," *Mercure de France*, June 15, 1938, pp. 369–370. In the *Livre secret de Gabriele d'Annunzio et de Donatella Cross* (Padova: Edizioni letterarie "Il Pellicano," 1947), p. xci, it is suggested that D'Annunzio's first conception of the saint came from "la nudité de Donatella," which offered him "le premier symbole visuel et charnel," in 1908.

5. Robert de Montesquiou, *Mémoires* (Paris: Émile Paul, 1923), III, 158. See also Ida Rubinstein, "Ma première rencontre avec Gabriele d'Annunzio," *Conferencia*, Sept. 20, 1927, p. 326.

6. See Gustave Cohen, "Gabriele d'Annunzio et le *Martyre de Saint Sébastien*," *Mercure de France*, June 16, 1911, p. 688.

7. D'Annunzio always needed a "living exemplar" to stimulate his creative activity.

8. Léon Blum, *op. cit.*, IV, 253.

9. "Le *Martyre de Saint Sébastien*," *La Revue*, June 1, 1911, p. 685.

10. *Op. cit.*, IV, 257.

11. "Gabriele d'Annunzio et le *Martyre de Saint Sébastien*," *Mercure de France*, June 16, 1911, p. 708–709.

12. May 20, 1911, p. 404.

13. *Chronique de la Grande Guerre* (Paris: Plon, 1935), VIII, 192.

14. "La Musique," Aug. 1, 1911, p. 625.

15. "A Propos du *Martyre de Saint Sébastien*," July 5, 1911, p. 16.

16. *Op. cit.*, p. 625.

17. "Claude Debussy; souvenirs," *Revue des Deux Mondes*, May 15, 1938, p. 804.

18. *Les Idées de Claude Debussy* (Paris, 1944), p. 246.

19. *Quelques souvenirs d'un éditeur de musique* (Paris, 1925), p. 25.

20. "Est-ce une renaissance de la musique religieuse?" *Excelsior*, Feb. 11, 1911.

21. *Tutte le opere; Prose di ricerca di lotta . . .* (Milan: Mondadori, 1950), II, 913: "Claude of France understood me when I first read to him the parts of the poem eagerly seeking expression in his music, and he was enchanted at loving me and giving himself, entire and pure, to me" (this writer's translation).

22. *D'Annunzio et Debussy; correspondance*, ed. Guy Tosi (Paris: Denoël, 1948), p. 70.

23. *Ibid.*, p. 32; T. Antongini, *op. cit.*, pp. 404–405.

24. *Op. cit.*, p. 6.

25. D'Annunzio's play was often compared to Wagner's *Parsifal*, because of the blending of the pagan spirit and Christian mysticism prevailing in both works.

26. This "mansion" seems to have been inspired in part by Flaubert's *Tentation de Saint Antoine.*

27. The work is dominated by the idea of Beauty as independent of any ethical norm. For this reason *Saint Sébastien* was likened to *Faust* (see A. Rémond de Metz and C. Soula, *"Faust* et *Saint Sébastien,"* *Mercure de France*, Feb. 1, 1913, pp. 524–535).

28. *Op. cit.*, IV, 256.

29. *D'Annunzio et Debussy; correspondance*, p. 77.

30. *Tutte le opere; Teatro*, II, 385. See also Barrès, *Mes Cahiers* (Paris: Plon, 1935), IX, 100–101.

31. See Tom Antongini, *op. cit.*, p. 381. Barrès intended to dedicate to D'Annunzio, in reciprocation, *Le Mystère en pleine lumière*, when he died in 1923.

32. See *D'Annunzio et Debussy; correspondance*, pp. 41–42.

33. "Le *Martyre de Saint Sébastien* à l'Opéra," *Nouvelle Revue française*, Sept. 2, 1922, p. 245.

34. "*Saint Sébastien* de Gabriele d'Annunzio, musique de Claude Debussy," *Mercure de France*, Oct. 1, 1922, p. 234.

35. See P. Le Flem, "Le *Martyre de Saint Sébastien*," *Paris-Midi*, June 17, 1941.

36. *D'Annunzio et Debussy; correspondance*, p. 43.

37. The metrical form of the play (blank verse) was borrowed from a comedy by Honoré d'Urfé, *Sylvanire ou la morte vive.* The long prologue uses the tale of a mysterious statue of Venus from Mérimée's *Venus d'Ille.*

38. *Op. cit.*, 1913, p. 302.

39. See Angelo Sodini, *Ariel Armato* (Milan: Mondadori, 1931), p. 416 (this writer's translation).

40. *Correspondance à Hérelle*, p. 414.

41. "La *Pisanelle ou la mort parfumée*," *Nouvelle Revue française*, July 2, 1913, p. 128.

42. "La *Pisanelle,*" *Annales politiques et littéraires*, June 22, 1913, p. 535.

43. "La *Pisanelle,*" *L'Éclair*, June 13, 1913.

44. Guillaume Apollinaire, "La Vie anecdotique," *Mercure de France*, June 13, 1913, p. 661.

45. "La *Pisanelle,*" June 13, 1913.

46. *Le Théâtre des autres* (Paris: Ollendorff, 1919), p. 4.

47. See Stoullig and Noël, *op. cit.*, 1913, p. 303.

48. Paris: Éditions de France, 1932, II, 122.

49. "La *Pisanelle ou la mort parfumée*," *Revue des Deux Mondes*, July 15, 1913, p. 450.

50. *Ibid.*, p. 446.

51. New York: Brentano, 1942, pp. 74–75.

52. See in *Études italiennes, 1939–1940* (Paris: Droz, 1942) a review by Guy Tosi critical of Bellessort's judgment concerning *La Pisanelle.*

53. I. de Casa-Fuerte, "Comment naquit le *Chèvrefeuille* de Gabriele d'Annunzio," *Revue mondiale*, Dec. 15, 1933, pp. 17–20.

54. *Il Ferro* was presented simultaneously in Milan, Turin, and Rome in Jan. 1914, without success.

55. See T. Antongini, *op. cit.*, p. 241.

56. "Le *Chèvrefeuille*," *Nouvelle Revue française*, Feb. 11, 1914, p. 347.

57. "Le *Chèvrefeuille*," *Revue des Deux Mondes*, Jan. 15, 1914, p. 445.

58. "Le *Chèvrefeuille*," *Revue du mois,* Jan. 10, 1914, p. 136.
59. "Le *Chèvrefeuille*," *Annales politiques et littéraires,* Dec. 28, 1913, p. 588.
60. *Nouvelle Revue française,* Feb. 11, 1914, p. 348.

12. After the First World War

1. *Livre secret de Gabriele d'Annunzio et de Donatella Cross* (Padova: Edizioni letterarie "Il Pellicano," 1947), p. 61.
2. *Ibid.,* p. 63.
3. *Ibid.,* p. 223.
4. *Ibid.,* p. 217.
5. See Ricciotto Canudo, *Mercure de France,* July 16, 1909, p. 375.
6. Issues of Aug. 15, Sept. 1, and Oct. 1.
7. See *Dossier de presse: Phèdre,* Collection Rondel.
8. "La *Phèdre* de d'Annunzio à l'Opéra," July 2, 1923, p. 114.
9. *Essai sur d'Annunzio,* p. 185.
10. See G. Saint-Aubin, "Le Nouveau drame de Gabriele d'Annunzio: la *Torche sous le boisseau*," *La Revue,* May 1, 1905, p. 115; Ricciotto Canudo, "La dernière tragédie de Gabriele d'Annunzio," *Mercure de France,* June 1, 1905, p. 460.
11. *Revue des Deux Mondes,* Dec. 15, 1927, p. 946.
12. Dec. 12, 1927.
13. Dec. 12, 1927.
14. Dec. 12, 1927.
15. Dec. 12, 1927.
16. Dec. 12, 1927.
17. *Le Figaro,* Dec. 12, 1927.
18. Dec. 12, 1927.
19. Gérard d'Houville, *Le Figaro,* Dec. 12, 1927.
20. Étienne Rey, *Comoedia,* Dec. 12, 1927. See also Martial-Piéchaud, *Revue hebdomadaire,* Dec. 17, 1927, p. 486.
21. See Critile, *Mercure de France,* Jan. 15, 1928, p. 426. Also, Martial-Piéchaud, *Revue hebdomadaire,* Dec. 17, 1927, p. 486.
22. Dorothy Knowles, *op. cit.,* p. 475.
23. *Nouvelles littéraires,* Dec. 10, 1927.

13. Conclusion

1. *Op. cit.,* I, 43.
2. *Dossier de presse:* la *Gioconda,* Jan. 27, 1905. Collection Rondel.
3. *Op. cit.,* p. 470.
4. *Comoedia,* June 13, 1913.
5. "L'horrible concret dans le théâtre de d'Annunzio," *Études italiennes, 1939–1940,* pp. 175–189.
6. Dorothy Knowles, *op. cit.,* p. 220.
7. *L'Action française,* May 19, 1911.
8. Ricciotto Canudo, *Mercure de France,* July 16, 1909, p. 376.
9. See *Caffaro* (Genoa), Nov. 11, 1908.
10. *Le Temps,* Dec. 12, 1927.
11. *Op. cit.,* I, 26.
12. *Op. cit.,* IV, 215.

13. *Quinzaine*, Sept. 2, 1902, p. 141.

14. Guy Tosi, "Introduction," *Correspondance à Hérelle*, p. 52.

14. The Volume of *Poésies*

1. *Correspondance à Hérelle*, pp. 403–404.

2. *Ibid.*, p. 404.

3. July 1, 1912, p. 184.

4. *Mercure de France*, July 16, 1912, p. 144.

5. *Correspondance à Hérelle*, p. 403.

6. *Ibid.*, p. 403.

7. "Les Quatorze lévriers de Gabriele d'Annunzio," *Annales politiques et littéraires*, June 15, 1913, p. 512.

8. "Les poésies de Gabriele d'Annunzio," *Les Livres du temps* (Paris: Émile-Paul Frères, 1929), pp. 104–105.

9. Quoted from *L'Enfant de volupté* (Calmann-Lévy), p. 138.

10. *Les Livres du temps*, p. 145.

15. Before the Publication of *Poésies*

1. "Au poète André Sperelli" (*La Chimera*), "Les Mains" (*Poema paradisiaco*), "Villa Chigi" (*Elegie romane*), "Le Voeu" (*ibid.*).

2. "Consolation," "En vain," "Un souvenir" (*Poema paradisiaco*); "Le Voeu" (*Elegie romane*).

3. "D'Annunzio poète chrétien?" Mar. 16, 1898, p. 209.

4. "Artifex gloriosus" (*Intermezzo*), "Hortus larvarum" (*Poema paradisiaco*).

5. Feb. 7, 1904, p. 93.

6. See Joseph G. Fucilla and Joseph M. Carrière, *D'Annunzio Abroad: A Bibliographical Essay* (New York: Institute of French Studies, 1935–37), I, 162–173; II, 51–54.

7. Les *Livres du temps*, p. 109.

8. Jean Dornis, "Les Poésies de d'Annunzio," *Revue de Paris*, Feb. 1, 1908, p. 627.

9. *Correspondance à Hérelle*, p. 173.

10. "Ballata delle donne sul fiume" (*Isottèo*). Only the first two stanzas are translated. D'Annunzio unquestionably spoiled his beautiful lines by transposing them into a language which he did not possess at that time. However, Hérelle's rendering of the same stanza is more prosaic than D'Annunzio's:

> Les riches marchands d'Alexandrie, parfumés
> d'hysope et de cinnamone, sur la rivière de canope
> buvaient dans des calices de lotus les vins rosés.

The stanza seems to have been drawn from some lines of Flaubert's *La Tentation de Saint Antoine*: "Les marchands d'Alexandrie naviguent les jours de fête sur la rivière de Canope, et boivent du vin dans des calices de lotus" (p. 7, Conard ed.).

The other two translations are "Psyché endormie" (the first two and the last stanzas of "Psiche giacente"—*Poema paradisiaco*) and "Petite ballade de l'absence" (first part of "Ballata e sestina della lontananza"—*Isottèo*).

11. "Certainement, ces sonnets—en fin d'année—sont une curiosité littéraire. Le *Figaro* —qui est en quête de curiosités—ne pourrait-il les publier?" *Correspondance à Hérelle*, p. 304.

12. *Ibid.*, p. 305. The friend who had requested the French verse from D'Annunzio was probably Sarah Bernhardt, to whom Sonnet IX, "Melpomène à Sarah Bernardt," was originally dedicated.

13. *Ibid.*, p. 304.

14. *Ibid.*, p. 316. In sending the manuscript to Hérelle, D'Annunzio quite seriously had expressed the intention of writing a book of French poems, "puisque j'ai brisé, désormais," he said, "ma lyre italienne" (*Correspondance à Hérelle,* p. 303).

15. *Ibid.*, p. 317.

16. Sonnet VIII, "Aestus erat," in *Le Figaro;* Sonnet V, "Les Donatrices," in *Le Gaulois.* "Aestus erat" must have been considered more characteristic of D'Annunzio's estheticism because of the ardent sensuality with which it is permeated. This perhaps is the reason for its choice for publication. In France D'Annunzio was known primarily as the author of the trilogy of the "Novels of the Rose." Here is the sonnet:

> Les paupières couvraient lourdes ses yeux ardents
> toutes rouges encor des voluptés fiévreuses;
> et je croyais sentir battre en ses tempes creuses
> la secrète fureur des rêves obsédantes.
>
> Je lui cueillis alors un des fruits mûrs pendants
> sur nos fronts, par pitié des lèvres douloureuses.
> Du bout de ses doigts blancs comme des tubéreuses
> elle écrasa le fruit de pourpre sur ses dents.
>
> Du bout de ses longs doigts doux comme des pétales
> (quel poison dans sa pulpe avait le fruit vermeil?)
> elle effleura ses cils alourdis de sommeil.
>
> Et son âme rêvait les voluptés fatales.
> "Donne, ô Mort, à sa chair le repos sans réveil."
> Et tout mon cœur puissant bondit vers le soleil.

The last two lines seem to echo Jean Lorrain's sonnet "La Coupe" (*La Forêt bleue*):

> Bois l'engourdissement et la mort sans réveil,
> Bois la volupté lente et l'oubli du soleil ... .

17. *Correspondance à Hérelle,* p. 305.

18. *Ibid.*, p. 305.

19. *Ibid.*, p. 303.

16. *Le Laudi*

1. Dec. 10, 1912, p. 730.

2. For a complete treatment of the subject, see J. Th. Paolantonacci, *Gabriele d'Annunzio et l'humanisme méditerranéen; Doctrine et poésie dans Maia* (Marseille: Jean Vigneau, Éditeur, 1943).

3. See, for a detailed treatment of the subject, Henri Bédarida, "Sur le livre d'*Alcyone,*" *Études italiennes, 1939–1940* (Paris: Droz, 1942), pp. 49–88.

4. *Correspondance à Hérelle,* p. 411.

5. *Ibid.*, p. 413.

6. *Ibid.*, p. 410.

7. *Ibid.*, p. 411 (note by Guy Tosi). René Dollot, in "Souvenir sur Gabriele d'Annunzio" (*Études italiennes, 1939–1940,* pp. 146–147), asserts that the poet was dissatisfied with Hérelle's translation of *Poésies* and that, as a result, he abandoned the idea of having *Laus Vitae* published in French.

8. *Ibid.*, p. 406.

9. André Doderet, *Vingt ans d'amitié avec Gabriele d'Annunzio,* p. 66.

10. See Fucilla and Carrière, *op. cit.,* I, 162–173; II, 51–54.

11. *Revue de Paris,* Sept. 1, 1917, p. 154.

12. "Accetta" in Italian means "axe," not "sickle" (French: "faucille").

13. See Fucilla and Carrière, *op. cit.,* I, 165; II, 52. See also: *Oeuvres libres* (1935), No. 168, pp. 5–14; *Revue de Paris,* Apr. 1, 1936, pp. 630–640; *Revue des Deux Mondes,* Dec. 1, 1938, pp. 576–581.

14. Paris: Droz, 1942, pp. 20–24, 89–128.

15. *Mercure de France,* Sept. 15, 1939, p. 592.

16. *Ibid.,* p. 593.

17. Poetic Homage to D'Annunzio

1. *Revue de Paris,* Mar. 15, 1938, p. 458.

2. *Annales politiques et littéraires,* June 10, 1923, p. 601.

3. *Ibid.,* p. 601.

4. *Dante* (Paris), May–June 1938, p. 184.

5. *Ibid.,* p. 173.

6. *Ibid.,* p. 170.

7. *Ibid.,* p. 185.

18. Before the French "Exile"

1. *Correspondance à Hérelle,* p. 125. *Revue hebdomadaire,* June 24, 1893, p. 599.

2. June 6, 1897, p. 363.

3. "Une visite à Gabriele d'Annunzio," *Annales politiques et littéraires,* Mar. 1, 1896, p. 132.

4. *Le Correspondant,* Jan. 25, 1898, p. 269.

5. *Le Figaro,* Oct. 2, 1897

6. *Le Correspondant,* Jan. 25, 1898, p. 269.

7. *Correspondance à Hérelle,* p. 320.

8. "D'Annunzio et la Duse," *Oeuvres libres* (1947), No. 246, p. 13.

9. Romain Rolland, *op. cit.,* p. 29.

10. Sergines, *Annales politiques et littéraires,* Feb. 27, 1898, p. 136.

11. See Maurice de Waleffe, "Opinions et souvenirs sur Gabriele d'Annunzio," *Dante* (Paris), May–June 1938, pp. 187–188.

12. *Ibid.,* p. 188.

13. Feb. 1, 1898, p. 647.

14. *Annales politiques et littéraires,* Feb. 7, 1904, p. 83.

15. See Henri Bordeaux, *Pèlerinages littéraires* (Paris: Fontemoing, 1905), p. 361.

16. Quoted in Italian by Angelo Sodini, *Ariel Armato,* p. 285 (this writer's translation).

17. "En Regardant chevaucher M. d'Annunzio," Nov. 15, 1908, p. 28.

18. Dec. 16, 1908, p. 716.

19. The French "Exile"

1. See Romain Rolland, *op. cit.,* p. 34.

2. See Tom Antongini, *op. cit.,* p. 264 ff.

3. See André Germain, *La Vie amoureuse de d'Annunzio* (Paris: Fayard, 1954), p. 225.

4. Albert Flament, "Gabriele d'Annunzio," *Revue de Paris,* Feb. 15, 1934, p. 933.

5. "Gabriele d'Annunzio e la società fiorentina," *Quaderni dannunziani,* 1959, XVI–XVII, 498. See also G. Gatti, *Gabriele D'Annunzio, studi e saggi* (Bologna: Cappelli, 1959), pp. 153–156.

6. *Tutte le opere; Prose di ricerca, di lotta* . . . , II, 771 (this writer's translation).

7. *Correspondance à Hérelle*, p. 45.

8. *Tutte le opere; Versi d'amore, di gloria*, I, 1027.

9. *Tutte le opere; Prose di ricerca, di lotta* . . . , I, 183 and 196 (this writer's translation).

10. *My Life* (Garden City: Garden City Publishing Co., 1927), pp. 5–6.

11. *Ibid.*, p. 256.

12. *Ibid.*, p. 6.

13. See Tom Antongini, *op. cit.*, pp. 148–149.

14. See Albert Flament, *op. cit.*, p. 937.

15. Paris: Grasset, 1929, II, 259.

16. Albert Flament, *op. cit.*, p. 931.

17. "Vingt ans de Paris," *Oeuvres libres* (1925), No. 52, p. 63.

18. *Ibid.*, p. 67.

19. Albert Flament, *op. cit.*, p. 939.

20. See Tom Antongini, *op. cit.*, p. 81.

21. Sergines, "D'Annunzio à Paris," *Annales politiques et littéraires*, June 3, 1923, p. 562.

22. See Tom Antongini, *op. cit.*, p. 240.

23. See *ibid.*, p. 241.

24. The touching story of Donatella is found in the *Livre secret de Gabriele d'Annunzio et de Donatella Cross* (Padova: Edizioni letterarie "Il Pellicano," 1947); and in André Germain's *La Vie amoureuse de d'Annunzio* (Paris: Fayard, 1954), pp. 172–224.

20. The War

1. *Curriculum Vitae, 1910–1914* (Rome: Casa del libro, 1934), II, 241–242.

2. *Quarant'anni con d'Annunzio* (Milan: Mondadori, 1957), pp. 364–366.

3. Mme Caillaux had murdered Calmette, the editor of *Le Figaro*, on March 16, 1914, and the trial was held July 20 through July 28. She was acquitted.

4. See Maurice Paléologue, "Musiques," *Revue de Paris*, Apr. 1947, p. 82. See also A. Caraccio, *D'Annunzio dramaturge*, p. 24; and G. Tosi, *D'Annunzio en France au début de la Grande Guerre* (Florence: Sansoni, 1961), p. 16. In this work Tosi traces, through unpublished notebooks (presented in his French translation), the life and the role of the poet in France at the beginning of the war, that is, from about June 1914 to May 1915.

5. See letter to Luigi Albertini dated July 27, 1914, in *Il Mondo*, Mar. 5, 1949; and G. Tosi, *D'Annunzio en France* . . . , p. 19.

6. The *Ode* is part of the fifth book of *Le Laudi*. It was published again in the *Revue hebdomadaire*, Feb. 20, 1915. For the enthusiasm of the poet's friends, see Tosi, *D'Annunzio en France* . . . , p. 24.

7. See Marie de Régnier, "Adieu à d'Annunzio," *Revue des Deux Mondes*, Mar. 15, 1938, p. 465. The poet called Marie de Régnier "Suora Notte" for the love of "notre cher Saint François"; and she called D'Annunzio "Frate Foco."

8. *Ibid.*, p. 465.

9. *Envoi à la France*, *Revue hebdomadaire*, Oct. 8, 1921, p. 140.

10. *Ibid.*, p. 147.

11. *Ibid.*, Oct. 15, 1921, p. 299.

12. Henry Bordeaux, *La Claire Italie* (Paris: Plon, 1929), p. 357.

13. See Antongini, *Vita segreta di Gabriele d'Annunzio*, pp. 415–416; Guy Tosi ques-

tions the authenticity of the interview with Gallieni. See his *D'Annunzio en France* . . . , p. 40.

14. *Envoi à la France, Revue hebdomadaire,* Oct. 15, 1921, p. 295.

15. Gheusi was the director of the Opéra-Comique.

16. Antongini, *op. cit.,* p. 460.

17. Gallieni wrote in his *Carnets* on the date of Sept. 16: "Visite de Gabriele d'Annunzio, enthousiaste."

18. *Le Figaro,* Oct. 10, 1914.

19. See Jean Dornis, *Essai sur d'Annunzio,* p. 205.

20. *Revue hebdomadaire,* Feb. 20, 1915, p. 280. The speech was published together with the *Ode.*

21. Paris: Plon, 1938, XI, 412.

22. At the start of the war the son of Giuseppe Garibaldi, Ricciotti (who had fought, with his brother Menotti, at the side of their father in France in 1870), arrived in Paris to form a legion of Garibaldini. His project was approved and the corps of Italian volunteers was placed under the command of his elder son, Peppino Garibaldi, who had already distinguished himself in Greece against the Turks, in Africa on the side of the Boers, in Venezuela, in Mexico, and again in Greece. (He was in the United States at the outbreak of the war.) The Garibaldini regiment, in which the four brothers of Peppino Garibaldi were also enlisted, had its baptism of fire in December 1915 on the Argonne front, where it distinguished itself for bravery and where one of the Garibaldi brothers, Bruno, was killed in combat. A week later another brother, Costante, met with heroic death in action. In a hand-to-hand battle on January 8, 1915, the regiment lost five hundred men, and it was sent back to rest for the moment. Later the decision was made not to rebuild the regiment but to use it for the projected landing in Genoa. In a letter from Marcel Boulenger to D'Annunzio, the bravery of the regiment is exalted:

> J'ai dîné ce soir avec un des amis (De Soria), qui revient de l'Argonne. Il y a vu, de ses yeux, le jeune colonel Garibaldi charger à la tête de son régiment, marchant réellement en tête, le premier de tous, et armé simplement d'une badine! (Aucun autre colonel ne marche en avant de ses hommes, pour une attaque: c'est d'une audace folle). Les Italiens de Peppino Garibaldi sont, paraît-il, si braves qu'on les met le moins possible dans les tranchées. Mais on les réserve pour toutes les attaques, et, le moment venu, on les lâche. ...

(See Tosi, *Gabriele d'Annunzio en France* . . . , pp. 104–105.

23. *Ibid.,* pp. 104–105.

24. *Le Figaro,* May 5, 1915. The sonnets were reprinted in the *Anthologie des poèmes de la Grande Guerre* in 1921 (Paris: Chapulot), and in *Yggdrasil,* Mar. 1938; finally they were included in the anthology *Poètes contemporains* (Paris: Firmin-Didot, 1938). They are now collected in book V of *Le Laudi.* After their publication in *Le Figaro,* they were to appear in a volume entitled *Pour la douce France* comprising the *Ode pour la résurrection latine* and some articles and speeches by the poet. The volume, which was to be printed by Champion to the benefit of the Italian military hospital in Paris, was never published.

25. This line is similar to line 11 of the first sonnet.

26. Line taken from Victor Hugo's *Élégie des Fléaux* (*Légende des Siècles*):

> France, l'univers a besoin que tu vives,
> Tu vivras. L'avenir mourrait sous ton linceul.
> France, France, sans toi, le monde serait seul.

27. *Avec d'Annunzio en mai 1915* (Abeville: Paillart, 1925).

28. "Italia cara," *Mercure de France,* June 1, 1919, p. 429.

29. *Chronique de la Grande Guerre* (Paris: Plon, 1932), IV, 317.

30. *Ibid.,* p. 230.

31. *Ibid.,* p. 231.

32. "Le miracle italien," p. 669.

33. "Pensées vers d'Annunzio," *Annales politiques et littéraires,* June 6, 1915, p. 703.

34. "Gabriele d'Annunzio et son rôle actuel," *Revue de Paris,* June 15, 1915, p. 837.

35. Antongini, *op. cit.,* p. 687 (this writer's translation).

36. *Chronique de la Grande Guerre,* VIII, 198.

37. *Ibid.,* VII, 302.

38. *Ibid.,* p. 303.

39. *Ibid.,* VIII, 192.

40. Antongini, *op. cit.,* p. 698 (this writer's translation).

41. *L'Illustration,* Mar. 12, 1938, p. 289. The manuscript of the message was preserved by a French officer, Jean Guibul. He sent it to *L'Illustration* for publication at the death of the poet.

42. Jacques Boulenger, "Visite au Commandant d'Annunzio," *Revue des Deux Mondes,* Dec. 15, 1918, p. 816.

43. *Ibid.,* pp. 815–816:

> Quand je me rappelle [says D'Annunzio to his friend] ce que la France a fait en 1914! ... Savez-vous que c'est moi, et j'en suis très fier, qui ai pour la première fois écrit ces mots: "Le miracle français," dans un article du *Gaulois,* au début de ce tragique août '14? ... Quand donc j'évoque la Marne, l'Yser, l'incroyable sursaut d'énergie de Verdun, et toute l'épopée; et lorsque aussi je songe à notre Italie, lancée soudain dans la plus monstrueuse guerre, sans préparation suffisante, manquant de tout ... au splendide arrêt sur le Piave, à la reprise héroïque et furieuse de soi-même à laquelle tout un peuple aura su se contraindre, car c'est notre miracle italien, le Piave! Dès que je réfléchis enfin à ces merveilles de l'histoire humaine, il me semble que nos deux patries fraternellement unies seraient capables, à elles seules, de soulever l'univers. ... L'Italie et la France représentent la latinité, c'est-à-dire la fleur du monde.

21. After the Victory

1. July 1, 1920, p. 69.

2. This was the more unfortunate and regrettable since the victory at Vittorio Veneto was one of the most decisive of the war. It was there that the Austro-Hungarian Empire was brought to its knees on the battlefield. Taking part in the offensive were fifty-one Italian, three British, two French, and one Czechoslovak divisions faced by seventy-three Austro-Hungarian divisions. And while it is true that there were six foreign divisions to help the Italians, it is equally true that Italy had three divisions on the French front, five in Albania, three in Macedonia, and other troops in Siberia, in Syria, and elsewhere to help the Allies. The Vittorio Veneto battle ended with the total disintegration of the Austrian army. The menace to Bavaria and to the rear of the German front, resulting from the collapse of Austria, sped the surrender of Germany. It is not improbable that without Vittorio Veneto the war could have lasted another winter. D'Annunzio's anger against the other allies' calculated undermining of the Italian victory was not completely unjustified.

3. *Tutte le opere; Prose di ricerca, di lotta* . . . , I, 817. Harsher words were said in the letter also against England and the United States as the following passage shows (translation of passages is the writer's):

> The People of the Revenge, intoxicated with victory, display all their colors, tune their bugle bands, quicken their steps to surpass the most resolute and speedy; and

we readily draw aside to make way for them. The People of the five meals, finished with their bloody task, reopen their jaws wide to devour as much as they can; and we tighten our belt by one more notch around our frugality. The People of the starry flag do not conceal that they carried out the best of their business under the cover of eternal ideals; and we let foreigners muddy the sources of our wealth. We are preached modesty, prudence, renunciation, mortification. . . . What peace will finally be imposed upon us, the destitute. . . . Pax gallica? Pax britannica? Pax stelligera? Miserere nostri.

He returned to the subject with increased bitterness in a speech he wrote for the anniversary of Italy's entry into the war (May 24, 1919) which the government did not allow him to deliver. In it he pointed out the wrongs of the "Latin sister," emphasizing the generosity of Italy in overlooking them in the moment of danger for France:

We forgot Nice and Corsica, we forgot Mentana, we forgot the bitterness of him who fought and won at Dijon, and the stupefaction of those who naively let themselves be tricked concerning Tunis. We forgot the military supplies given to our enemy in Abyssinia—loaded in Marseilles and unloaded in Obuk. We forgot the open and the hidden hostility against our overseas exploits, our war in Libya, the war smuggling against us, and the loads of shells going from Tunisia to the Turks. We forgot our dead in Amba Alagi and Adua, stretched on the sand by the weapons arriving in Ethiopia through French and English ports. We forgot also the episode of the two ships in our Tyrrenian, one of which bore a name evoking the hostile arrogance of the old Censor. All of this we forgot, and remembered only the "gentle Latin blood" and obeyed only the necessity of saving France and Europe, as was asserted in sudden psalms of love and praises by those who now despoil and vilify us. How many were the rewards promised to us!

And in defending Italian victory in the war D'Annunzio said:

How did the Allies win the war? They fought on one front, the French, against only one country of sixty-seven million inhabitants, pounding at her with all of the forces of France, the British Empire, and the United States, as well as auxiliary Italian, Portuguese, Polish forces, colonial troops of every color and creed. How did we win the war? Alone, always alone, from year to year, with a faith which became stronger and stronger as the Allies reduced and suppressed the promised help. We remained alone to face a military empire of fifty-two million inhabitants now freed from the task of facing its enemy in the East.

4. The letter appeared as a pamphlet in 1919. Paul Souday reviewed it in *Le Temps*, Apr. 11, 1919.

5. See René Dollot, "Souvenirs sur Gabriele d'Annunzio," *Études italiennes, 1939–1940* (Paris: Droz, 1942), p. 156.

6. *Tutte le opere; Prose di ricerca, di lotta* . . . , I, 821.

7. *Ibid.*, pp. 824–825.

8. The Caporetto episode, undoubtedly a sad and frightful one, was unduly stressed for political reasons—primarily to undermine Italy's contribution to the common cause and, therefore, to deny her any territorial gain beyond the two provinces under the Austrian yoke. The defeat at Caporetto was in the over-all view no more serious than the French defeat in 1914 when the Germans reached the Marne, or that of the spring of 1918 when the enemy was again near Paris. If the French had their "miracle" on the Marne, it is fair to say that the Italians had theirs on the Piave, where they, alone, stopped the enemy, to the great surprise of the Allies who had wanted the organization of the resistance line on the Po River, several miles back. During the whole war Italy had to fight on two fronts—

the defeatist social-communist propaganda within and an enemy far superior both in number and armaments (also favored by the terrain) without. At the time of Caporetto, Austria, free from the task of facing the Russians in the East, had moved all her might on the Italian front, where heavy German reinforcements joined the Austrian troops. (It was, in fact, the Germans who broke through Caporetto.) In addition, the configuration of the Italian front (in the form of a semicircle) was such that a break at one point would force the entire line of defense to fall back, in order to prevent being taken from behind. However, although Italian losses were extremely heavy in the retreat, the enemy was unable to cross the Piave. In June 1918 the Austrians launched their most powerful offensive to break the Italian line but with no success, and four months later they were totally defeated in the battle of Vittorio Veneto. The Allies' propaganda at the time of the Peace Conference at Versailles constantly brought up the Caporetto episode and deliberately ignored Vittorio Veneto. D'Annunzio, therefore, cannot be blamed for his denunciation of the Allies' ingratitude.

9. *Tutte le opere; Prose di ricerca, di lotta* . . . I, 824.

10. *Ibid.*, p. 903 (this writer's translation).

11. *Ibid.*, p. 829.

12. *Ibid.*, p. 965.

13. *Ibid.*, p. 1053.

14. "Gabriele d'Annunzio à Fiume," *Revue de Paris,* Oct. 1, 1920, p. 551. See also second installment in the Oct. 15 issue.

15. This was a malicious accusation. In the *Mercure de France* (Feb. 1, Mar. 1, and Apr. 15, 1920) three articles had already appeared on the question of the poet's name—"Généalogie dannunzienne"—one anonymous, one by Georges Hérelle, and one by Paul Guiton, with the reproduction of D'Annunzio's birth certificate. Despite this, it is amusing to notice that the infallible *Dictionnaire Larousse* (edition of 1922 in two volumes) enters thus his name: "Annunzio (Gaetano Rapagnetta dit:), littérateur italien, . . ."; and *Biblio,* published by Hachette, still lists the author as: "D'Annunzio, Gabriele Rapagnetta."

16. Feb. 1, 1921, p. 576.

17. *Ibid.*, p. 578.

18. *Mercure de France,* Mar. 15, 1921, p. 571.

19. *Revue des Deux Mondes,* Oct. 1, 1922, p. 638.

20. June 3, 1923, p. 561.

21. June 10, 1923, p. 597.

22. *Ibid.*, p. 598.

23. These comments appeared on p. 601.

24. June 17, 1923, p. 614.

25. "D'Annunzio au Vittoriale," *Oeuvres libres* (1938), No. 203, p. 111.

26. *Ibid.*, p. 113.

27. See Robert de Beauplan, "La *Torche sous le boisseau* à la Comédie-Française," *La Petite Illustration,* Dec. 31, 1927, p. 31.

28. *Ibid.*, p. 31.

29. Henry Bordeaux, "De Locarno à d'Annunzio," *Revue de Paris,* Apr. 1, 1929, p. 540.

30. *Ibid.*, p. 530.

31. Constantin Photiadès, "Gabriele d'Annunzio au Vittoriale," *Revue des Deux Mondes,* Apr. 1, 1938, p. 611.

32. *Ibid.*, p. 612.

33. *Ibid.*, p. 634.

34. *Ibid.*, p. 636.

35. *Mercure de France*, Sept. 6, 1932, p. 706.

36. *Tutte le opere; Prose di ricerca, di lotta* . . . , III, 560–561.

22. French Friendships

1. *Journal*, trans. J. O'Brien (New York: Knopf, 1947), I, 51.

2. *André Gide–Paul Valéry; correspondance, 1890–1942* (Paris: Gallimard, 1955), p. 210.

3. See entries for Dec. 28, 1895, and Jan. 6, 1896, in Gide's *Journal* (Vol. I).

4. *Gide–Valéry; correspondance*, p. 300.

5. Besides the article on D'Annunzio there was one critical of Mallarmé. These two pieces so displeased Gide that the entire first issue was in a sense disavowed and the next brought out as number one.

6. Entry for Apr. 16.

7. Oct. 1938 issue.

8. *Journal*, III, 410.

9. "D'Annunzio et la Duse," *Oeuvres libres*, 1947, No. 246.

10. *Ibid.*, p. 6.

11. *Ibid.*, p. 3.

12. *Ibid.*, p. 47.

13. See Guy Tosi, "D'Annunzio visto da Romain Rolland," *Il Ponte*, Jan.–June 1963), XIX, 508.

14. "D'Annunzio et la Duse," *Oeuvres libres* (1947), No. 246, p. 47.

15. See *ibid.*, p. 48.

16. See Guy Tosi, *op. cit.*, pp. 512–513.

17. "D'Annunzio et la Duse," *Oeuvres libres* (1947), No. 246, p. 48.

18. "Au-dessus de la mêlée," *Journal de Genève*, Sept. 15, 1914.

19. *Journal des années de guerre, 1914–1919* (Paris: A. Michel, 1952), pp. 352–353.

20. *Ibid.*, p. 365.

21. See Guy Tosi, *op. cit.*, p. 514.

22. *Journal des années de guerre*, p. 415.

23. *Ibid.*, p. 1617.

24. *Ibid.*, p. 1846.

25. *Ibid.*, p. 1846.

26. See Guy Tosi, *op. cit.*, p. 518.

27. See *ibid.*, p. 519.

28. "D'Annunzio et la Duse," *Oeuvres libres* (1947), No. 246, p. 50.

29. *Journey Within*, trans. Elsie Pell (New York: Philosophical Library, 1947), p. 165.

30. *Les Pas effacés* (Paris: Émile-Paul Frères, éditeurs, 1923), III, 147.

31. *Ibid.*, pp. 151–152.

32. *Ibid.*, p. 152.

33. *Ibid.*, p. 149.

34. *Ibid.*, p. 169.

35. See Luigi Salvatorelli, "D'Annunzio e Barrès," in *Studi sulla letteratura dell' Ottocento, in onore di Pietro Paolo Trompeo* (Naples: Edizioni scientifiche italiane, 1959), pp. 472–480. The intellectual kinship between the two writers was also outlined by Jean Anglade, "Barrès, d'Annunzio et l'universel," *La Table ronde*, Mar. 1957, pp. 201–207.

36. *Les Pas effacés*, III, 149.

37. *Ibid.*, p. 153.

38. *Ibid.,* p. 154.

39. Maurice Barrès, *Mes Cahiers* (Paris: Plon, 1938), VIII, 193.

40. Robert de Montesquiou, *Les Pas effacés,* III, pp. 165–166.

41. See Preface to the *Martyre de Saint Sébastien.*

42. Lucia Culcasi, "Les Rapports de d'Annunzio et de Barrès," *Letterature moderne,* 4 (1953), 449–464.

43. "De Locarno à d'Annunzio," *Revue de Paris,* Apr. 1, 1929, p. 537.

44. See *Mes Cahiers,* Vol. XII.

45. *Ibid.,* p. 47.

46. *Mes Cahiers,* XIII, pp. 182–183.

47. See Lucia Culcasi, *op. cit.,* p. 461.

48. Marcel Boulenger, "Gabriele d'Annunzio à Fiume," *Revue de Paris,* Oct. 15, 1919, p. 862.

49. See Guy Tosi, "Anna de Noailles et Gabriele d'Annunzio (d'après une correspondance inèdite)," *Quaderni Dannunziani,* 1958, XII–XIII, 199. The brief outline of the relations between Anna de Noailles and D'Annunzio is based on Tosi's article.

50. See *ibid.,* p. 200.

51. Constantin Photiadès, "Gabriele d'Annunzio au Vittoriale," *Revue des Deux Mondes,* Dec. 15, 1939, p. 626.

52. See Tosi, "Anna de Noailles et Gabriele d'Annunzio (d'après une correspondance inédite)," *Quaderni Dannunziani,* 1958, XII–XIII, 202.

53. *Ibid.,* p. 202.

54. *Ibid.,* p. 203.

55. *Ibid.,* p. 203.

56. *Ibid.,* p. 204.

57. *Ibid.,* p. 205.

58. See Guy Tosi, *Gabriele d'Annunzio et Paul Valéry* (Florence: Edizioni Sansoni Antiquariato, 1960), p. 9. This writer has utilized Tosi's article in this brief outline of the relations between D'Annunzio and Valéry.

59. André Doderet, *Vingt ans d'amitié avec Gabriele d'Annunzio,* p. 93.

60. *Ibid.,* p. 65.

61. See *ibid.,* p. 68, and Tosi, *D'Annunzio et Valéry,* p. 14.

62. See Tosi, *D'Annunzio et Valéry,* p. 15.

63. Ugo Ojetti, *As they seemed to me (Cose viste),* trans. Henry Furst (New York: Dutton, 1927), p. 191.

64. See Tosi, *D'Annunzio et Valéry,* p. 16.

65. *Ibid.,* p. 19.

66. *Ibid.,* p. 22.

67. "Un Prince de la terre," *Nouvelles littéraires,* June 20, 1963, p. 11.

23. The Last Years

1. Paris: Librairie de France, 1932, V, 356.

2. Mar. 11, 1933, p. 290.

3. "Gabriele d'Annunzio," *Revue de Paris,* Feb. 15, 1934, p. 944.

4. See José Germain, "Réception au Vittoriale," *L'Illustration,* Oct. 17, 1936, p. 225.

5. Mar. 10, 1938, p. 245.

6. Mar. 15, 1938, p. 465.

7. Mar. 15, 1938, p. 455.

8. Mar. 12, 1938, p. 283.
9. *Dante,* May–June 1938, p. 176.
10. "Adieu à d'Annunzio," *Revue des Deux Mondes,* Mar. 15, 1938, p. 468.
11. "Gabriele d'Annunzio," *Annales politiques et littéraires,* Mar. 10, 1938, p. 245.

Bibliographical Note

A COMPLETE BIBLIOGRAPHY, listing the translations of D'Annunzio's works into French and the biographical and critical studies devoted to him in France, would run into a considerable number of pages. No necessity was felt for such a bibliography, since it would be in large part a duplication of the extensive bibliographical information given in the numerous footnotes and in the text itself.

An exhaustive bibliographical coverage of the subject until about 1935 is found in Joseph G. Fucilla and Joseph M. Carrière's *D'Annunzio Abroad: A Bibliographical Essay* (New York: Institute of French Studies, 1935–37, 2 vols.), to which this writer is deeply indebted. The work, excellently organized, contains a little over two thousand five hundred entries (translations and criticism), approximately half of which appeared in France. For the period between 1935 and 1940 the reader is referred to the 1939–40 volume of *Études italiennes* (Paris: Droz, 1942) which is devoted to D'Annunzio and contains a great deal of bibliographical material in addition to unpublished texts, new translations, and biographical and critical essays. For the years 1940–55 one may consult the *Rassegna della letteratura italiana,* and Umberto Bosco's *Repertorio bibliografico della letteratura italiana* (Florence: Sansoni, 1953–60, 2 vols.) which covers the period 1948–53. Needless to mention also are the *Publications of the Modern Language Association,* whose annual bibliography (in the April issue) is well known. The period from 1955 to the present is thoroughly covered by *Quaderni Dannunziani* (Fondazione de "Il Vittoriale degli 'Italiani,'" Gardone Riviera, Brescia) which carries in each issue the most minute and complete bibliography, both Italian and foreign, concerning the author.

The main general bibliographical sources are Roberto Forcella's *D'Annunzio: Guida bibliografica* (Rome: Fondazione Leonardo, 1926–28, Vols. I, II; Florence: Sansoni, 1936–37, Vols. III, IV), Giulio De Medici's *Bibliografia di Gabriele d'Annunzio* (Rome: Edizioni del Centauro, 1929), Enrico Falqui's *Bibliografia dannunziana* (Rome: Ulpiana, 1939), and Marino Parenti's *Bibliografia dannunziana essenziale* (Florence: Sansoni, 1940).

Index